Vico and Plato

Emory Vico Studies

Donald Phillip Verene
General Editor

Vol. 8

PETER LANG
New York • Washington, D.C./Baltimore • Bern
Frankfurt am Main • Berlin • Brussels • Vienna • Oxford

Nancy du Bois Marcus

Vico and Plato

PETER LANG
New York • Washington, D.C./Baltimore • Bern
Frankfurt am Main • Berlin • Brussels • Vienna • Oxford

Library of Congress Cataloging-in-Publication Data

Marcus, Nancy du Bois.
Vico and Plato / by Nancy du Bois Marcus.
p. cm. — (Emory Vico studies; v. 8)
Includes bibliographical references and index.
1. Vico, Giambattista, 1668–1744. 2. Plato—Influence.
3. Platonists. I. Title. II. Series.
B3583 .D8   195—dc21   00-056758
ISBN 0-8204-5178-9
ISSN 0883-6000

Die Deutsche Bibliothek-CIP-Einheitsaufnahme

Marcus, Nancy du Bois:
Vico and Plato / Nancy du Bois Marcus.
–New York; Washington, D.C./Baltimore; Bern; Frankfurt
am Main; Berlin; Brussels; Vienna; Oxford: Lang.
(Emory Vico studies; Vol. 8)
ISBN 0-8204-5178-9

The paper in this book meets the guidelines for permanence and durability
of the Committee on Production Guidelines for Book Longevity
of the Council of Library Resources.

Printed in the United States of America

For Fred

O Plato, the soul and pupil of the eye of all the wise.
—Vico, *Oration* II

. . . a metaphysics compatible with human frailty, which neither allows all truths to men, nor yet denies him all, but only some.
—Vico, *Ancient Wisdom*

Contents

Preface   .   xi

Introduction   Vico's First Author and the Family of Plato   1

PART I   **The Dignity of Pico**   13
Introduction   Vico's Praise of the Renaissance   15

Chapter 1   History: Poetic Wisdom and Chronology   21
                     Poetic Wisdom   22
                     Chronology   32

Chapter 2   Poetry: Maker and Molder of Thyself   39
                     De hominis dignitate   40
                     Born for Wisdom   48

Chapter 3   Eloquence: Wisdom Speaking   59
                     Pico as Eloquent Critic of Untruthful Rhetoric   60
                     Vico's Eloquence as the Flower of Wisdom   64

PART II   **The Piety of Augustine**   75
Introduction   Vico's Particular Protector   77

Chapter 4   Rational Civil Theology   81
                     Augustine and Varro on Types of Theology   82
                     Vico's Division of Theology   91

Chapter 5   Divine Providence: Certain and True   103
                     Augustinian Providence in the *City of God*
                     and the *New Science*   104

Vichian Providence: Poetic and Philosophical   111
The Certainty of Poetic Providence   115
The Truth of Philosophical Providence   120

Chapter 6   Educating the Fallen Image of God   129
Augustinian Humility and Platonic Pride   130
Vico's Pious Humanism   136

PART III   The Philosophical Heroism of Plato   149
Introduction Vico's Ideal Philosopher and the Search
for the True Plato   151

Chapter 7   Ideal Eternal History   157
Plato's Ideal City and History   159
Vico's Form of History   190

Chapter 8   The Serious Poet: Divine and Human   199
Plato's Poetic Metaphysics   199
Vico's Frontispiece as Platonic *Eikon*   208

Chapter 9   Conclusion: Socrates as Philosophical Hero   221

Notes   237

Index   255

Preface

Giambattista Vico (1668–1744) holds as an axiom of his *New Science* that "the nature of things is nothing but their coming into being at certain times and in certain guises." Like all human things, this study of the kinship of Vico and Plato has specific origins. The importance I attach to Vico's references to Plato and Platonism arises from my conviction that philosophy must begin with Plato. The impetus to read Plato with a modern philosopher arose from my persistent sense of the incompleteness of focusing on Plato alone. My interest in Plato raised the following fundamental question: how can Plato be brought to life in philosophical conversation today?

Before discovering Vico, I immersed myself the work of Alasdair MacIntyre. I thought MacIntyre had found a way to revive the themes of ancient philosophy, especially moral philosophy, while acknowledging the history of ideas between Plato's time and our own. I defended MacIntyre from charges of historicism, but ultimately that defense unravelled. I had to accept that MacIntyre was conceding too much on the nature of truth to the modern epistemological skeptics. At this juncture, I was introduced to Vico. Providentially, MacIntyre and the Vico scholar Donald Phillip Verene had a published debate that clarified for me that Vico's project was exactly what I had sought and could not find in MacIntyre's work. I saw that Vico was the way back to the high road of Platonism for which I had been searching, and the fruit of that discovery is this work on Vico and Plato.

Investigating who Plato is for Vico both illuminates what wisdom is for Vico and provides a context for today's reader of Plato. I discovered the centrality of moderation in metaphysics as well as in moral life by studying Vico in light of Giovanni Pico della Mirandola, Augustine, and Plato. My approach is grounded in the history of Western philosophy, yet the philosophical insights which emerged could have been discovered in other guises, as they are timeless human and moral truths. That human beings can find the ideal and eternal in the particulars of history is one of Vico's greatest insights, and his most Platonic.

The references which Vico makes to Plato and Platonism dispel the illusion that Vico is an historicist and reveal a metaphysician and a moral philosopher in the Platonic tradition. In axiom 5, Vico says "to be useful to the human race, philosophy must raise and direct weak and fallen man, not rend his nature or abandon him in his corruption." Two conclusions immediately follow; first, he "dismisses from the school of our Science" the Stoics and Epicureans, and second, he "admits to our school the political philosophers, and first of all the Platonists, who agree with all the lawgivers on these three main points: that there is divine providence, that human passions should be moderated and made into human virtues, and that human souls are immortal. Thus from this axiom are derived the three principles of this Science."

The more familiar form of these three principles is the "certain" form, as religion, marriage, and burial, but each of these is also proven "true" by the philosophers. Philosophical wisdom grows out of poetic wisdom, metaphysics from poetry, and Vico is telling us that the philosophers he chooses for this task are the Platonists. My claim is that insofar as the Vichian scientist is a philosopher, that philosophy is Platonic, as opposed to Stoic or Epicurean. As Plato's *Republic* excluded untruthful poets from the ideal city, so Vico excludes immoderate philosophers from his Science. Vico makes this judgment on the same moral grounds as did Plato. For Vico as for Plato, philosophy is meant to be the guide of life.

If humility is endless, so is gratitude. No remarks here will adequately reflect the cooperation behind this work, but an attempt is necessary. I am grateful to my parents, Jere Edward and Joyann du Bois, to my brother David Michael du Bois, and to my grandparents, Robert L. and Mary E. Krabbe, for your endless love and your support of this mysterious endeavor called philosophy. To all my professors at Sewanee and Emory for your direction and encouragement. To James R. Peters, who introduced me to Plato and philosophy. To Donald Phillip Verene, who has been my primary guide, as will be evident to anyone familiar with his work, for showing me the Vico road and allowing me to be a fellow traveler. To Ann Hartle, for her insight into the human condition, and for her example, embodying the life to which I aspire. To all my friends, past and present, especially to Cameron W. Swallow, Susan E. Engelhardt, and James R. Goetsch who have accompanied me on my philosophical journey from its origin. And, most fundamentally of all, I am grateful to my husband, Frederick R. Marcus, who is a true philosophical friend and a constant source of insight and inspiration.

I am indebted to Phi Beta Kappa, whose motto *"philosophia biou kubernetes"* I have taken as my own, for the Mary Isabel Sibley fellowship in 1995–96 which enabled me to complete this work.

Introduction

Vico's First Author and the Family of Plato

Iris Murdoch seeks to make Plato more accessible by comparing him to Immanuel Kant. She writes that "Plato temperamentally resembles Kant in combining a great sense of human possibility with a great sense of human worthlessness. Kant is concerned both with setting limits to reason, and with increasing our confidence in reason within those limits."[1] This Platonic understanding of the duality of human nature, and the consequences of this self-knowledge for drawing the limits of philosophy, finds a better analogy in the thought of Giambattista Vico.

The analogy between Vico and Plato is suggested by Vico himself. Plato is the first of the four "authors" Vico had "ever before him in meditation and writing."[2] The degree to which Vico's kinship to Plato and the family of thinkers identified with Platonism can shed light on the philosophical significance of Vico's *New Science* has not been explored in detail. Many scholars acknowledge Vico's references to Plato and the Platonists in passing or even to some extent, but there is no book-length study devoted to the complexity of the relationship between the two thinkers.[3]

Several scholars acknowledge that relative to other topics Vico's first author has been passed over in silence. G. L. C. Bedani, for instance, writes that "one of the real lacunae in Vico studies is a convincing account of the true meaning of his declared indebtedness to Plato."[4] This neglect is surprising since reading Vico with Plato directly illuminates the heart of his philosophical thought. Other routes to understanding Vico either through important themes or other authors reveal significant dimensions of Vico's thought as well, and have been more well-travelled by scholars. But the crucial question of his integrity as a metaphysician and a moral philosopher in the Platonic tradition remains for the most part unasked.

If the connection between Vico and Plato is the key to discovering Vico's philosophical significance, as I am arguing, why has this been neglected even among Vico scholars? It may be that a philosopher acknowledging a debt to Plato seems a matter of course, so readers of the *Autobiography* move on to the more unusual authors: Tacitus, Bacon, and Grotius.[5] Another explanation may be found in the mutually reinforcing misreadings of both Plato and Vico. The prevalent caricature of Vico as an historicist epistemologist may be the most important factor. From the other side, the reading of Plato as a rationalist more like René Descartes contributes to the paradoxical ring of the claim that there is a significant kinship between Vico and Plato. If Vico is an historicist, how could he be significantly related to Plato, who is an idealist metaphysician and a realist concerning truth? If Plato banishes the poets and thinks rhetoric is the opposite of philosophy, how could he have anything in common with a professor of rhetoric whose great discovery is that poetic wisdom is the genesis of thought? The initial implausibility of a kinship of Vico with Plato arises from misinterpretations of both thinkers, which are reflected in such dismissive questions, and can be overcome by carefully reading their texts together. The strongest connections are often at first unapparent; as Heraclitus teaches: "an unapparent connection is stronger than an apparent one."[6]

Vico himself provides clues about how to think about the way scholars have interpreted his thought. The obvious way to think about most of the errors in Vico scholarship is to define them as a species of making the unfamiliar familiar.[7] Instead of the less helpful critique that much scholarship on Vico commits this basic error, I will review the landscape of Vico scholarship in terms of the more specific philosophical errors which Vico delineates. Vico distinguishes two sets of distortions of the ideal, one for metaphysics and moral philosophy and the other for epistemology. In both cases Vico locates his own thought as a moderate position between the two extremes which he rejects. Just as Aristotle locates for every virtue a vice of defect and a vice of excess, so Vico articulates his philosophical ideal in contrast to deficiency and excess.[8] The location of the ideal for human wisdom and the distortions at either extreme are invaluable to understanding Vico's own philosophical perspective. These claims orient a study of Vico's metaphysics, moral philosophy, and epistemology by providing a standard internal to Vico's thought instead of imposing a foreign standard. Errors occur when Vico's thought is brought too close to one or the other of these distortions, and away from the balance of the midpoint. Inadvertently, many scholars distort Vico's thought toward the extremes which he explicitly rejects, and in so doing they miss the balanced philosophy Vico presents.

Vico establishes a metaphysics which acknowledges the limits of human knowledge in the early work *On the Most Ancient Wisdom of the Italians Unearthed from the Origins of the Latin Language*. Vico concludes this work by telling his friend Paolo Mattia Doria, to whom it is dedicated, that it is "a metaphysics compatible with human frailty, which neither allows all truths to men, nor yet denies him all, but only some" (*metaphysicam humana imbecillitate dignam, quae homini neque omnia vera permittat, neque omnia negat, sed aliqua*).[9] This work of metaphysics is ironically most often cited as the basis of the historicist readings, for it is here that Vico discovers in the Latin language that "the true is the same as the made" (*verum esse ipsum factum*) (*AW* 46). But the context reveals that human making and knowing are modeled on the perfect knowing and making of God. In conclusion, Vico reaffirms that his work is one of metaphysics, and "it is a metaphysics consonant with Christian piety because it distinguishes divine from human truth and does not set up human knowledge as the rule for divine knowledge, but divine science as the rule for human knowledge" (*AW* 109). By drawing such limits Vico's metaphysics steers the middle way between the knowledge claims of dogmatism and skepticism. He states plainly that "the dogmatics do not know everything nor the skeptics nothing" (ibid.).

An interpretation of Vico must fall within these extremes of skepticism and dogmatism which Vico rejects in favor of "a metaphysics compatible with human frailty" (ibid.). A reader of Vichian secondary literature will find that this is not always the case. Skepticism in the twentieth century has often taken the form of historicism, and considering Vico an historicist is the most common distortion.[10] I am using skepticism in the sense that Vico does: as denying to human beings all truths, drawing the limits of human reason such that human beings cannot know truth at all, and cannot even grasp the idea of transcendent truth or wisdom in any timeless sense. This kind of historical relativism is a species of skepticism that has nothing in common with Vico's philosophical study of history.[11]

Alasdair MacIntyre makes the claim that Vico is "Plato historicized."[12] This partial truth reveals more about the contemporary philosophical interpretation of Vico as an historicist than it does about Vico's relationship to Plato.[13] It expresses the common assumption that if Vico has a relationship to Plato it is one of inversion.[14] Vico's interest in history does not betray philosophy as MacIntyre's charge of historicism suggests. The relationship of philosophy to its past, including its birth from poetic wisdom, is not genetic in any reductive sense.[15] MacIntyre does qualify the portrait of Vico as an historicist by reformulating his epithet as more appropriately

"Plato philologized."[16] He is closest to the truth in his third version, when he says Vico is "philology Platonized."[17] "Philology Platonized" is more accurate because Vico's "new critical art" (*la nuova arte critica*) requires philosophy to "undertake to examine philology" (*qui la filosofia si pone ad esaminare la filologia*), and this implies that philosophy is the governing art (*NS* 7). For Vico, philosophy and philology are related as strophe and antistrophe, as Aristotle observes about dialectic and rhetoric (*Rh.* 1354a). Whatever MacIntyre intended by associating Vico with historicism, his epithet "Plato historicized" is emblematic of many contemporary interpretations of Vico which Peter Burke associates with the powerful "myth of the forerunner, the John the Baptist."[18] On this view, Vico anticipates, for instance, Hegel or Herder. This error illustrates both the general one of the conceit of scholars and the specific one of making Vico too much of a skeptic.

On the other hand, one finds in the Vico literature those who read Vico as a dogmatic theologian. Some who see Vico this way are themselves theologians in the sense Vico would call dogmatic. Those who read Vico as a theologian like themselves often read more into Vico's claims about Christianity, and Catholicism in particular, than is in fact there, and as a result they miss the complex relationship of philosophy and religion in Vico. Such interpreters make Vico too much of a dogmatist. For instance, John Milbank writes that he aims "to disclose how Vico's apparently modern, 'scientific' concern with the history of religion, is, in reality, still subsumed within the framework of an Augustinian *theology*."[19] I show how Vico is not a dogmatic theologian, but a philosopher who gives "a rational civil theology of divine providence" that relies not on revelation but on the study of human nature and history (*NS* 2, 342). Only by a distortion of Vico's own claims can one read him as a dogmatic theologian.

Other commentators, who have a secular not a theological metaphysical orientation, make Vico more like themselves by reading his philosophy as secular. The translators of the *New Science*, Thomas Goddard Bergin and Max Harold Fisch, show an affinity for this way of reading Vico, when they write that "it is not possible to trace with any assurance the precise steps by which Vico moved toward a resolution of the conflict between his Catholic piety and his eminently secular if not heretical philosophy."[20] Accepting the Kantian revolution that metaphysics in the traditional sense is no longer possible, contemporary philosophers tend to assume that a thinker writing about God and providence must be a theologian (and dogmatic is the only type of theologian in this view) not a philosopher. To save Vico from this unphilosophical categorization, sympathetic commentators emphasize the secular and unorthodox aspects of Vico's thought. Such commentators, who deny there is a place in philosophy for any reference to the divine, extend their skepticism over Vico like a cloak, hiding his genuine, non-dogmatic, philosophical piety.

That Vico's philosophical ideal, his mean between extremes, is Platonic is made explicit in the *New Science*, where he criticizes the Stoics and Epicureans repeatedly and includes in his Science instead "the political philosophers, and first of all the Platonists" (*NS* 130). Vico identifies the Stoics with a metaphysics of fate and a moral philosophy which mortifies the senses, and the Epicureans with a metaphysics of chance and a moral philosophy which makes pleasure the criterion (ibid.). Vico offers a mean between these extremes. In Vichian metaphysics, human beings are not completely determined, but events are not entirely the product of chance; instead divine providence governs free human beings, turning the evil they do into good. Likewise, in moral philosophy Vico takes the middle stance on the passions, holding that moderation is what is required. Vico says that on these grounds the political philosophers, not the solitaries, are admitted to the Science, and he names as first among these the Platonists (ibid.).

Despite this clear statement of his judgments of the relative merits of these three schools of philosophy, there are interpreters who read Vico not as Platonist, as the *New Science* suggests most closely resembles his view, but as an Epicurean or a Stoic. In both cases they must posit an esoteric teaching beneath the exoteric, which they acknowledge has religious content incompatible with their readings. Those who read him as an Epicurean emphasize his early Lucretian poem.[21] They suggest that it was only because Vico's friends were imprisoned by the Inquisition for heresy that he feigned any theological or religious dimension to his thought. For an example of this reasoning, consider *The Political Philosophy of Giambattista Vico* by Frederick Vaughn.[22] Vaughn applies Leo Strauss's thesis about writing and persecution to Vico. Vaughn writes that "it is our conviction that the *New Science* is exoteric book which means that it contains two levels of meaning: one which conveys a popular and orthodox message, and another which conveys a philosophical message to philosophers."[23] As I noted above, the presumption is that philosophers do not take religious ideas seriously at a literal level.

Leon Pompa exemplifies an interpretation which makes Vico's ideal eternal history resemble Stoic fate. On this view, human beings cannot act in the face of the barbarism which Vico describes.[24] Pompa's comments on Vico's description of the barbarism of reflection are the most revealing.

Pompa writes that "both the tone of the passage, and the inconsistencies which it involves, give the impression that Vico is trying either to avoid or to conceal the deterministic character which his view of history derives from the emphasis which it places upon social conditioning. But if the *Scienza nuova* were truly deterministic, of course, even were it to enable us to diagnose our state of health as a nation, it would be unable to offer any serious practical suggestions as to how to avoid our ultimate fate. Certainly, nothing that Vico has so far offered can be thought of as a serious practical suggestion, since none seem to be in our power to control."[25] In this way Pompa moves Vico toward this metaphysical extreme of fate and the moral incapacity it entails. Pompa further claims that "the reason for Vico's failure to publish the *Practica* is almost certainly to be found in his realisation that its more optimistic prescriptions are incompatible with the basically deterministic character of the rest of the *Scienza Nuova*."[26]

Even though, unlike Pompa, Isaiah Berlin sees that Vico's providence is not deterministic, he also misses the ethical dimension of Vico's thought.[27] Berlin compares Vico to Spinoza, and he denies that Vico's philosophy has an integral moral dimension. Berlin writes that "Vico is not primarily concerned with morality, or value judgments. Like Spinoza—the adversary often in his thoughts—he seems content to understand. He does, of course, in fact make moral judgments, and in them unhesitatingly takes for granted the validity of the values embodied in his own faith and civilization; but this is quite consistent with his 'historicist', conservative thesis."[28]

In this study, I will interpret the *New Science* as expressing Vico's own stated position: that he opposes Stoicism and Epicureanism and favors social or political philosophers like the Platonists. I will also maintain the relevance of Vico's claims at the end of the *Ancient Wisdom* for understanding what he means by metaphysics in the *New Science*. When the *Ancient Wisdom* and the *New Science* are taken together, the main question is: in what way can Vico's *New Science* be understood as "a metaphysics compatible with human frailty"? If the Platonists are the example of the kind of metaphysics Vico accepts, then the question becomes what does Platonism mean to Vico, and are the connections as significant as these passages suggest?

It is not as easy to say who Plato is for Vico as it is for his other authors because there are many generations of Platonists between Plato's dialogues and Vico. Fausto Nicolini suggests a kinship metaphor for their relationship when he writes, "we must begin with a consideration of Vico as the greatest spiritual son . . . [of the] philosophical father (Plato)" (*il Vico quale grandissimo figlio spirituale . . . [del] padre filosofico (Platone)*).[29] My study affirms the kinship Nicolini asserts. Vico himself calls Socrates "the father of all philosophers," so perhaps it would be better to consider Plato as his brother.[30] However the details of the metaphor are understood, there is a deep spiritual kinship among the members of "the family of Plato."[31]

The way to understand who Plato is for Vico is not to regard the mediations of intervening Platonists as irrelevant. Paul O. Kristeller comments that much of contemporary Plato scholarship commits what Vico calls "the conceit of scholars," when it exaggerates the differences between Plato and the later Platonists because of its own anti-religious and scientific prejudices. Kristeller is right that Platonic philosophers have combined the insights of the dialogues "with notions of diverse origin, and these accretions, like tributaries of a broadening river, became integral parts of the continuing tradition." He warns modern interpreters who want "to cleanse the genuine thought of Plato from the mire of the Platonic tradition" that the "archaeologist who tries to remove the crust of later centuries from a Greek statue must be careful not to damage its incomparably subtle surface." Whereas earlier interpreters erred on the side of too closely identifying Plato and the Neoplatonists, the temptation now is "to overlook certain genuine features in Plato's thought that may be alien to modern science and philosophy but served as a starting point for his earlier interpreters."[32]

Vico does sometimes blur the identity of Plato with that of Neoplatonists, and these references will be identified. What Vico most shares with the other "earlier interpreters," from Plotinus to Pico, is the commitment to self-knowledge and the love of wisdom that goes beyond the logical and the historical or philological interpretations of Plato that dominate recent Plato scholarship. As an historian, Kristeller does not explore the sense in which a full reading of Plato involves moving from historical to philosophical questions, much less moving from contemplation to action within the philosophical domain. Vico illuminates Plato by serving as a basis for correcting rationalistic interpretations of Plato and for reopening the poetic and the paideutic nature of the dialogues. Plato also illuminates Vico; Vico was still feeling the force of the river of Platonism that is drying up in our time.

Given the complexities of Platonism, what is the best method for uncovering the layers of Vico's Platonism? How can one read Vico with Plato across so many centuries? The answer lies in Vico's own method of discovering the truth in history. Vico's account of the relationship between philosophy and history dictates that I must end, rather than begin, by reading Plato's dialogues with Vico's *New Science*. I have already mentioned Vico's method, which is summed up in the claim that "philosophy must undertake to examine philology" (*NS* 7). Using this method to answer the question of who Plato is for Vico involves seeing how Vico discovers the true (*il vero*) in the certain (*il certo*) for the family of thinkers that has its birth with Socrates, the hero of Plato's philosophical poetry. Such a method views Platonism as a human thing (*cosa umana*) that is born, lives its life, declines, and dies. And yet the human soul is immortal, so there is an analogous transcendent teaching of Platonism in its many embodiments which is its soul.

My study considers the kinship of Vico and Plato by focusing on the major mediating influences on Vico's view of Platonism as well as on the dialogues themselves. I will consider the major texts which influenced Vico's understanding of Plato and Socrates: Pico's *Oration on the Dignity of Man*, Augustine's *City of God*, and Plato's dialogues, in particular, the *Republic*, the *Timaeus*, the *Critias*, the *Statesman*, the *Laws*, and the *Symposium*. Mediation of earlier philosophers' views of shared predecessors is not in any way an exact science, nor do I pretend it is. It is impossible to know for certain whether Vico knew a particular line of a dialogue from having read that dialogue or from a later Platonic commentary. Delineating these ideas cannot result in the sort of exactitude the genre of source criticism desires, nor does this study engage in such historical research for its own sake. I do argue that seeing Vico in the context of such predecessors makes visible elements in his thought that do not stand out when reading him alongside Hegel or Herder, to choose two notable examples. Above all my subject is a family of thinkers who as such will have more in common than not. This does not mean that they are without significant disagreement among themselves over the nature of humanity, philosophy, divinity, and other central shared questions. Through exploring such differences, the unique nature of Vico's Platonism will emerge.

The best way to think about this study's descent through the history of Platonism is Vico's *la storia ideale eterna*; the best way to imagine this study's descent is to turn to the poet W. B. Yeats's image of history as a "widening gyre."[33] River metaphors for history, such as Kristeller's, are too simplistic to account for the complexities of cyclical history. Yeats himself made the connection between his philosophy of history and Vico's, so it is not surprising that his images for history can be helpful in understanding Vico's central insight about the cycles of history.[34] Drawing on one of Yeats's most famous images, we can imagine Platonism as a gyre or spiral that has Socrates as its origin and center. As in Vico's *New Science* history is divided into *corso* and *ricorso*, so in Yeats's philosophy of history there is an ancient cycle and a Christian cycle.[35] In the *ricorso* Socrates is mediated through

Christianity as the new age of gods and heroes precedes the new age of humans and with it the *ricorso* of philosophy. The farther from the origin of philosophy in the figure of Socrates the more complex the genealogy of the Platonist. Augustine can still be seen as connected to the circles of Socrates and Plato, but Augustine considers two origins, that of philosophy and of Christian theology. Pico encompasses the circles of Augustine, Plato, and the origin of Socrates. Vico, the furthest circle I will consider in the history of Platonism, sees Plato through the mediation of Pico and Augustine, and continues to see Socrates through the mediation of Plato. By tracing the spiral backwards to Socrates, the reader can reconnect the disconnected references to Platonism in Vico as well as gain insight into a fundamental conversation of kindred souls across centuries.

My search for the true nature of Vico's kinship with Plato and Platonism is a Vichian project, but not one Vico himself undertook. Vico gives us many clues about the importance of Plato for his thought, but he does not as clearly separate the true Plato from confused memories as he does in his discovery of the true Homer. As Vico found with Homer, so with Plato, the errors are as instructive as the truth, both about human knowing and human nature. In the end, finding out who Plato is for Vico goes a long way toward discovering who Vico is as a philosopher.

Plato is especially important for any philosophical study of Vico because part of the answer to who Plato is for Vico is that he identifies Plato with philosophy itself. Philosophy and Plato consider human beings as they "ought to be."[36] In this way, Plato plays a role in Vico's *New Science* more analogous to Homer than to his other authors. Alfred North Whitehead is famous for claiming that Western philosophy is "a series of footnotes to Plato," and Ken Wilber has made the insightful addition that these are "fractured footnotes."[37] Platonism has been fractured almost to complete destruction since the Renaissance, and Vico can be seen as extending to another generation the family of Plato. Plato is the intellect of the Greek people as Homer was the sense; his is the rational metaphysics that builds on the poetic. Vico's *New Science* gives renewed life to this Platonic metaphysics.

I am aware that, stated in this way, my study may seem to be another instance of taking a part of Vico for the whole. The proof that my study is not merely another act of interpretive alchemy will lie in the reader's assessment of the correctness of the textual exegesis.[38] The strength of my approach is that it avoids the extremes Vico himself criticized: skepticism and dogmatism in epistemology, and Stoicism and Epicureanism in metaphysics and moral philosophy. Vico himself invites the Platonists into the school of the *New Science*, and calls Plato his first author. Vico may not have noticed some of the links between his thought and the details of the family of Plato that I locate in this study, but he does point the reader in this direction.

Further, this study is conducted with Vico's own method rather than imposing an external one. There is no way for me to defend against those who insist upon an esoteric reading in which Vico's direct claims become useless, other than to ask them to consider the coherence of his thought without the hypothesis of an esoteric meaning. While I acknowledge that the study of Vico's other three authors as well as specific studies of his original ideas illumine his thought, my inquiry begins to remedy the neglect of Vico's relationship to his first author which has distorted his philosophical significance. To ignore Vico's Platonic roots is to miss the heart of Vico. If this attention to Plato is interpretive alchemy, then at least it converts lesser metals into gold.

This study requires the reader to follow the subtle interplay of Vico's ideas with previous generations of the family of Plato, whose father, Socrates, lived over two thousand years before Vico, so a description of the topics of each of the book's three parts may help to orient the reader.

The first part of my study, "The Dignity of Pico," focuses on Pico's *Oration on the Dignity of Man* in order to provide a concise introduction to a humanist reading of Vico's *New Science*. Its order follows the three aspects of the Renaissance which Vico admires: history (chapter 1), poetry (chapter 2), and eloquence (chapter 3). Vico's answer to the question of the relationship between history, poetry, and wisdom is only intelligible against the background of Renaissance poetic theology. His rejection of this tradition is the source of his doctrine of poetic wisdom. Although Vico criticizes the Renaissance understanding of poetic theology, he shares the idea that poetry is definitive of human nature. Reading Vico's inaugural orations with Pico's *Oration* reveals that both philosophers emphasize the dignity of human beings as makers of themselves and the necessity of moral education or *paideia*. In chapter 3, I introduce Pico's correspondence on eloquence in order to dispel the misconception that eloquence and wisdom are incompatible, and to remove this obstacle to seeing Vico's kinship to Plato. Finally, I consider the eloquence of the writings of Pico and Vico. I show that, instead of criticizing both thinkers for random eclecticism, one should praise them for embodying "wisdom speaking copiously," which Vico calls "the flower of wisdom."

The second part, "The Piety of Augustine," shows that Vico balances the sense of human dignity which he shares with Pico with a humility arising from an acknowledgment of the fallen condition of human beings and a belief in divine providence which he shares with Augustine. Most of this part is devoted to understanding the Augustinian roots of Vico's "rational civil theology of divine providence." Both Vico's typology of theology (chapter 4) and his idea of divine providence (chapter 5) are indebted to Augustine's *City of God*, yet Vico's conclusions differ from Augustine's in both cases. In Vico's mixture of natural (or rational) with civil (or poetic) theology, he distinguishes between the certain and the true, and generates correlative notions of poetic and philosophical providence. Finally, in chapter 6, I consider Vico's acceptance of the idea that human beings are fallen as a counterpoint to the human dignity emphasized in the first part. Vico agrees with Augustine's critique of Platonic pride, but humbles philosophy by placing it in the larger context of human life and history rather than subordinating it to theology. Vico is unique in responding to Augustine's critique of Platonic pride while remaining a philosopher who is committed to the ability of *paideia* to cure corruption. Reading Vico in light of Augustine reveals his pious humanism.

In the third part, "The Philosophical Heroism of Plato," I explore Vico's references to Plato's dialogues themselves. In this part, I address the commonality between Plato and Vico which is not mediated through later Platonists. I show that the connection between the thought of Vico and Plato involves their most original and central ideas. In chapter 7, I elucidate how the philosophy of history contained in Plato's dialogues, in particular the relationship between the ideal and the historical, "what ought to be" and "what is," anticipates elements of Vico's ideal eternal history. I conclude that ideal eternal history can be described as a new Platonic form, that of history itself. Moving from history to poetry, as in the previous two parts, in chapter 8, I address the quarrel between philosophy and poetry. The key to seeing that Vico and Plato are not far apart even on poetry is that Plato does not reject all uses of the imagination, but makes a division between true and false images. In this way, the solution to the compatibility of philosophy and poetry is analogous to the one for eloquence. The discussion of Plato as a serious poet and his truthful image or *eikon* leads to an interpretation of Vico's frontispiece to the *New Science* as a Platonic *eikon*. As Vico's frontispiece is the summary *eikon* for the *New Science*, so Plato's *eikon* of Socrates contains the wisdom of the dialogues. In conclusion, in chapter 9, I return for a third time to *paideia*, and explore the significance of Vico's praise of Plato for inventing philosophical heroism, (*NS* 515, 1041). The ideas of Plato and Vico on philosophical heroism reveal their kinship more than any other aspect of their thought, for it is the shared educational goal of their philosophy. This dimension of Vico's Platonism, which he also calls "heroic mind," comes directly from Plato and takes the reader all the way back to the origin of philosophy in Socrates.

We live in an age when philosophical falcons have difficulty hearing their falconer; yet Vico teaches that through memory we can imagine a heroism suited to our times, a philosophical heroism. The reader is asked to follow a circuitous path, descending through the spiraling generations of the family of Plato in the anticipation that the call of the falconer will become more audible. As we descend, we recall from Pico a confidence in the dignity of the human mind, from Augustine, a humble piety which acknowledges both human corruption and divine providence, and from the serious poetry of Plato, a desire to imitate the philosophical heroism of Socrates. When all the textual details are delineated, what emerges as the heart of the kinship of Vico and Plato is the shared educational ideal of the heroic mind. This heroic desire to know, to make, and to govern oneself is the faintly heard call of the philosophical falconer, Socrates.

PART ONE

THE DIGNITY OF PICO

If strength fails, there shall surely be praise for daring;
and to have wished for great things is enough.

Propertius, quoted by Pico in his *Oration*.

Introduction

Vico's Praise of the Renaissance

Vico praises the Renaissance philosophers and shares their commitment to poetry, history, and eloquence. Ironically, seeing through their mistakes about poetry and history left an even greater mark on Vico's philosophy. Vico shares their humanist ideal of eloquence, but completely rethinks the relationship of wisdom and philosophy to their poetic origins. All of these themes become clearly visible when one considers Vico in relation to Giovanni Pico della Mirandola.

In the column for Greece on the Chronological Table prefacing the *New Science*, Vico marks the birth of philosophy, saying, "Socrates originates rational moral philosophy," "Plato flourishes in metaphysics," and "Athens is resplendent with all the arts of the most cultivated humanity." Seen in the light of Vico's central insight of "ideal eternal history," fifteenth- and sixteenth- century Italian art and thought is aptly named the "Renaissance" by historians, for it is the return of the philosophers in the *ricorso* of the third age, a rebirth of the human times. In Vico's *Autobiography*, he writes that the Renaissance "contributed so much to poetry, history, and eloquence that all Greece in the time of its utmost learning and grace of speech seemed to have risen again in Italy" (*A* 132). Before turning to Pico specifically, it will be helpful to recall Vico's narrative of the development of his thought and how the Renaissance Platonists are portrayed in his *Autobiography*.

Following the complex narrative of Vico's study and thought leading up to the *New Science*, one is not presented, as some scholars have thought, with a radical break. When Vico returned from his reading of classical and Tuscan poetry at Vattolla, his study guided by his first two authors, Plato and Tacitus, he cast himself as "a stranger in his own land" (ibid.). Cartesianism had made Aristotle's physics "a laughingstock" and "as for metaphysics, which in the sixteenth century had placed in the highest ranks of literature such men as Marsilio Ficino, Pico della Mirandola, Agostino Nifo and Agostino Steuchio, Giacopo Mazzoni, Alessandro Piccolomini, Matteo Acquaviva, and Francesco Patrizi . . . was now thought worthy only of being shut up in the cloisters and as for Plato, an occasional passage was turned to poetic use, or quoted to parade an erudite memory, and that was all" (ibid.). Hopes were raised temporarily by "a great and sudden revolution in literary affairs in Naples" credited in part to the founding of an academy by the Duke of Medinaceli (*A* 137). But just as later Vico would not have the distinguished morning law chair despite all indications pointing toward his success, so "just when it was thought that the best literature of the sixteenth century was to be reestablished there for a long time to come, the departure of the duke-viceroy gave rise to a new order of things which cast it down in a very short time and contrary to every expectation" (ibid.).

When metaphysics began to be taken up again, the style followed Descartes not the Renaissance Platonists; the modern metaphysicians "studied it not, as Marsilio and others had done, in the works of men like Plato and Plotinus (which had made fruitful so many great men of letters in the sixteenth century), but in the Meditations of René Descartes and its companion piece his book On Method, wherein he disapproves the study of languages, orators, historians and poets" (*A* 138). The three achievements of the Renaissance—poetry, history, and eloquence—are precisely those that Descartes excludes from his metaphysics (*A* 132, 137). Vico's praise of the Renaissance excellence in poetry, history, and eloquence signals his rejection of the modern disdain for these arts by modern philosophers preferring less imaginative more ratiocinative sciences.

These remarks are instructive for discerning the differences Vico came to see between Renaissance Platonism and modern, especially Cartesian, metaphysics. Vico implies that he had hoped for a reestablishment of literary models from the Renaissance, and perhaps saw his own "New Science or metaphysic" (*NS* 31) as the fulfillment of the anticipated revolution that was cast down by misfortune. The fact that Vico does not point out that he once thought with Doria that Descartes might be an ally not an enemy, either is ignored out of a desire to conceal his mistake, or to underscore the gulf he eventually saw. Vico tried to convince Doria, as he had himself become aware, that all that was good in Descartes he shared with the Platonists, and what Descartes rejected was essential for fruitful metaphysics (*A* 138).[1] "What Doria admired . . . as sublime, great and new in Descartes, Vico remarked to be old and common knowledge among the Platonists" (ibid.). The Renaissance Platonists serve as important mediators of Plato for Vico, and there is no hint that he thinks they betray Plato as he came to believe Descartes does.

The most obvious allusions to the Italian Platonists in Vico's writings, in particular Ficino and Pico, are in the inaugural orations.[2] The *Autobiography* provides the context for understanding the enduring presence of Plato in Vico's thought, including how Plato's ideas were mediated by the Renaissance. The significance of the inaugural orations for understanding Vico's thought as a whole is often obscured by interpreting the metaphysics of the orations as merely Cartesian rather than Platonic essentially and Cartesian only incidentally in the formulation of some arguments, such as the immortality of the soul and the nature of mind. The Cartesian reading of the inaugural orations is based more on the contemporary association of Plato and Descartes made possible by putting both under the epistemological label "rationalist" than any evidence in Vico. There is no indication that Vico rejects the Platonism of these inaugural orations along with the Cartesian formulations. That Vico did not always see clearly that the differences between the Cartesian and the Platonic metaphysics overshadowed the similarities may account for the hyperbole in the *Autobiography*. There are aspects of the early admiration of Descartes in the inaugural orations, but there is no reason to think the Platonism in the inaugural orations is reducible to the Cartesian.

Vico himself saw the inaugural orations as lacking a unifying principle, but this does not imply a complete rejection. Consider the similarities between the philosophy of education in these first orations and the last orations; "On the Heroic Mind" and "The Academies and the Relation between Philosophy and Eloquence" retain the themes of self-knowledge and wisdom characteristic of the Platonic claims of the early orations. Vico summarizes the inaugural orations in the *Autobiography*, showing their Platonic themes clearly, so he did not intend to conceal his early Platonism as he rejected the Cartesianism. He preserved what was good in the inaugural orations in his summaries. Vico was glad he did not publish these, not because all of what he said was false, but because the orations lacked a single principle that would unite all the knowledge of things divine and human. Vico acknowledges that what he said was not yet new, heightening the sense that he is moving toward the heroic discovery of *New Science* which will provide such a new principle.

All of Vico's studies had been leading up to a single heroic moment, just as Pico proposed the disputation at Rome as the crown of his education. Consider the following summary of Vico's insight that inspired first the *Universal Law* and culminated in the *New Science*. Vico writes that "prepared by all these studies and the knowledge he has acquired, and by these four authors whom he admired above all others and desired to turn to the wise of the Catholic religion, Vico finally came to perceive that there was not yet in the world of letters a system so devised as to bring the best philosophy, that of Plato made subordinate to the Christian faith, into harmony with a philology" (*A* 155). This new system of reconciling philosophy and philology, the contemplative and the active, things and words, was a new way of ordering all of his previous thought. Vico sees this project as the culmination of his earlier thought, saying that "by this insight Vico's mind arrived at a clear conception of what it had been vaguely seeking in the first inaugural orations and had sketched somewhat clumsily in the dissertation *On the Method of Studies of Our Time*, and a little more distinctly in the *Metaphysics*" (*A* 155-56). Far from rejecting his earlier *Metaphysics*, the *Ancient Wisdom*, which concludes with the statement that it is "a metaphysics compatible with human frailty," Vico remarks that he was closest to the new insight in that work (*AW* 109). As in the events in his life, in his writings there is a gradual movement, with occasional setbacks, to a heroic moment. The description of Vico's irenic goal of seeking harmony of many ideas and practices sounds very much like what Pico sought in his *Nine Hundred Theses*.[3]

The comparison between Vico's *New Science* and Pico's *Nine Hundred Theses* has a basis in the text of the *Autobiography*, which suggests it is possible that Vico viewed their projects as comparable, at least in scope. Vico quotes from "a solemn public opening of studies" in 1719 in which he sets out his idea for a New Science, and reports that "some considered the argument, particularly in the third part, more magnificent than effectual, saying that Pico della Mirandola had not assumed such a burden when he proposed to sustain 'conclusions concerning all the knowable,' for he left aside the great and major part of it, namely philology, which, treating of countless matters of religions, languages, laws, customs, property rights, conveyances, sovereign powers, governments, classes and the like, is in its beginnings incomplete, obscure, unreasonable, incredible, and without hope of reduction to scientific principles" (*A* 157). Despite Pico's interest in philology, and mastery of Greek, Hebrew, and Aramaic or Chaldean, Vico would consider him as among the philosophers who failed by half in not confirming philosophy with philology (*NS* 140). Vico's initial articulation of his discovery was greeted with skepticism, if not the open hostility Pico faced. Because of the reaction he received, Vico decided to write a prospectus which would give the preliminary idea of his *Universal Law*, which he would write next, and circulate it in the North, from whose scholars he always sought approval. "A New Science is Essayed" (*nova scientia tentatur*) would be a chapter of this jurisprudential work, and when considered with his application of his ideas to interpreting Homer's *Iliad* and *Odyssey*, it contains recognizable origins of the *New Science* (*A* 158; 160).[4]

Following this developmental view, without rigid breaks from early metaphysical writings, we can see that for Vico the *New Science* is the culmination of the project explained as the union of Plato subordinated to Christian faith and in harmony with philology. An obvious parallel for this system of Platonic metaphysics subordinated to Christian faith is Ficino's *Platonic Theology*. But Vico has much more in common with the approach of Giovanni Pico della Mirandola than any of the other Italian Platonists. Pico, of course, shared many ideas with Ficino, but was not hesitant to disagree with him. Both Pico and Vico proudly proclaimed that they were members of no one school, and what they knew they taught themselves, like Epicurus.[5] Pico and Vico have certain characteristics in common beyond what Ficino and Pico share; there is a boldness of thought, in sheer scope, as well as specific parallels. In particular, the complex relationship between philosophy and eloquence in Pico clarifies what is at stake for a Platonist to advocate eloquence as an ideal while trying to remain invulnerable to Plato's criticisms of the abuse of rhetoric. Pico highlights aspects of Vico not illuminated by other Italian Platonists, as well as the ones shared by all of them.

Chapter 1

History: Poetic Wisdom and Chronology

What is the relationship between history, poetry, and wisdom? The Renaissance humanists, and even more so the Italian Platonists, answered this question very differently than previous thinkers.[1] Aristotle judged history to be less philosophical than poetry, since history only dealt with particulars not universals (*Po.* 1451b). The Neoplatonists and Stoics gave allegorical interpretations of the Greek fables to illustrate their philosophical ideas, but without the same sense of historical anticipation or confirmation. Until Augustine history was not a philosophical problem, and for him it was sacred history that was the primary concern. In contrast, the Renaissance articulated a sense of history as a philosophical problem which we find prominently in Vico as well. In the *New Science* ideal eternal history (*la storia ideale eterna*) is universal as well as particular (*NS* 349).

In the Renaissance the boundaries of history and poetry, like that of rhetoric and poetry, became indistinct.[2] A commonplace held that the first theologians were poets. Orpheus, Hermes Trismegistus, and Zoroaster were seen as important sources, worthy of being placed alongside the great philosophers and saints in the transmission of wisdom down through the ages. As a striking witness to the belief in such a transmission of wisdom, the narthex of the cathedral at Sienna displayed a mosaic of Hermes Trismegistus with a deferent Moses.[3] Vico's references to these poetic theologians can puzzle a reader unfamiliar with Renaissance texts and become a significant obstacle to understanding the *New Science*. But far from being esoteric in his references to such figures, Vico assigns them a less mysterious, though in some ways equally significant, role in his chronology and in his account of poetic wisdom.

According to the Renaissance commonplace, these first poets hid philosophical wisdom beneath poetic veils. Vico is responding to this view of poetic wisdom in the longest book of the *New Science* (Book 2, "Poetic Wisdom"), the application of which is another book (Book 3, "The Discovery of the True Homer"). Without the Renaissance errors about poetic theology, the *New Science* would have been a very different book, if it would have been written at all. Vico founded the New Science with its new vision of history, poetry, and wisdom at least in part because he saw through the errors of the Renaissance poetic theology, or *prisca theologia* as it is also called. I will first explain further the Renaissance commonplace of poetic theology by focusing on Pico's use of it, and then turn to Vico's criticism of this error or conceit, as he calls it, and his alternative.

Poetic Wisdom

Pico's *Oration* has enjoyed an unusual fame, though no one ever seems to read much beyond the opening fable, which explains the traditional addition of "on the dignity of man" (*de hominis dignitatis*) to the simple title "Oration" (*Oratio*).[4] As typically interpreted, the first half contains the philosophical expression of the humanist idea of "the dignity of man" and the second half Pico's unique syncretism or doctrine of "the unity of truth."[5] This simple division is one imposed by scholars, not a natural division. The *Oration* does open with a striking view of human nature and its wondrousness, and does in its second half indicate that truth can be found from many sources, but these ideas are not the ones Pico used to structure his speech. Reading Pico's *Oration* as primarily about the dignity of man began early. Bartolomeo Facio and Giannozzo Manetti had already established a tradition of answering *De Misere Hominis Conditionis* by Lothario Dei Segni, Pope Innocent III, written in 1195.[6] The father of humanism himself, Francesco Petrarch, was explicitly asked by the Grand Prior of the Carthusians to fulfill the Pope's promise to present the other side of the human condition.[7] In this context, it is likely that Pico was viewed by Renaissance contemporaries as continuing this project, which the future Pope himself indicated was incomplete without an account of the dignity of human beings to balance his account of their misery.

On the model of an inaugural oration, Pico wrote a preface for a disputation in which he proposed to defend nine hundred theses at Rome, which he was never allowed to give. An inaugural oration had two parts; the first was an often hyperbolic defense of one's chosen discipline, and the second was a proposal for a course of studies.[8] Following this model, Pico wrote the *Oration* as a defense of philosophy as well as an explanation of the course of study, in this case, the content of the nine hundred theses, why he should dispute at all, and why this number was required. Pico's transitional questions reveal that he sees himself as defending philosophy from her detractors throughout the *Oration*, and that he himself stands accused with her. Pico argues that he must call on as many authorities as possible from various schools, since he is defending philosophy herself and not only one school.

Poetic theology is not itself argued for in the *Oration*, but is a presupposition of Pico's view of the opinions of various authorities marshaled to defend his idea of the importance and the dignity of philosophy. In particular, he finds many sources among the poetic theologians for the idea that through philosophy human beings can learn to use their free will to become like angels instead of like beasts (*O* 226–27, 229). He also uses poetic theology to argue that if wisdom is something that has flowed from one continent to another, then to read only the Latin authors would not make sense if one were really a philosopher, really a lover of wisdom (*O* 244).

If one reads the *Oration* expecting neither a doctrine of the dignity of man nor the unity of truth or syncretism, one finds an eloquent speech about the purpose of philosophy. The author himself is an example of the resistance genuine philosophers encounter. His plans were thwarted by the envy of doctors who, as Pico makes clear, did not deserve the name philosopher (*O* 238). Pico emphasizes in his *Oration* that his youth was a major factor in not letting him entertain so many theses. Gianfrancesco Pico in his *Life of Pico* concurs that the charges of heresy should be attributed to the envy of his enemies.[9]

In the *Oration* Pico makes several references to poetic theology, one explicitly about the idea of it, saying he will write a work proving Homer used fables as veils for philosophical ideas. "Homer persevered, whom I shall sometime prove, in my Poetic Theology, to have concealed this philosophy beneath the wanderings of Ulysses, just as he concealed all others" (*O* 248). This claim is significant because it shows great self-consciousness about his own allegorical interpretations of myths, such as in his *Commentary on the Canzone of Benivieni*.[10] On the birth of Venus, for instance, he writes "under the veil of fable the ancient theologians of the gentiles tell how she was born of him."[11] In fact, the *Commentary* contains all we have of Pico's intended work on poetic theology.[12] This projected future treatise on poetic theology was meant to be a better account of the subject than Ficino had given, just as he intended his commentary on the *Symposium* to be read against Ficino's *De Amore*. Pico's references to poetic theology also demonstrate that he did not think his *Oration* was proving "the unity of truth" based on the poetic theology.

Pico's own estimate of Hermes Trismegistus as one authority among many is indicative of his attitude toward poetic theology in general (*O* 223). Pico knows he is not breaking completely new ground with his use of poetic theology, saying "I have not been content to add to the tenets held in common many teachings taken from the ancient theology of Hermes Trismegistus, many from the doctrines of the Chaldeans and of Pythagoras, and many from the occult mysteries of the Hebrews" (*O* 245). Pico believes such appeals to poetic theology are legitimate, yet he does not want merely to repeat what has been said already. This commonplace of poetic theology, which Pico isolates by distancing himself from it, is what is essential for understanding Vico's poetic wisdom.

Since Pico is not the origin of this idea of poetic theology, and we do not have the promised treatise, it may be helpful briefly to consider the claims of the earlier proponents of this idea to clarify what Pico meant before turning to Vico's criticism. Petrarch anticipates his reader's question about poetic theology, asking rhetorically "who is the source of these ideas?"[13] His answer is Varro, and also Suetonius. Petrarch writes that "the first theologians among the gentiles certainly were the poets," adding that "among these Orpheus was especially ennobled, whom Augustine mentions in the eighteenth book of the *City of God.*"[14] Petrarch's admiration of Augustine is well known, so his view of the theological poets is most likely from the discussion of Varro in the *City of God.* Turning to Boccaccio, we see how firmly established this commonplace was; for in *The Genealogy of the Gentile Gods* Boccaccio sums up saying that only a fool does not see that the fables are poetic veils.[15] Marsilio Ficino gives an elaborate chronology which details how, as Pico said, "wisdom flows from the East, to the Greeks, to us"(*O* 244). In the *argumentum* to Ficino's translation of *Poimander* his genealogy of sages places Hermes, the supposed author of this text, first: "He [Mercurius Trismegistus] is called the first author of theology: he was succeeded by Orpheus, who came second amongst the ancient theologians: Aglaophemus, who had been initiated into the sacred teaching of Orpheus, was succeeded in the theology of Pythagoras, whose disciple was Philolaus, the teacher of our Divine Plato. Hence there is one ancient theology (*prisca theologia*) . . . taking its origin in Mercurius and culminating in the Divine Plato."[16] The *Poimander* is one of the texts Vico names as fraudulent, as will be discussed below (*NS* 128). Nevertheless, in the *Theologia Platonica* Ficino adopts a chronology more like Pletho's, and ranks Hermes Trismegistus second to Zoroaster.[17] The details of the variations in genealogies are not as important as understanding the idea of the ancient theology. Even Boccaccio admitted he was confused about the chronologies, though he was certain that these gentile poets were guided by divine providence.[18]

For Ficino, Plato was the descendent of an ancient wisdom passed down from Hermes or Zoroaster to Orpheus to Pythagoras, and the Neoplatonists like Iamblichus and Proclus had understood the hidden wisdom of Plato. Ficino writes to Bessarion that Plato, who is for Ficino the last *priscus theologus*, was to be read as containing hidden wisdom.[19] That Pico moves quickly from interpreting Greek poetry allegorically to doing the same for the fable of the birth of *Eros* in the *Symposium* in the *Commentary* suggests that he too considered Plato one of these poetic theologians. In the *Oration* he declares that "Pythagoras, Democritus, and Plato all traveled to study the latter [good magic]" and cites praise of "the science of the Divine of Zoroaster" in Plato's *Alcibiades* and "the magic of Zamolxis" in the *Charmides* (*O* 247–48). For Vico, unlike Ficino and probably also unlike Pico, saying that a philosopher conceals philosophical wisdom is not at all the same as saying a poet does (especially one as early and important as Homer). Paying attention to Plato's images is good, but the problem arose when these Platonists wanted to read every author as if he were Plato, or at least as if the poet were a philosopher as clever as themselves. This projection of philosophical ideas on pre-philosophical poetry is what Vico calls the conceit of scholars.

With the commonplace of poetic theology recalled to memory, one can see more clearly the centrality of Vico's critique of this tradition. Vico knew from the historian Isaac Causabon that a second century Christian Neoplatonist, not the Egyptian Hermes, conceived as contemporary of Moses, wrote *Poimander* (*NS* 47). So Vico knows why when Ficino read the *Poimander* he saw in Hermes a link between Christianity and Moses. The poetic theology had been based on misdated Hellenistic Neoplatonic texts, which generated the correspondences that so fascinated Renaissance thinkers from Petrarch to Giordano Bruno. Vico does not remain untouched by ideas which grew out of this error, but he is aware of the historical obstacles to any claims of a continuous succession of sages all teaching the same wisdom. Frances Yates observes that "this huge historical error was to have amazing results."[20] Vico stands on the other side of this fruitful illusion; yet the *New Science* was also its last fruit.

Eugenio Garin holds that in Vico's "clear affirmation of the fallacy of the most ancient knowledge set at the origins, of a *prisca philosophia* or *theologia*, or an original revelation . . . one immediately sees Vico's clear detachment from those very Renaissance positions—Platonic or neo-Platonic—to which the historiography of this century has so often wanted to bring him back."[21] I agree with Garin that Vico is rejecting the *prisca theologia* as formulated by Ficino, Pico, and Steuco, but I am emphasizing how Vico transforms this tradition rather than simply rejecting it. Vico certainly rejects the claims made for the esoteric wisdom of Hermes, Orpheus, and Zoroaster, but he does not dismiss the questions of poetic wisdom and chronology. The reason Vico must provide such a reinterpretation is apparent once one sees the important role these figures played in solving a basic conflict of the Renaissance, that of the continuity of wisdom given the disparities between sacred and gentile histories. The differences between Vico and the Renaissance thinkers should not prevent one from exploring how Vico takes their views of poetic wisdom and chronology as a starting-point for his own search for the ideal and eternal in history.

The *New Science* is punctuated by references to the conceit of scholars, and some of the most crucial ideas are presented as alternatives to the characteristic errors in chronology and poetic wisdom. Vico both opens and closes the longest book of the *New Science*, "Poetic Wisdom," by contrasting his conception of poetic wisdom with the errors of those suffering under the conceit of scholars and nations. The axiom he cites is a clear rejection of the tradition of poetic theology with its genealogies of wisdom: "To this conceit of nations is added that of scholars, who will have it that what they know is as old as the world" (axiom 4, *NS* 127). Vico immediately applies this axiom to the texts of the poetic theology and the modes of interpretation of its advocates: "This axiom disposes of all the opinions of the scholars concerning the matchless wisdom of the ancients. It convicts of fraud the oracles of Zoroaster the Chaldean, of Anacharsis the Scythian, which have not come down to us, the *Poimander* of Thrice-great Hermes, the *Orphics* (or verses of Orpheus), and the Golden Verses of Pythagoras, as all the more discerning critics agree. It further condemns as impertinent all the mystic meanings with which the Egyptian hieroglyphs are endowed by the scholars, and the philosophical allegories which they have read into the Greek fables" (*NS* 128). Vico cannot accept their solution, but he keeps the question, and makes it central as axiom 4.

In a similar passage Vico says that "in this way the later discoveries of esoteric wisdom were attributed to the first authors of vulgar wisdom; and [poetic characters like] Zoroaster in the East, Thrice-great Hermes in Egypt, Orpheus in Greece, Pythagoras in Italy, originally lawgivers, were finally believed to have been philosophers, as Confucius is today in China" (*NS* 427). In the explanation of the column of Zoroaster, Vico makes his most explicit statement that whereas Zoroaster and the others are really poetic characters, through the conceit of scholars, they are made over in the image of Pythagorean-Platonic philosophers: "But the conceit of scholars, who will have it that whatever they know is as old as the world, has made of them [poetic characters] one individual man brimming with the highest esoteric wisdom, and has attached to him the oracles of philosophy, which do nothing but palm off as old a very new doctrine, namely that of the

Pythagoreans and the Platonists" (*NS* 59). Vico concludes the book on "Poetic Wisdom" with the claim that by attempting to elevate the earlier poets to our age's standards for wisdom, scholars "have in effect denied it this honor by their very efforts to affirm it" (*NS* 779). This passage leaves us with many questions. If the Renaissance was wrong about the relationship of wisdom to history and poetry, then what is right? What does Vico mean that these figures were really poetic characters? Vico's reinterpretation has three interrelated aspects: a new understanding of poetic wisdom, a new chronology, and a new way in which the Egyptians provide the model for chronology.

The introduction to "Poetic Wisdom" (*NS* 361) recalls the axiom that "all histories of gentile nations have had fabulous beginnings" (*NS* 202). To this connection of history and poetry, he adds wisdom; the first sages were theological poets. Until now this poetic wisdom was admired for the wrong reasons, the main one being the conceit of scholars that led them to think that the poets' wisdom was philosophical. The errors are important, for Vico maintains that providence allowed such deceptions in order for philosophy to arise (*NS* 362). Pico and the others did not commit these errors because they were not clever enough; rather they were too refined, for to understand "the way in which this first human thinking arose among the children of the human race, characterized above all by robust imagination, [we had] to descend from these human and refined natures of ours to those quite wild and savage natures, which we cannot at all imagine and can comprehend only with great effort" (*NS* 338). Vico emphasizes in the *New Science* the difficulty of discovering that the first humans were poets who communicated by imaginative universals (*NS* 34). The Renaissance advocates of poetic theology were right that there is a continuity to be found in ancient wisdom, but their assumptions about the nature of language kept them from seeing the true relationship of poetry, history, and wisdom.

Consider Pico's claim in the *Oration* that "all wisdom has flowed from the East to the Greeks to us" (*O* 244). The metaphor of a fountain of wisdom assumes that wisdom, like water, is the same at any time or place (*O* 252). Vico instead employs an organic metaphor that acknowledges the temporal development of human wisdom, in accordance with his view that all things move in cycles, with a beginning and an end. "And it may be said that in the fables the nations have in a rough way and in the language of the human senses described the beginnings of this world of sciences. . . . the theological poets were the sense and the philosophers the intellect of human wisdom" (*NS* 779). The mistake of the Renaissance thinkers was to see the poetic theology as linear, like Catholicism's apostolic succession. Vico transforms the poetic theology by learning from the Egyptians that history is marked by a cyclic movement of ages. The wisdom of an early age is not the same as the later, and ignorance of the historical, epochal development of nations and consciousness is what made the error of the poetic theology so blatant to Vico, and made criticizing it at length a dialectically suitable way to present his new insight.

The doctrines of wisdom in both the Renaissance conception of poetic theology and Vico's revised notion of vulgar wisdom depend on basic assumptions about the nature of language. Vico's position is summed up in the axiom of the conceit of scholars which condemns the allegorical interpretation of theological poetry (NS 127). Such allegorical interpretations require the ability to convey a non-literal meaning through the literal that is not yet developed in the age of theological poets. In this way, allegorical interpretation of ancient poetry rests on the false assumption that prose is the primary mode of language. Vico argues that, on the contrary, "by a necessity of human nature, poetic style arose before prose style, just as, by the same necessity, the fables, or imaginative universals, arose before the rational or philosophic universals, which were formed through the medium of prose speech" (NS 460, cf. 409). This mistake about the development of language is manifested in the presumption that philosophic meaning is the literal or true meaning and the poetic is only embellishment or guise. This conviction is the source of the Renaissance's frequent use of the metaphor of "the poetic veil" for the hidden wisdom of the poets.

In contrast, Vico's metaphor for the discovery of the truth in ancient poetry is not the poetic veil but the poetic tree of knowledge. Imagination for Vico is a productive power which is crude and completely sensory. All the arts and sciences have their roots in imagination (*fantasia*), and so are entirely poetic. Since metaphysics is the governing science, "the wisdom of the ancients was that of the theological poets," and because "the origins of all things must by nature have been crude: for all these reasons we must trace the beginnings of poetic wisdom to a crude metaphysics. From this, as from a trunk, there branch out from one limb logic, morals, economics, and politics, all poetic; and from another, physics, the mother of cosmography and astronomy, the latter of which gives their certainty to its two daughters, chronology and geography—all likewise poetic" (NS 367). The crude, vulgar wisdom of the poets and lawgivers made possible the arts and sciences. These heroes of the poetic theology are wrongly ascribed philosophical, esoteric wisdom.

The idea itself of concealing meanings which can be teased out by allegorical interpretation is incompatible with the nature of the language available to the early poets. Vico discusses allegory first in the axioms, contrasting its analogical meanings with the univocal meaning of fables (*NS* 209, 210). He returns to allegory in the "Poetic Logic," saying "allegory is defined as *diversiloquium* insofar as, by identity not of proportion but (to speak scholastically) of predicability, allegories signify the diverse species or the diverse individuals comprised under these genera"(*NS* 403). Vico concludes from this definition that "they must have a univocal signification connoting a quality common to all their species and individuals (as Achilles connotes an idea of valor common to all strong men, or Ulysses an idea of prudence common to all wise men); such that these allegories must be the etymologies of the poetic languages, which would make their origins all univocal, whereas those of the vulgar languages are more often analogical. We also have the definition of the word 'etymology' itself as meaning *veriloquium*, just as fable was defined as *vera narratio* " (*NS* 403). In allegory there is an intrusion of interpretative distance between what is said and what is meant that is absent in the real poems and the metaphors of the first humans.

The reflection required to say one thing and mean another has not yet developed in the first poetry of humanity; this sophistication of expression is the most philosophical trope, namely, irony. Vico explains that "irony certainly could not have begun until the period of reflection, because it is fashioned by dint of reflection which wears the mask of truth. Here emerges a great principle of human institutions, confirming the origin of poetry disclosed in this work: that since the first men of the gentile world had the simplicity of children, who are truthful by nature, the first fables could not feign anything false; they must therefore have been, as they have been defined above, true narrations" (*NS* 408). The first poets could not have intended the sort of philosophical meanings the later philosophers attribute to them because they were incapable of the duplicity of irony.

For Vico, the faculty of *fantasia* is ascendant in the ages when intellect is descendant and vice versa (*NS* 185). The allegorical interpretation of the first poems is an attempt to impose the intellect of the third age on the *fantasia* of the first. It is a category mistake, and like most category mistakes, the error is instructive. This mistake is precisely the sort which a philosopher would make if knowledge were conceived according to Descartes's very different tree of knowledge in his author's letter to the *Principles*.[22] Vico is telling us much more than how not to interpret certain poets; he is founding a new epistemology and a metaphysics based on *fantasia* instead of *ratio*.

The opening claim of the "The Discovery of the True Homer" reveals the scope of Vico's criticism of previous philosophers. "Although our demonstration in the preceding book that poetic wisdom was the vulgar wisdom of the peoples of Greece, who were first theological and later heroic poets, should carry as a necessary consequence that the wisdom of Homer was not at all different in kind, yet, as Plato left firmly fixed the opinion that Homer was endowed with sublime esoteric wisdom (and all the other philosophers have followed in his train with [pseudo-] Plutarch foremost, writing an entire book on the matter), we shall here examine particularly if Homer was ever a philosopher" (*NS* 780). Vico's book on Homer is an example of how a poet-founder is a poetic character for a nation and not an individual sage. Homer was wrongly interpreted allegorically, and so Vico offers a rival interpretation that does not depend on the conceit implicit in the notion of the poetic veil. Since Vico sees his discovery of the True Homer as correcting an error made by Plato and all other philosophers, this statement is a serious charge and a bold claim to originality.

The question for my inquiry into the kinship of Vico and Plato is what to make of Vico's claim that "Plato left firmly fixed the opinion that Homer was endowed with sublime esoteric wisdom (and all the other philosophers have followed in his train . . .)" (*NS* 780). On this passage Nicolini has two comments; on the claim about Plato he says, "just the opposite is true" (*é vero proprio il contrario*), and about the claim that all philosophers believed in Homer's esoteric wisdom, he writes "not everyone" (*non tutti*).[23] In essence, Vico is overgeneralizing and not being just to Plato's complexity.

What evidence of the conceit of scholars is there in Plato's dialogues? There are places that one can point to where Plato commits the conceit of scholars. For instance, in the *Theatetus* Homer is listed as one of the Ionians on the side of the giants, putting him alongside the philosopher Heraclitus.[24] The idea that Homer's Oceanus means that he advocates the philosophy of flux also appears in the *Cratylus* (402a–c). Vico quotes the *Cratylus* where Plato glosses "all things are full of Jove" as the philosophical doctrine of ether (*NS* 379). In these instances, Plato does commit the conceit of scholars, but Plato does not encourage in any systematic way, as his successors would, reading the early poets allegorically to uncover esoteric, philosophical wisdom. By implication, perhaps, Plato is opening the door for philosophical categorization of Homer, but it is significant that Plato considers Homer on the other side from "the friends of the forms," the material side of the battle over what is real in the *Sophist* (248a). The idea that the poets conceal an esoteric wisdom does not appear in Plato as prominently as it does in the Neoplatonists, who may have derived their increased interest in it from the Stoics. There is nothing in Plato's dialogues comparable to Plotinus's spiritual interpretation of the *Odyssey* in the *Enneads*; "we shall put out to sea, as Odysseus did, from the witch Circe or Calypso—as the poet says (I think with a hidden meaning)."[25]

Consider the contrary evidence in the dialogues about poetry in general and Homer in particular. The *Republic* and the *Apology* make clear that poets, especially understood as rhapsodes of Homer, are far from concealing any wisdom. Fausto Nicolini rightly points to *Republic* Books 2 and 3 as an indication that the opposite of Vico's claim is true.[26] The ethical critique of Homer and the rhapsodes who claim wisdom on his behalf is arguably more firmly fixed by Plato's dialogues. For instance, this moral critique is what Augustine remembers in *The City of God*. Overall, I think it is fair to say that Plato more often thinks that poetry does not contain wisdom despite claims made for it, and needs to be corrected by philosophy. So despite the instances where one can find the conceit, the wisdom of Homer is hardly something Plato leaves "firmly fixed."

Given that Plato's dialogues do not unequivocally claim Homer has philosophical wisdom, why does Vico claim that Plato left this conceit "firmly fixed"? Why would Vico make such a strong criticism of his first author? There are several possible explanations, but the most plausible explanation of Vico's criticism of Plato is that it is a result of the mediation of Plato's views through Italian Platonists like Pico who highlighted his occasional esoteric use of myth. Ficino and Pico, influenced by Neoplatonists such as Plotinus, drew attention to the instances in Plato where the conceit occurs, and gave poetic theology an even more central role than it had in Plotinus. It makes sense that Vico is seeing Plato through the mediation of the Platonic tradition in which allegorical interpretations of Homer were the rule. It is in this manner that Nicolini suggests that Vico is thinking not of Plato himself but of Platonists or Neoplatonists. This explanation is at least partially satisfying, since Plato's followers, from Plotinus to Pico, do read Homer allegorically.

Another explanation is that Vico viewed "Plato" as an imaginative universal for philosophy itself. Considering human beings as they *ought* to be instead of how they *are*, poets become better teachers of virtue and vice in the hands of later philosophers than they really were. Ignorance of the humble origins of humanity is the archetypal philosophical mistake. When one reads carefully what Vico writes, it amounts to saying that whereas Vico has proven Homer to be a poetic character and not a philosopher,

Plato got all the philosophers off on the wrong track because he did not know this. Plato is guilty of not having invented the *New Science*. Criticizing Plato and all the philosophers after him does have the significant rhetorical effect of elevating the originality of Vico's discovery. On this interpretation, Vico is overstating the centrality of the esoteric view of poets in Plato to emphasize how revolutionary his discovery is. It is stronger to say that every one from Plato on makes this mistake, and Vico sees what poetic wisdom really is, than to be precise about Plato's ambivalence.

That Plato does not discover Vichian poetic wisdom is not really a fair criticism, since Plato was much closer to this discovery than later Platonists. Vico's arguments that the stories must be corrupted versions of the original true stories are themselves versions of Plato's ethical arguments against the portrayal of the gods and heroes as immoral in *Republic* Books 2 and 3. In light of these possible explanations, Vico's critique of Plato (*NS* 780) does not close the door to examining the parallels between their thought.

Chronology

Regardless of whether "all the philosophers" (*NS* 780) so far have missed the true connection between history, wisdom, and poetry, what is Vico's alternative? Vico's conception of poetic wisdom is the heart of his alternative, as has already been maintained. Now Vico's discovery is worth exploring from another angle, focusing on history. Historian Edwin Thiele wrote a sentence that could have been taken from Vico's *New Science*: "chronology is the backbone of history."[27] Rarely is the Chronological Table made central to anyone's interpretation of the *New Science*, but it is crucial for understanding fully Vico's alternative to Renaissance poetic theology.

In his explanation of the Zodiac signs in the *Dipintura*, or the Frontispiece, Vico writes "thus from Saturn (whose Greek name Chronos means time) new principles are derived for chronology or the theory of times" (*NS* 3). This gloss suggests two crucial aspects of Vico's new conception of chronology, namely that it is poetic and historical. In the description of the tree of knowledge, poetic chronology is described as one of the two eyes of poetic history, the other being poetic geography (*NS* 741).[28] Each of these eyes of history must be cleansed to discover universal history. The Chronological Table contains a summary of the materials which the *New Science* is trying to give form through its elements, including the two conceits enumerated as axioms 3 and 4. "Now, in order to make trial whether the propositions hitherto enumerated as elements of this Science can give form to the materials prepared in the Chronological Table at the beginning, we beg the reader to consider what has hitherto been written concerning the principles of any subject in the whole of the gentile knowledge, human and divine. Let him then see if it is inconsistent with the above propositions"(*NS* 330). The discovery of the two conceits makes all other histories useless, because "all that has been written so far is a tissue of confused memories" (ibid.). Vico specifically distinguishes his "rational poetic chronology" from some other recent attempts at intellectual chronology (*NS* 736), just as his "rational civil theology of divine providence" will replace "poetic theology" (*NS* 342).

The discovery of the poetic character is presented as the way out of the confusion surrounding chronology. "As for the rough chronological tempests, they will be cleared up for us by the discovery of the poetic characters, one of whom was Orpheus, considered as a theological poet, who through the fables, in their first meaning, first founded and then confirmed the humanity of Greece" (*NS* 81). The confusion of the scholars was to collapse the founding and the confirming of wisdom. The poetic character Homer did found Greek wisdom, but he did not cloak in it philosophical ideas; that was read into him by later philosophers who, ignorant of the fact that poetic origins of their own wisdom were vulgar not esoteric, made the poetic wisdom resemble their own. On Vico's view of chronology, it does not matter that "these men and deeds either did not have their being at the time or in the places to which they are commonly assigned, or never existed at all" (*NS* 43). But the purpose of his Table and the notes that follow it is "to show how uncertain, unseemly, defective, or vain are the beginnings of the humanity of the nations" (ibid.). These defects are why Vico refers to the Chronological Table as "the museum of credulity" (*NS* 49).

Vico knows from the historian Casaubon that Hermes Trismegistus is not the author of the Hermetic texts given such importance in the Renaissance (*NS* 47), yet despite this knowledge Vico gives these poetic theologians an important place as "poetic characters." Vico's chronology is an act of imagination in the sense of memory. Vico wants to provide "universal history," and since he learned from the Egyptians that the world moves through stages, his chronology has to reflect these different ways of perceiving and ordering reality. This observation raises the question of the continuing importance Vico places on the Egyptians, despite his rejection of the *Hermetica* as a fraud.

The Chronological Table itself depicted the place of the Egyptians in the *New Science*. The heading states that it is "based in the three epochs of the times of the Egyptians, who said all the world before them had passed through three ages: that of the gods, that of the heroes, and that of men." This heading in conjunction with placing Hermes in the fifth place in the genealogy shows how Vico reconceived the real wisdom of the Egyptians. Vico looks to the Egyptians for their insight into history, rather than for the philosophical claims made in the name of Hermes: "in this undertaking we shall be greatly helped by the antiquity of the Egyptians, for they have preserved for us two great fragments not less marvelous than their pyramids, namely those two great philological verities" (*NS* 52). The Egyptians have preserved the poetic origins of wisdom, and since origins are indicative of nature for Vico, the Egyptians provide the key to all gentile wisdom. "The first is narrated by Herodotus: that the Egyptians reduced all the preceding time of the world to three ages, the first that of the gods, the second that of the heroes, the third that of men. The other (as related in Scheffer's *De Natura et constitutione philosophiae italicae seu pythagoricae*) is that, with corresponding number and sequence, through all that period three languages had been spoken: the first hieroglyphic, with sacred characters; the second symbolic, with heroic characters; the third epistolary, with characters agreed on by the peoples" (*NS* 52). Vico says that Varro must have chosen only to consider Roman history whereas the principles Vico is developing are universal, "true of all the ancient nations" (ibid.). This Egyptian view of the historical pattern of ages and languages provides Vico with a crucial axiom (*NS* 173).

If one looks at the *Hermetica*, despite its inauthenticity, there are passages that Vico may have thought truly represented Egyptian wisdom about history. For instance, the following "lament" sounds very much like Vico's description of the final remedy of providence to end the barbarism of reflection (*NS* 1106): "The pious man will be thought mad, the impious, wise . . . Such will be the old age of the world, irreligion, disorder, confusion of all goods . . . God . . . will annihilate all malice, either by effacing it in a deluge or by consuming fire. . . . Then he will bring back the world to its first beauty, so that this world may be again worthy of reverence and admiration, and that God also, creator and restorer of so great a work, may be glorified. . . . that is what the rebirth of the world will be; a renewal of all good things by God's will."[29] The rebirth of the world leads to a moral restoration among the remaining people, "the men who shall live then in continual hymns of praise and benedictions" (ibid.). Vico very similarly describes that "people who have reached this point of premeditated malice, when they receive this last remedy of providence and are thereby stunned and brutalized . . . and the few survivors in the midst of an abundance of the things necessary for life naturally become sociable and, returning to the primitive simplicity of the first world of peoples, are again religious, truthful, and faithful. Thus providence brings back among them the piety, faith, and truth which are the natural foundations of justice as well as the graces and beauties of the eternal order of God" (*NS* 1106).

In addition to this striking parallel about providence, Vico's central idea of ideal eternal history (and that in particular human things, like all things, are born, live a life, decline, and die) is present in the following: "those things which cannot be eternal as individuals . . . are eternal as species . . . the earth changes all its parts from time to time and in a certain order and so renews itself . . . And we ourselves and the things pertaining to us come and go, pass and repass."[30] This vision of the history of the world, including human history, is strikingly similar to Vico's *corso e ricorso*. Such passages which go beyond the division of the three ages make one doubt that he was basing his admiration for the Egyptian view of history only on the odd collection of sources he lists, from Herodotus to Censorinus.

Regardless of why Vico thinks the Egyptians point the way toward a true chronology of the past, he is also clear that they themselves illustrate one of the two most important errors he is exposing, that of the conceit of nations. The Egyptians articulated the pattern of ideal eternal history, which is universal, but then claimed that their Jove was the oldest and that the Egyptian Hercules gave the name to those of other nations. The Egyptians emerge as Vico's inspiration, though not at all in the same way that they inspired a thinker like Giordano Bruno. Vico emphasized that "certainly such boundless antiquity did not yield much recondite wisdom" (*NS* 45). In fact their books "contained the greatest errors in philosophy and astronomy . . . their morality was dissolute . . . their theology was full of superstition, magic and witchcraft" (ibid.).

In tension with the truth Vico discovers in Egyptian wisdom, the claims made for Hermes are minimized even relative to the other poet theologians. Hermes is placed fifth in antiquity. Vico's position on Hermes is summed up as follows: "Now as to what touches on that great theme of the Christian religion—that Moses did not learn from the Egyptians the sublime theology of the Hebrews—there seems to be one great obstacle, chronology, which places Moses after Thrice-great Hermes. But this difficulty, besides being met by the reasons set forth above, is completely overcome by means of the principles expressed in a really golden passage of Iamblichus, *On the Mysteries of the Egyptians*, where he says that the Egyptians ascribed to this same Hermes all they discovered that was necessary and useful to human civil life" (*NS* 68). Vico concludes that "he must therefore have

been, not an individual man rich in esoteric wisdom who was subsequently
made a god, but a poetic character of the first men of Egypt who were wise
in vulgar wisdom and who founded there the first families and then the
peoples that finally composed that great nation . . . this Hermes must
embrace the entire Egyptian age of gods" (*NS* 68). Notice that, based on
what Iamblichus said, Vico could deduce from the principles of his Science that Hermes could not have been the author of the *Hermetica,* and no
other such work attributed to one of the poetic characters could be au-
thentic either.

Emanuele Riverso suggests how Vico's conclusion based on the nature
of language "enlarges the one reached by Casaubon" and "is much more
binding as it is no longer a simple assessment of a matter of fact but rather
the result of a strictly scientific inference."[31] This highlights how Vico
generalizes Casaubon's conclusion in terms of a Science of cultural development that in principle precludes such exceptional figures. Vico has explained why Hermes could not have written the Neoplatonizing text mis-
takenly ascribed to him, which is more than saying merely that as a matter
of fact he did not. As Frances Yates notes, there was resistance to rejecting
the Hermetic texts even after Casaubon's textual discovery.[32] Vico's chronology in this way does not depend on exposing all such texts as fraudulent. He has shown from an examination of the nature of language and the
stages it proceeds through, correlative to the ages of gods, heroes, and humans, that a conception of ancient wisdom that requires a philosophical
consciousness in the age of gods or heroes is false. Ironically, the Egyptian
wisdom about the ages and the types of language dethrones Hermes. Vico's
admiration of the Egyptians leads him to discover the conceit of scholars
and to reject the cult of Hermes.

The wisdom of the Egyptians is unlike anything the Renaissance humanists or Platonists imagined. The central insight of the *New Science* is
precisely the otherness of the vulgar, poetic wisdom. Vico denies the distance that allegorical interpretations interpose, and he exposes the conceit
by which philosophers make the fables mere metaphors, as they would use
to adorn their own writing. So understood, the poetic theology illustrates
all of the first four axioms of the *New Science* (*NS* 120–128). When in
ignorance, human beings make themselves the measure, and in this way
they make the unfamiliar familiar. Likewise, each nation's philosophers
proclaim its own poetic theologian primary out of the conceit of nations.
Finally, the advocates of poetic theology illustrate the conceit of scholars,
for they make their own wisdom as old as the world, reading their own
thoughts back into the earliest poets.

The conceit of scholars, as has been shown, is characteristic of Renaissance poetic theology, and the correction of this error leads to Vico's own doctrine of poetic wisdom. At the end of the *New Science* Vico states that the desire for wisdom can be corrupted, as for those who sought an esoteric wisdom in the poets. It was misplaced veneration, Vico reiterates in conclusion, that led to the conceit of scholars. "But providence, through the order of civil institutions discussed in this work, makes itself palpable for us in these three feelings: the first, the marvel, the second, the veneration, hitherto felt by all the learned for the matchless wisdom of the ancients, and the third, the ardent desire with which they burned to seek and attain it. These are in fact three lights of divine providence that aroused in them the aforesaid three beautiful and just sentiments; but these sentiments were later perverted by the conceit of scholars and by the conceit of nations—conceits we have sought throughout this work to discredit. The uncorrupted feelings are that all the learned should admire, venerate, and desire to unite themselves to the infinite wisdom of God" (*NS* 1111).

The Platonists who believed in the ancient poetic theology did so out of an "ardent desire," but one Vico sees as a corrupted sentiment. The Platonists were not wrong that there is a wisdom in poetry, but it is not a hidden esoteric wisdom as they assumed. Plato is blamed for leading the rest of the philosophers in this direction with his occasional esoteric reading of a myth, but the reason Vico sees the conceit of scholars in Plato is because the Italian Platonists highlighted the instances in the dialogues where it occurs. Plato did not discover the true Homer, or understand how the quarrel between philosophy and poetry is made possible by poetry; but the idea that Plato seriously read Homer as a philosopher concealing wisdom in his poetry has little evidence. With the Italian Platonists, however, "the ardent desire" for "the matchless wisdom of the ancients" fueled the quest for a poetic theology to establish a continuity between diverse traditions in a way foreign to Plato himself. This distinction between Plato and the Italian Platonists is the first of several instances where one must know the Platonic tradition in addition to Plato's dialogues to understand who "Plato" is for Vico.

Chapter 2

Poetry: Maker and Molder of Thyself

The allegorical interpretation of poems is not the only sense of poetry in the Renaissance or in Pico's *Oration*. *Poiein* in Greek can have either the narrow sense of composing verse or the broader meaning of making anything. In the *Symposium* (205b–c) Diotima explains to the young Socrates that *eros* has a narrower and a broader meaning by referring to the more familiar parallel double meaning of *poiein*. Vico makes this same observation in the *New Science*; "the same ones who invented it, created it, whence they were called 'poets,' which is the same in Greek as 'creators'" (*essi medesimi che fingendo le si criavano, onde furon detti 'poeti', che lo stesso in greco suona che 'criatori'*) (*NS* 376, my trans.). In the last chapter, I considered poetry's relevance to history and wisdom; now, I will explore the broader meaning of poetry as definitive of human nature.

For Pico, human beings are unique because we make ourselves. Self-making and self-knowing enable human beings to possess the dignity and the wisdom that they were created to have as the image of God. Nicholas of Cusa's epithet "created god" is a useful formula to amplify Pico's account of human nature in the *Oration*, since it sums up the double meaning involved in understanding human beings as primarily poetic; human beings are both creatures and creators.[1] The *Heptaplus*, Pico's commentary on *Genesis*, reveals that Pico too sees human beings as creatures of God's making as well as creators of themselves.[2] Vico draws on this Christian Neoplatonic tradition in his description of human beings. The Renaissance emphasis on the dignity of human beings as creators, as artists and as makers of themselves, is evident in Vico's inaugural orations especially.

To see how Pico illuminates Vico's ideas of human nature and education or *paideia*, one first must understand what Pico's position is. I will consider the famous part of Pico's *Oration*, the one rightly labeled "on the dignity of man," in light of the *Heptaplus*. Some think, on the basis of

Pico's *Oration*, that he rejects one of the central ideas of Renaissance Platonism, the idea that human beings are "the bond" of the universe and its microcosm.[3] Evidence from the *Heptaplus* (and from the *Oration* itself) will show that this is not the case. Pico does not reject it; he enriches it. Turning to Vico, I will compare these ideas from Pico to Vico's ideas of human nature and *paideia* in his inaugural orations. For Vico and Pico alike the most important poetics is the making of humanity itself.

De hominis dignitate

Pico wrote the *Oration* with the righteous indignation of a talented young man who would not be able to prove his genius because of the envy of others. There is a daring and boldness in Pico's tone that accords very well with the human dignity he praises. Forgetting this side of human beings is as serious an obstacle to being wise as ignoring the other side, human weakness. Pico emphasizes the uniqueness and the dignity of human beings in his *Oration*, and he defends the dignity of philosophy as a tool to actualize this potential human greatness. When one reads the *Heptaplus* one sees some of the same quotations used in the *Oration* now in a different context, including the opening quotation from Hermes Trismegistus. Since Pico himself neither gave nor published his *Oration*, the *Heptaplus* should be given at least equal or more weight as Pico's account of human dignity. In the *Oration* he was primarily defending philosophy and himself, but in the *Heptaplus* he is meditating on *Genesis,* on the creation of the world and especially of human beings. Human beings are given an absolutely central and dignified position in the universe in both works. Reading passages in the *Heptaplus* (where it is clear that Pico considers human beings as microcosmic) counters exaggerated readings of the *Oration* as a complete rejection of that Renaissance Platonic idea.

Pico begins his *Oration* with a report that Abdala the Saracen, when asked "what on this stage of the world, as it were, could be seen most worthy of wonder," asserted that "there is nothing to be seen more wonderful than man" (*O* 223). Pico adds the confirming authority of Hermes Trismegistus, who said "a great miracle, Asclepius, is man" (ibid.). Pico takes these two sayings about human nature as a point of departure for his own reflections. After listing the typical claims for human excellence, Pico says, "admittedly great though these reasons be, they are not the principal grounds, that is, those which may rightfully claim for themselves the privilege of the highest admiration" (ibid.). In fact, from the *Heptaplus* one can see that Pico does believe in these other reasons as listed here. Moreover,

Pico's position does not question the truth of the claims for human excellence, only the weight assigned to those claims (ibid.).

Yet even in the *Oration*, Pico does not dismiss the idea of the Chain of Being or the microcosm. He is not denying that human beings occupy an intermediary position in the universe, residing a little lower than the angels, ruling over the lower world, and serving as the bond between time and eternity. His question is: why not admire the angels more? What is it about human beings that make them "the most fortunate and consequently worthy of all admiration and what precisely is that rank which is his lot in the universal chain of Being—a rank to be envied not only by the brutes but even by the stars and by minds above this world"? (ibid.). Pico gives his own version of God's reason for creating Adam as his answer to the question of human excellence. If one had to choose one phrase from this famous section to sum up what Pico thinks is the principal reason for human excellence and admiration, it would be that, unlike any other creature, as a human being you are "the maker and molder of thyself" (*O* 225). Unlike lower animals, ruled by instinct only, or angels, ruled by reason or love of God by nature, human beings alone must "become what they are to be" (ibid.). This ability to change oneself makes human beings distinctive.

Consider the words of God to Adam as Pico imagines them: "'Neither a fixed abode nor a form that is thine alone nor any function peculiar to thyself have we given thee, Adam, to the end that according to thy judgment thou may best have and possess what abode, what form, and what functions thou thyself shalt desire. The nature of all other beings is limited and constrained within the bounds of laws prescribed by Us. Thou, constrained by no limits, in accordance with thine own free will, in whose hand We have placed thee, shalt ordain for thyself the limits of thy nature" (*O* 224–25). This limitless vision of human freedom is usually where commentators stop. But notice how Pico prefaces God's speech: "He therefore took man as a creature of indeterminate nature and, assigning him a place in the middle of the world, addressed him thus" (*O* 224). Pico holds that the indeterminate nature and the middle position are compatible, not contradictory. The limitless freedom is not seen as incompatible with being set "at the world's center," since from that vantage point we will be able better to "observe whatever is in the world," observation that will result in using our freedom to move either up or down the Chain of Being (*O* 224–25). It makes sense that, to go up or down, we would be placed in the middle as a starting-point. Abdala's question "what on the world's stage is most worthy of wonder" is answered with the rhetorical question: "who would not admire this our chameleon. Or who could more greatly admire aught else whatever?" (ibid.). The Protean nature of human beings is what is most to be wondered at, our "self-transforming nature" (*O* 225). Pico cites authorities from Greek and Hebrew sources that testify to our transformative nature (*O* 226).

Pico sees clearly that not being given fixed limits to one's nature is a challenge. Being given power over one's life is only good if it is used well. If we fail to live up to our divine potential, then we are worse off than the creatures with fixed natures, for Pico is clear that we can sink below as well as rise above other creatures. Pico explicitly states the ambivalence of our power, having God tell Adam, "thus thou shalt have the power to degenerate into the lower forms of life, which are brutish. Thou shalt have the power, out of thy soul's judgment, to be reborn into the higher forms which are divine" (*O* 225). Judgment becomes a matter of being most worthy of praise or falling into brutishness.

Seeing how essential right judgment is, one now must ask how does one come to right judgment? How do we learn how to govern our souls? As Plato answers this question in the *Republic*, philosophy teaches us how to govern our souls, and the philosopher is the one who masters his manifold nature (588c) and becomes a friend to the gods and himself (621c; 443d). In the *Oration* Pico does not directly refer to the *Republic*'s image of human beings making themselves into beasts, if they let appetites rule; lions, if they let spirit rule; and truly human, if they let reason rule (588c). In the *Heptaplus* Pico does refer to the *Republic* on the soul; "in Plato's *Republic* we learn that we have various kinds of brutes dwelling within us" (*H* 123). Recall that Pico's purpose in the *Oration* is to defend philosophy itself and his own activity as a philosopher. His account of the freedom which human beings have to transform themselves makes the acquisition of right judgment urgent and, as a result, raises the dignity of philosophy. Philosophy so understood is not only knowledge in the sense of contemplation, but an active shaping of ourselves to reveal the divine rather than the bestial within us. Philosophy is the education into who we truly are. Without cultivating that which is divine in us, we will sink to our bestial nature instead; so there is a great urgency. A heroic effort is required to be truly human. Amplifying Pico's metaphor, human beings are not only Proteus, but their higher self is the hero trying to hold him still, to figure out the truth he knows (*O* 225).

The saying from the Chaldeans reveals the inconstancy that is part of this unique nature that Pico must emphasize lest human beings think that they have dignity without effort. "'Man is a being of varied, manifold, and inconstant nature.' But why do we emphasize this? To the end that after we have been born to this condition—that we can become what we will—we should understand that we ought to have especial care to this, that it should never be said against us that, although born to privileged position, we failed to recognize it and became like unto wild animals and senseless beasts of burden" (*O* 227). Pico continues to explore this theme, adding another authority "the saying of Asaph the prophet should apply: 'Ye are all angels and sons of the Most High,' and that we may not, by abusing the most indulgent generosity of the Father, make for ourselves that freedom of choice He has given into something harmful instead of salutary. Let a certain holy ambition invade our souls, so that, not content with the mediocre, we shall pant after the highest and (since we may if we will) toil with all our strength to obtain it" (ibid.).

In the next section, Pico asks "but how shall we go about it, and what in the end shall we do?" (ibid.). This transition reveals that the preceding description was not an abstract exercise in cosmology or in anthropology, without practical consequences. Showing who we are also reveals that we must do something in response to this new self-knowledge. So Pico rightly adds that to achieve the goal of our "holy ambition," we should try to be like angels, to "emulate their dignity and glory. And if we have willed it, we shall be second to them in nothing" (ibid.). The uniqueness of human beings willing to imitate the angels makes their achievement surpass that of angels themselves who do not have to struggle against part of themselves pulling them down and away from God.

In a manner as impressive as the speech to Adam, Pico uses the division of angels into Seraphim, Cherubim, and Thrones, as models for human perfection. Each serves as a model for a different expression of the higher soul; the Seraph for love, the Cherub for knowledge, and the Throne for judgment. Pico makes the Cherub the intermediary, asking "by what means is one able either to judge or to love things unknown . . . the Cherub as intermediary by his own light makes us ready for the Seraphic fire and equally lights the way to the judgment of the Thrones. . . . This is the one for us first to emulate, to court, and to understand; the one from whence we may be rapt to the heights of love and descend, well taught and well prepared, to the functions of active life" (*O* 228). This division of angels makes philosophy, especially moral philosophy, but also natural philosophy, the necessary preparation for either loving or judging correctly.

To praise and urge us to imitate the Cherubic way of life is to praise philosophy. Moral philosophy involves governing the passions, whereas natural philosophy or metaphysics instructs us in the knowledge of divine things. Pico writes, "let us . . . by emulating the Cherubic way of life on earth, by taming the impulses of our passions with moral science, by dispelling the darkness of reason with dialectic, and by, so to speak, washing away the filth of ignorance and vice, cleanse our soul, so that her passions may not rave at random nor her reason through heedlessness be deranged. Then let us fill our well-prepared and purified soul with the light of natural philosophy, so that we may at last perfect her in the knowledge of things divine" (O 229). Once the passions are tamed and the darkness of reason is lifted, then the soul is able to know the divine things perfectly. That this is not the last step in the soul's progress is clear from the ladder metaphor.

Moral philosophy is a necessary preparation for the perfection of the soul; just as in climbing a ladder the earlier rungs are ineliminable. "If this is what we must practice in our aspiration to the angelic way of life, I ask: "Who will touch the ladder of the Lord either with fouled foot or with unclean hands?" . . . lest we be hurled down from the ladder as impious and unclean, let us bathe in moral philosophy as if in a living river . . ." (ibid.). It is significant for evaluating the pride attributed to Pico in his *Oration* that impiety is one of the vices eliminated through moral philosophy. Pico then develops the ladder metaphor: "Once we have achieved this by the art of discourse or reasoning, then, inspired by the Cherubic spirit, using philosophy through the steps of the ladder, that is, of nature, and penetrating all things from center to center, we shall sometimes descend, with titanic force rending the unity like Osiris into many parts, and we shall sometimes ascend, with the force of Phoebus collecting the parts like the limbs of Osiris into a unity, until, resting at last in the bosom of the Father who is above the Ladder, we shall be made perfect with the felicity of theology" (O 230). In the ladder image in Plato's *Symposium* (211c), the final step beyond philosophical speeches into the vision of the Beautiful itself is still the perfection of philosophy, the love of wisdom. For Pico that final step off the ladder goes beyond philosophy into theology, the love of God.

Philosophy is not the most perfect of human sciences, just as the Cherub is not the highest rank of angel. Yet Pico defends the necessity of philosophy, since as he said about the Cherub, one must know in order properly to judge and to love. One has to bathe in moral philosophy and be pious to climb the Cherubic ladder at all. But one should not stop at the top rung of the ladder, but step beyond philosophy into theology, which is to go beyond the imitation of the Cherub to the Seraph. Theology in this analogy must be conceived as an expression of love, not primarily of knowledge, for the Cherub is said to have perfect knowledge of divine things. Love is perfected in the highest mystery of the ladder. In *De Ente*, Pico stops himself in the middle of a sustained philosophical argument to re-mind himself and his reader that knowledge of God, however noble, is inferior to love of God. "But see, my Angelo, what madness seizes us. While we are still in the body we can love God more than we can speak of him or know him. In loving we profit more, we labour less, we obey him more. Yet we prefer to be always seeking him through knowledge and never finding what we seek, rather than to possess by loving that which would be found in vain without loving."[4] In the *Oration*, Pico is clear that "it is not . . . in the power of natural philosophy to give us in nature a true and quiet and unshaken peace, but that this is the function and privilege of her mis-tress, that is, of holiest theology. She will show us the way . . . When we have been so soothingly called, so kindly urged, we shall fly up with winged feet, like earthly Mercuries" (*O* 231–32). Pico is defending not only phi-losophy, but also theology; he clearly places theology above philosophy, while giving philosophy an essential preparatory role.

From this survey of the crucial passages in the first half of the *Oration*, it is evident that human dignity is something attained only through "holy ambition" and with great difficulty. The *Oration*'s focus is primarily to be a defense of the dignity of philosophy and theology as the means to achiev-ing the angelic nature that would be our perfection as human beings if we could attain it. The praise of human beings is meant to inspire us by show-ing us the greatness which can be ours. Nevertheless, Pico is not blind to the obstacles to such perfection.

Despite the great freedom of the will that we have as the essence of our nature, we cannot "become who we are to be" completely through our own efforts (*O* 225). In the passage quoted above, human beings become angelic through the peace of God, and earlier Pico says explicitly "it is not permitted for us to attain this through our own efforts" (*O* 228). This reference to grace seems to contradict the earlier claim that "thou mayest fashion thyself in whatever shape thou shalt prefer . . . thou shalt have the power, out of thy soul's judgment, to be reborn into the higher forms, which are divine" (*O* 225). But the key to the reconciliation of such pas-sages is that God was speaking to Adam at his creation, before the Fall. We do not share with Adam the power to transform ourselves. This interpreta-tion accords well with the ideas in the *Heptaplus* about the necessity of Christ as the second Adam through whom human beings again have the power to become angelic. Combining Platonic philosophy with Chris-tianity may place one close to the Pelagian heresy about human freedom, but the Renaissance Platonists such as Pico did consider themselves ortho-dox Christians. That the doctors at Rome found thirteen of Pico's nine hundred theses suspect of heresy should not diminish the fact that the other eight hundred and eighty-seven were judged orthodox.

Between the *Oration* and the *Heptaplus*, I see only a difference of emphasis. In the *Oration*, Pico's goal is to defend the importance of reason to justify his disputation. In the *Heptaplus*, Pico is more apt to emphasize human weakness over dignity. He writes, for instance, that philosophers even more than others should devote themselves to piety. Pico says that "it is neither ridiculous nor useless nor unworthy of a philosopher to devote great and unremitting care to holy prayers, rites, vows, and hymns jointly sung to God. If this is helpful and proper for the human race, it is especially useful and proper for those who have given themselves up to the study of letters and the life of contemplation. For them nothing is more necessary than to purify by an upright life those eyes of the mind which they turn repeatedly up toward the divine, and to enlighten them more amply with the light obtained from above through the use of prayer and, mindful always of their own weakness, to say with the Apostle, 'Our sufficiency is from God'" (*H* 144).

Philosophy can provide only natural happiness: "In regard to man, although different philosophers hold different opinions, nevertheless all have kept within the narrow bounds of human capacity, limiting the felicity of man either to the mere search for truth, as the Academics do, or to its attainment through the study of philosophy, as Alfarabi said" (*H* 149). Much like Thomas Aquinas, Pico holds that nature is completed by grace, and specifically human nature and happiness. "Therefore, I pray, let us listen to the holy theologians reminding us of our dignity and of the divine goods freely promised us by the most generous of fathers, lest, cruel to our own souls and ungrateful to God the creator, we reject them. . . . the highest felicity lies in the attainment of God . . . We have shown, and we shall show, that through their own powers, created things cannot achieve this ultimate felicity, but only the former [natural happiness]. The former, if we look closely, is rather the shadow of felicity than true felicity" (*H* 150).

Pico also shows how our freedom of choice can affect not only our own happiness, but also the whole universe. First he reminds us of the honor we have been given as a microcosm. "Earthly things are subject to man and the heavenly bodies befriend him, since he is the bond and link between heaven and earth; but they cannot both have peace with him unless he who in himself sanctifies their peace and alliance is at peace with himself" (*H* 136). Human beings are the middle as center whereas God is middle as origin; "the difference between God and man is that God contains all things in Himself as their origin, and man contains all things in himself as their center" (*H* 135). As in the *Oration*, Pico follows this exalted view of human dignity with a warning. "But let us beware, I pray, that we do not misunderstand the greatness of the honor we have been given. . . . Let us always hold it in our mind's eye as a sure, proven, and indubitable truth that just as all things favor us when we keep the law which has been given to us, so if through sin or evasion of the law we forsake the beaten path, they will all be unfriendly, hostile, and dangerous" (*H* 136). Given the microcosm-macrocosm relationship between human beings and the whole creation, Pico concludes that "it is reasonable that to the same extent that we do injury not only to ourselves but also to the universe, which we encompass within us, and to almighty God, the creator of the world itself, we should also experience all things in the world as the most severe punishers and powerful avengers of injuries and, with God among the foremost. Therefore let us dread the penalties and torments which await transgressors of divine law" (ibid.).

Pico does say in the *Oration* that being the middle, being the microcosm, is not the main reason that humanity is most worthy of wonder on the world's stage, but instead that "it is granted to him to have whatever he chooses, to be whatever he wills" (*O* 225). The perfectly optimistic and enthusiastic passages are all within or about the speech of God to Adam, and from the *Heptaplus* we can see that Pico would not retell Moses's creation story lightly, nor would he conveniently forget Adam's Fall. From Pico's gloss on his own account of the creation of human beings, what is amazing is that we are free to live up to our angelic nature or to sink to the bestial. So the source of our dignity is also the source of our wretchedness. There is no one-sided naïve optimism in Pico. To the praise of human beings as created completely free is added a solemn warning not to repay this generosity of God by using that freedom to become bestial instead of angelic. The fact that human beings must expend so much effort to make and mold ourselves supports rather than negates the importance of grace in actually achieving happiness.

Pico may commit the sin of pride in his *Oration* (as his nephew thought he did in the *Vita*), but his humility in the *Heptaplus* seems much too thorough-going to be feigned. The idea behind the conventional subtitle "*de hominis dignitatis*" can be saved, as Peter Burke said, "at the price of a qualification."[5] It is misleading only if one does not know that the exalted position human freedom gives us in the universe can lead to misery as well as happiness. Pico does state well the dignity which human beings have been created to achieve, but he does not ignore the dark side of this freedom as many of his interpreters have. With a more complete sense of what

human nature is for Pico, we can now turn to Vico's allusions to Pico in his
inaugural orations and see in Vico a similar emphasis on human dignity,
with a similar acknowledgment that human nature tends toward corruption.

Born for Wisdom

In the introduction to this part, I explained the relevance of Vico's inaugural orations to his thought as a whole. Certain Platonic themes are developed which remain central, such as self-knowledge and *paideia*. These interrelated themes depend on the broader sense of poetry as making in
general. In this section I will highlight the similarities between Pico and
Vico on human dignity and the need for moral education to know oneself.
Vico's claims about the human capacity to perfect ourselves through wisdom reveal a confidence in moral philosophy and human nature as seen in
Pico, with a similar sense that we have to make ourselves into a worthy
likeness of God through education.

As a professor of rhetoric, Vico certainly always took into account his
audience when he gave a speech, and so should we as readers. Vico was
addressing an audience of "privileged youth, who by natural disposition
have turned away from folly and have directed your mind to the study of
wisdom" as well as "those of you who have made the search for wisdom
your professions—you the highest authorities holding public responsibili-
ties" (*IO* 2.4). The youth are his primary concern, since he sees in them
potential philosophers and rulers, and perhaps that rare potential philosopher-king. Performing this annual duty of giving the convocation speech,
Vico has a slightly different purpose than Pico had in his *Oration on the
Dignity of Man*.

Vico's inaugural orations were meant to inspire students to become better human beings through education, to rouse in them the courage to pursue difficult studies. Vico confidently tells the young students that they are
"born for wisdom" (*IO* 1.4). The emphasis throughout the inaugural orations is on the free choice to become wise through purifying the mind and
the spirit, or to be a fool through allowing the passions to rule. Only individuals who can rule themselves first can rule others. What Vico would say
to such an audience would be very different from what he might have said
in a published work or to a less elite audience. Vico's task is to encourage
these students by conveying his confidence in their capacity to become
wise. In order to persuade them, Vico draws on ideas from a remarkable
array of sources from both Latin and Greek traditions. I will be concerned
here only with the echoes of Pico's *Oration*.

The reader of Vico's first oration is immediately struck by Vico's use of exclamations. One finds many lines echoing Pico's "O supreme generosity of God the Father, O highest and most marvelous felicity of man!" (*O* 225). Vico summarizes the goal of the first oration in the imperative "let us constantly cultivate the divine force of our mind" (*IO*, *Appendix*, 141). What is celebrated in the first oration is that the human mind is among the divine things, and self-knowledge involves knowing the divinity of one's mind. Vico repeatedly conveys his excitement about the depths self-knowledge can uncover: "O wonderful knowledge of oneself! How high you exalt and honor us! For each one of you, O listeners, the mind is to you your own god" (*IO* 1.12).[6] In his enthusiasm, Vico even modifies Cicero's famous claim about Socrates: "Socrates is said to have derived his moral philosophy from the heavens. On the contrary, he raised man's spirit up to the heavens" (*IO* 1.12).

Like Descartes, Vico holds that the "divine things . . . are the human mind and God" (*IO* 6.9). But for Vico this statement is more closely related to the ideas of the Renaissance Platonists than to those of the Cartesians. The Cartesian arguments echoed in the first oration should be read in the light of Vico's claim in the *Autobiography* that what was admired "as sublime, great and new in Descartes" was "old and common knowledge among the Platonists" (*A* 138). This "old and common knowledge among the Platonists" is precisely what the reader has to recall to understand the metaphysics beneath Vico's ideal method of studies, a method explicitly pitted against Descartes in the seventh oration, which was revised and published separately as *On the Study Methods of Our Times*. Echoing the goal of articulating " a metaphysics compatible with human frailty" in the *Ancient Wisdom*, the goal of oration seven is, "let us embrace the method of studies that corrupt nature dictates" (*IO*, *Appendix*, 142).

The metaphysical idea that the human soul is the microcosm of the universe is one of the most important Greek philosophical ideas revived by the Renaissance Platonists to express their vision of the human condition. Following this Platonic tradition, for Vico the relationship of God and the human mind is one of analogy (*IO* 1.5). God's relationship to the world as creator is imitated by human beings in their creation of arts, which they know as God knows nature; "finally, God is the master artist of nature: the mind, we may say, is the god of the arts" (ibid.). Human making, as well as knowing, is explained by God's creation of human beings in God's image, conceiving the divine nature as fundamentally creative. Vico explicitly declares, with the audacity of the style of Pico, "O matchless excellence of spirit that cannot be explained suitably and aptly except by its similarity to

almighty God! Once you have known to what the spirit is similar, you
have known its very nature. The spirit, indeed, is a certain divine force of
thought . . . Would that Minerva had given me a gift of language so profound and so rich that I could explain with my words as you have already
done with your thought!" (*IO* 1.5).

What characteristics of human beings suggest to Vico that only comparison with God is adequate? Vico says he will "only briefly mention
them" and let his listeners judge. "Divine is the faculty that sees; divine
that which hears; divine that which conceives ideas; divine that which
perceives; divine that which judges; divine that which reasons; divine that
which remembers" (*IO* 1.12). It is significant that for Vico human divinity
is not limited to reasoning, but extends to senses that require the body,
such as seeing, hearing, and recollecting. Remarkable in his list is "the
power that fashions images of things, which is called phantasy, at the same
time that it originates and produces new forms, reveals and confirms its
own divine origin" (*IO* 1.6). Imagination (*fantasia*) as well as reason makes
us divine. "To see, to hear, to discover, to compare, to infer, to recollect are
divine. Sagacity, keenness, cleverness, capability, ingenuity, and swiftness
are marvelous, great, and divine" (*IO* 1.12). After this brief survey he says
"be aware that these are the least wonders that we can express of the divine
force of the human mind!" (*IO* 1.7). In this section the repetition of "divine" operates as a charm to convince us of what lies hidden within us all.
But what does "divine" mean? Notice that Vico gives "marvelous" and
"great" as synonyms for the adjective "divine." The human mind is similar
to God, but this description does not collapse the difference between human beings with "divine" minds and God who is imitated. God is the
original and makes human beings capable of expressing an image of God
in themselves.

In "On the Heroic Mind," Vico concedes that the love of wisdom requires of the students "something surpassing the human condition itself,"
but he qualifies that it is "yet befitting that nature of yours" (*HM* 230).
There he uses "heroic mind" as he uses "divine" in the earlier orations, but
it amounts to the same thing. In oration four, he makes the similar point
that "the liberal arts and sciences are mastered only with effort . . . so much
effort is needed in their attainment that it often seems beyond the limits of
human nature . . . if, therefore, by exhortation, admonition, and entreaty,
man is persuaded to assume his duties, none of which is foreign to humanity but rather totally in conformity with it, how much more incentive is
necessary so that he will surpass his own nature" (*IO* 4.3). The goal of
education is to cultivate one's *daimonion*, the part of oneself that is more

than human, and resembles most closely God Himself. In both cases human beings are raising themselves up to the divine, as heroes are the offspring of gods and mediators of the gods and the humans.

In 1732 in "On the Heroic Mind" Vico makes *paideia* central as he does in his first oration of 1699. In addition to amplifying the claims in the earlier orations, "On the Heroic Mind" demonstrates that Vico persisted in viewing philosophy in the Platonic sense of *paideia* even after he discovered the *New Science*. "If heroes are those who, as poets say or as they invent, were wont to boast of their divine lineage from 'all-judging Jove,' this much is certain: the human mind, independent of any fiction and fables, does have a divine origin which needs only schooling and breadth of knowledge to unfurl itself. So you see, I do ask of you things greatly surpassing the human: the near-divine nature of your minds—that is what I am challenging you to reveal" (*HM* 230). Learning how to govern oneself, to make one's passions into virtues, is a Herculean task.[7]

Vico reformulates the crucial question for us, "What is it that brings man and God together?" His answer is that "it is but truth, which only the man of wisdom can comprehend and that abides in God" (*IO* 2.11). To know yourself is to know something divine, but this knowledge requires great effort. "Truly, indeed, divine philosophy constructs an extended series of long arguments . . . and thus explains (and this is almost too audacious to say!) how man, from the knowledge of himself, gradually ascends to that of God"(*IO* 1.9). Knowledge of the self is linked to knowing and imitating God. This is not a self-absorbed state of introspection or idleness; rather imitating God requires us to help others, for "what goal is more honorable than to wish to help the greatest number of men and in so doing become more like Almighty God, whose very nature is to help all?" (*IO* 4.8).

About the imperative of the Oracle at Delphi "know thyself," Vico says that it is the axis of the sphere of liberal arts. Vico states that "as a sphere rotates on its axis, so my argument"(*IO* 1.3). This is a clever metaphor, since a commonplace about education is its circularity; encyclopedia is the circle of *paideia*.[8] Vico argues that his argument would not have such force "if formulated to subdue pride of spirit and cast down human arrogance, since innumerable and almost infinite proofs of human frailty and misery are available everywhere" (*IO* 1.4). Vico continues that "man, who by lack of courage constrains his divine mind, by lack of confidence in himself debases it, and by despair of great accomplishments wears it down, may instead be incited and encouraged to undertake great and sublime endeavors for which he has more than ample capacity. Know thyself, therefore, O youth, so that you can attain wisdom, since you were born for wisdom" (ibid.). Vico learned this confidence from the Renaissance, and in particular from Pico's *Oration*. Vico's purpose as an educator is to encourage students so that they will not give up and take the easier road of pleasure described in the *Practica* of the *New Science*, rather than the road of virtue (*NS* 1411).

Vico builds up the *eros* of the students for the true and the good by telling them that they are "born for wisdom" in the first oration. He maintains this claim throughout the orations. Vico repeats this idea in the second oration, in the (even more Platonic) variation that "our reason is moved by the beauty of virtue, for which it has been born" (*IO* 2.10). And even amid references to original sin in the sixth oration, he still maintains "because man desires the true, he can do the good easily and when he is in the habit of doing it, he chooses over all else the true goals of all good things in the conduct of his life, that is, the virtues and the good arts of the spirit, and through them he cultivates the divinity of the mind, and by means of the mind, he reaches God" (*IO* 6.14). Although Vico does not abandon the first oration's goal, "to cultivate the divinity of the mind," the sense in which human beings are born for wisdom is more complex than the first oration suggests (cf. *IO* 1.14).

If it is right to see the human mind as divine, Vico says that what is astonishing is that the love of wisdom faces so many obstacles. It is unnatural for human beings to be ignorant of themselves, and "remain deprived and unenlightened concerning the highest truths because they have never ventured by using the faculties of the spirit as wings for soaring upward to divine things" (*IO* 1.13). Vico ends his first oration on self-knowledge by encouraging the students to try these wings, not to remain ignorant of themselves. The praise of human greatness as our natural potential spurs them to want to learn what Vico inspires them to believe is already theirs if they just look for it and accept the models offered to them for moderating the passions and cultivating virtue. Vico encourages them to be the "earthly Mercuries" Pico speaks of in his *Oration* (*O* 231, cf. 234). For Pico, one first must bathe in the living river of moral philosophy if one would climb the ladder to become angelic oneself. There are no shortcuts to wisdom, and those that "rush ahead" will fail to reach their goal (*IO* 6.14)

So far we have seen how Vico has considered human beings as they *ought* to be. Nevertheless, the account is not complete until this ideal is related to the way human beings *are*, not by nature but in actuality. Vico opens the second oration with a litany of the paradoxes of the human condition: "men are lovers of truth but surrounded by errors; they are gifted with reason but subservient to passions; they are admirers of virtue but full of vices; they are searching for happiness but oppressed by miseries; they have a desire for immortality but languish in their idleness of which, as of death, it is best not to speak" (*IO* 2.1). How does Vico hold both that the mind is divine and that most human beings are fools? The answer involves understanding that the dignity of human beings is a goal, not a given. Only through *paideia*, through the development of knowledge, judgment, and love in Pico's terms—knowledge, virtue, and eloquence in Vico's terms—are human beings "divine." Such wise beings rise above the usual human situation to realize the potential of their nature. As is evident from the selections from the orations, Vico embraces calling human beings "divine" and makes free will central in his thought in the orations, because as an educator he sees the importance of inspiring confidence in human potentiality.

As in Pico, freedom is what makes human beings great as well as miserable. Vico echoes Pico's claim that human beings have "to become what they are to be" in order to get the students to recognize their potential for greatness in the third oration (*O* 225; *IO* 3.1). Vico emphasizes that freedom is unique to human beings; "man alone is whatever he chooses to be. He becomes whatever he desires to become. He does whatever pleases him. . . . Because of his freedom, which no other created thing possesses, the world would recognize him as being, if not its lord, then nearly its lord" (*IO* 3.1). However, Vico is far from claiming that human beings are divine more often than bestial. We may be capable of becoming god-like, but we tend to fall short of our potential. Vico even exclaims that we would be better off without such extensive freedom; "O would that God Eternal had made man subservient to his own nature like all other creatures! With his will thus shackled man would then follow the course of right reason for which he was intended" (*IO* 3.2). It is best freely to choose to be wise, virtuous, and eloquent, but it would be better not to have such freedom than to live in the self-imposed slavery of the fool, or worse, the tyrant of Plato's *Republic*, Book 9.

This idea clearly echoes Pico's description of the fool waging war against himself as the most wretched state, worse than animals with no rationality at all (*IO* 2.2).[9] Far worse to be made in the image of God and to obscure that image than to have no such potential. Ficino sums up this idea when he writes: "O soul, you are something grand if you are not filled with petty things, you are the finest if evil displeases you, the most beautiful if ugly things horrify you, eternal if you disdain the temporal. Since you are of such qualities, if you wish to discover yourself, look for yourself there where those qualities exist."[10] Like Ficino and Pico, Vico holds that human beings are only truly deserving of praise when they are virtuous and wise.

Consider the second oration where the emphasis is on the work required to achieve this divine nature. Appropriating the Stoic idea of the sage as a citizen of the world, Vico says that, "man's privilege of citizenship is not by birth, nor by one's legitimate children, nor is it a reward earned in the fields of battle or at sea, but only by the possession of wisdom" (*IO* 2.11). Vico's summarizes the goal of this oration as "let us fashion our spirit by virtue and wisdom" (*IO*, *Appendix*, 141). Fashioning or making ourselves is explicitly linked to wisdom and virtue. By nature human beings desire to know, desire wisdom, since they long to be happy (*IO* 6.14). This Aristotelian idea is cast in a more Platonic and Stoic light when Vico makes clear that it is only through virtue, through the hard work of *paideia* or self-making, that human beings achieve wisdom, which is our nature and not our automatic birthright.

So "nature" is the ideal human being, what God created Adam to be as described by Pico, but after the Fall we have to toil to be wise and happy. Vico summarizes his position on wisdom as follows: "certainly those who think that wisdom is idleness have simply failed to understand it. Wisdom indeed is the improvement of man. And man is mind and spirit. While mind is misled by error, the spirit is corrupted by passions. Wisdom heals both ills, ordering the mind by truth and the spirit by virtue" (*IO* 5.2). Human beings can become divine or nearly divine, but in order to imitate God we have to tame the passions and cure the corruptions of human nature through education. "In fact, nature has unhappily established that we, by the impetuousness of our mind, fall into error and are brought around to that truth which we are born to reach by a direct path only by a tortuous one" (ibid.). On this path "while other created things must follow their nature, man instead must follow wisdom as his guide" (*IO* 2.2). Human beings differ from all other creatures in that wisdom, not nature, is our guide. The enthusiasm for our potential (as we saw in the first oration) is not eclipsed in the later orations, but the hard work of becoming virtuous and wise is emphasized.

The definition of wisdom that emerges as central to the account of *paideia* in the inaugural orations is from Plato's *Alcibiades*: "wisdom is the perfecter of man" (*Alc.* 1 124e). Different ages have remade who Plato is in large part by the dialogues they favor. The fact that Vico makes the *Alcibiades* one of the dialogues he cites or alludes to often suggests further the mediation of his interpretation of Plato through the Renaissance Platonists. Specifically, it is likely that Vico is following Pico who makes the *Alcibiades* an important source for Plato's views of self-knowledge and wisdom. Recall that in the *Alcibiades*, Socrates asks "what is a human being?" And Alcibiades answers, "I do not know what to say." (*Alc.* 1 129d). How one answers this most Socratic of questions is definitive of what one thinks philosophy as the love of wisdom is. The similarity between Pico's and Vico's answers to this question identifies them as part of the same spiritual family.

In the *Oration*, Pico cites Plato's *Alcibiades* to make the point that "he who knows himself in himself knows all things" (*O* 235). In the *Heptaplus* Pico's unique contribution to the traditional interpretation of the *Genesis* passage is "to interpret the whole passage again in relation to man, and to prove by the facts themselves that every mode of speech in the whole work includes such hidden sense and deep truths about human nature" (*H* 117). Pico defends this approach by referring to a passage from the *Alcibiades*; "How useful and necessary self-knowledge is to man was so demonstrated by Plato in *Alcibiades* 1 (to pass over the Delphic inscription) that he left nothing new for posterity to add on the subject. Shameless and rash is the study of that man who, still ignorant of himself and not yet knowing whether he is able to know anything, nevertheless boldly aims at a knowledge of things remote from himself. Let us turn therefore to ourselves and see (as the Prophet says) how many good things God has made for our souls" (ibid.).

Vico paraphrases from the same part of that dialogue when he defines wisdom in the *New Science* as "wisdom is the perfecter of man" (*Alc.* 1 124ff). In addition, he uses this definition in the prayer at the end of the Academy of Oziosi oration; "wisdom, which is mind and language, is the perfecter of man in his properly being man" (*PE* 90).[11] This account of wisdom as self-knowledge in Vico's later writings was first expressed in the fifth inaugural oration, as quoted above (*IO* 5.2). To be wise one must know who one is. This knowledge is creative as opposed to merely reflective since one must make oneself actually what one is potentially. Perfection is both the process and the goal of human nature, and wisdom is what makes the achievement of the human *telos* possible. For Aristotle human beings were distinguished primarily by reason, but also by their political and mimetic nature. It is this third definition from the *Poetics* that most Renaissance thinkers (at least the Platonists) adapt, that "human beings *by nature* delight in imitation" (1448b5–9, emphasis added). That both Pico and Vico select the dialogue that defines wisdom as perfecter of man reveals the commonality in their view of humanity.

What can be done to remedy the human corruption that obscures this divine nature? Pico answered this question of what we are to do given this paradoxical state of falleness and freedom with the division of angels. We imitate the Cherubim in order to know how to judge and what to love. Vico's answer involves another tripartite division. He clearly states that human beings are comprised of various parts, each of which has its own perfection and its own vice. "The punishments for corrupted human nature [are] the inadequacy of language, opinions of the mind and the passions of the soul . . . the remedies are eloquence, knowledge and virtue" (*IO* 6.5). These correspond to spirit, mind, and speech: "the spirit being the part of human beings perfected by virtue, as the mind by truth, and speech with eloquence" (*IO* 6.7). Only those who do the three "duties of wisdom" are compared to the gods; "those who do these things are indeed men much above the rest of mankind, and, if I may say, only a little less than the gods. A glory neither counterfeit nor transitory but solid and true follows such men" (*IO* 6.6). In this way Plato "has rightly merited the name of Divine" (*IO* 3.6; cf. *NS* 365). Such human beings have through the cultivation of the virtues embodied *humanitas*; they have expressed the image of God which is the potential of all human beings. Human beings can become divine or nearly divine, but in order to imitate God we must tame the passions and cure the corruptions of human nature through *paideia*.

Ernst Cassirer explains that for the Renaissance "the gap between them is closed; between the creative principle and the created, between God and creature, stands the spirit of humanity, *humanitas*, as something at once creator and created."[12] This sums up the metaphysics beneath humanistic education. The goal of *paideia* is *humanitas*. We are making ourselves into human beings. Self-knowledge involves making oneself into the image of God through governing one's passions, that is, by shaping them into virtues. The definition of wisdom as the perfecter of man is united with the more common definition from Cicero that wisdom is "the knowledge of things divine and human."[13] For the way one knows oneself is through education about both things divine and human. For the Platonists, the human mind has a divine element within itself that gives human beings dignity when perfected; but that divinity must be fostered or it will be obscured by vice.

In order to cure our failings we must have sufficient power to transform ourselves. We must believe we can change ourselves, and hence are capable of becoming virtuous, in order actually to become virtuous. After arguing that the fool is the most miserable of men, Vico encourages his audience to "take refuge in the sanctuary of wisdom," and to "obey the law of nature which commands each one of us to be true to himself" (*IO* 2.15). He concludes that "it is within our power because it is indeed within us. It is for our well-being because it is indeed within nature" (ibid.). The universe must allow for our freedom to change ourselves for *paideia* to be possible. Vico's metaphysics of providence is essential for this same reason; in a world of Stoic fate or Epicurean chance, *paideia* cannot be achieved.

The teaching of the inaugural orations is that corruption obscures the natural splendor of human beings and can be cured through knowledge, virtue, and eloquence. The humanist educational ideal could hardly be stated more strongly than Vico states it in these inaugural orations. Wise and virtuous human beings are rightly considered "divine" for such accomplishments. What tempers the optimism of Pico and Vico alike is the acknowledgment that humanity is the perfection of human beings, and that this is only achieved through making oneself virtuous and following wisdom as all other creatures follow nature. Vico's orations inspire students by showing them that their own minds are among the divine things. Education requires a genuine sense of one's freedom and dignity, a sense of the greatness of humanity at its best.

In the fourth oration Vico exhorts himself to live up to his ideal for philosophy, praying "God help me to force myself according to my ability to exhort them repeatedly every time I see them so that they do not lose courage and give up" (*IO* 4.3). The continued centrality of education in Vico's mature ideal for philosophy is evident in his axiom 5 of the *New Science* which states that philosophy must "raise and direct weak and fallen man, not rend his nature or abandon him in his corruption" (*NS* 129). The final perfection of the knowledge of the truth is the eloquent speech of this truth, so that others also will see the good and want to pursue it.

Chapter 3

Eloquence: Wisdom Speaking

In the last chapter on poetry, I pointed out that Vico counted eloquence among the cures for human corruption necessary to actualize human dignity. As knowledge cures false opinions of the mind, and virtue the untamed passions, so eloquence cures the inadequacy of language. Adding eloquence to knowledge and virtue as essential to *paideia* strongly signals Vico's inheritance from the Latin rhetorical and humanist tradition. Vico concludes the sixth oration, "I have done that in this oration because it is as much as I may seriously and diligently do for you *according to the proper object of my profession* and according to my part as a man in serving human society" (*IO* 6.15, emphasis added). As professor of Latin eloquence, Vico emphasizes that eloquence is the culmination of self-knowledge, which is the axis of humanistic education or *paideia*. But is not eloquence as an ideal in tension with the Platonic dimensions of Vico's philosophy which I am tracing?

Vico's appropriation of the Latin rhetorical tradition has been studied by other scholars.[1] My primary aim here is to explore how Vico can reconcile his commitment to eloquence with a Platonic conception of philosophy as the love of wisdom. To understand Vico's ideal of eloquence, we can again turn to Giovanni Pico della Mirandola whose thought has Platonic as well as rhetorical facets. Brian Vickers rightly cautions, "although rhetoric was often linked with philosophy in the Renaissance, it is not easy for us to estimate their true relationship, which was neither stable nor always clearly formulated."[2] In Pico, as well as other humanists, where they stand on the relationship between philosophy and eloquence is not always obvious, and Pico's position in the famous letter to Ermolao Barbaro is a particularly vexed question.[3] Yet in a question as fundamental as the quarrel between philosophy and rhetoric, complexity is a virtue. Pico's letter to Barbaro can shed light on the philosophical significance of Vico's claims about eloquence, in his inaugural orations as well as in later works, and on how a Platonic philosopher can have eloquence as an ideal. Furthermore, the writings of Pico and Vico embody this ideal of eloquence. What some call "eclecticism" in both thinkers is more appropriately understood as a manifestation of eloquence in Cicero's sense, as summed up in the sentence: "eloquence is nothing other than wisdom speaking copiously" (*nihil enim est aliud eloquentia nisi copiose loquens sapientia*)(*De part. orat.* xxiii. 79).

Pico as an Eloquent Critic of Untruthful Rhetoric

When considering Pico's position on the quarrel of philosophy and rhetoric, it is helpful to think in terms of the two pivotal Platonic dialogues on the question: the *Gorgias* and the *Phaedrus*. Many Renaissance humanists followed Cicero in seeing how Plato stands in a complex relationship to rhetoric (*De or.* i.11.47); Plato is both the greatest philosophical critic of rhetoric when divorced from truth as well as the most eloquent of the philosophers. Pico mirrors Plato's Janus-face toward rhetoric when he criticizes the degeneration of rhetoric into flattery and mere adornment and simultaneously embodies in his own language the ideal of the true orator. With one eye on each *topos*, Pico sees that the ideal is that of the true orator in the *Phaedrus*, yet he retains the caution of the *Gorgias*. In this way, Pico maintains in his famous letter to Barbaro the guarded endorsement of rhetoric, which is necessary for the philosopher to preserve the primary commitment to truth.

Pico writes to Barbaro defending the philosophy of the scholastics despite their lack of eloquence, not because he thinks there is no need at all for philosophers to be eloquent; rather he must respond because he cannot sanction valuing *verba* over *res*, words over things, even though his ideal is their union. Pico's ironic stance in the letter has made many scholars think he abandoned the humanist ideal of eloquence, whereas in fact he illustrates the way the philosopher can reconcile philosophy and eloquence without ceasing to be a philosopher. Pico's correspondent, Barbaro, playing on his own name, did not miss the irony, and neither should we; "what a ridiculous thing it is: a barbarous man defends eloquence, while you, an eloquent man, defend its want."[4]

Cicero provides another touchstone text which can further assist us in sorting out the complexity of Pico's simultaneous defense of the scholastics as well as an ideal of eloquence: "I have been led by reason itself to hold this opinion first and foremost, that wisdom without eloquence does too little for the good of states, but that eloquence without wisdom is generally highly disadvantageous and is never helpful" (*De invent. rhet.*, I. i. 1).[5] Whereas Plato considered only the failure of the rhetorician to be philosophical, Cicero considers the failure of the philosopher to be eloquent. In this way, Cicero opens the door for those who would identify moral philosophy and rhetoric, and have no use for philosophy apart from its issue in speech and action, even though he himself does not take this position.[6] Cicero himself vacillates, but still considers philosophy the higher activity, despite the claim that it is incomplete without eloquence. Pico and Barbaro, and (I will argue) Vico as well, are much more tolerant of the failure of the philosopher to achieve the ideal than the failure of the rhetorician. The scholastics fell short of the ideal of the true orator, the philosopher who speaks wisdom, but the way they failed is not as serious an error as an orator who fails to speak the truth and thus deceives.

Pico places his arguments for the scholastics and against rhetoric in a character's mouth, one of the more eloquent of the barbarians.[7] The opening points reduce eloquence to mere adornment, which is, he says, as inappropriate to the philosopher's wisdom as rouge for a maiden.[8] To a critic like Barbaro who finds the scholastics dull, Pico's character replies that the scholastics had "the god of eloquence not on the tongue but in the heart, and if eloquence they lacked, they did not lack wisdom; (let him find out), that eloquence should not have been joined to wisdom."[9]

Further into the letter, Pico's character weakens his stance toward a position which acknowledges that wisdom and eloquence can exist together. Pico's character gives us a helpful image for the relative merit of eloquence without wisdom and wisdom without eloquence. Ideally, a Roman would want a coin with a Roman stamp which is also pure gold, but if, as second best, one had to choose between a pure gold coin with a Teutonic stamp and a counterfeit Roman coin, everyone would choose based on the material not the stamp. The material is the wisdom, the substance of what is said, and the stamp is the eloquence, its form.[10] If the ideal is absent, and one must choose between wisdom and eloquence, then the philosopher's answer is clear; he must choose wisdom. Pico warns the humanists, like Barbaro, that their own greatest authority supports Pico's argument for preferring wisdom to eloquence in such a case; "Cicero prefers sagacity though halting in speech to stupid loquacity."[11]

As a persuasive final point, Pico's imaginary scholastic turns the humanists' own speciality of making us human against them: "we can live without a tongue, though not conveniently; but we cannot live at all without a heart. He is not cultured (*humanus*) who were alien to polite letters; he is not man (*homo*) who were destitute of philosophy. The most inarticulate wisdom can be of use. Unwise eloquence, like a sword in a madman's hand, cannot but be most dangerous."[12] Bringing the images back to the defense of the scholastic philosophers, Pico says Lucretius may be more pleasing than Scotus, but who would doubt Scotus is closer to the truth? He says, in effect, "who among you would really say it is better eloquently to explain that the universe is atoms in the void rather than say in imperfect speech the truth that it is governed by providence?" Pico knows his audience.

The key to unlocking the complexity of Pico's letter is to understand its irony.[13] Pico is explicit that Barbaro should not take all his criticisms of rhetoric separated from wisdom as an indictment of true eloquence. Pico distances himself before and after the speech of his fictional scholastic. Pico could not be more clear that he does not take his arguments for the divorce of philosophy and rhetoric entirely seriously. Especially Pico's parallel with Glaucon, the devil's advocate in Plato's *Republic*, would seem to make this unmistakably evident. Pico reveals that "my special aim was like that of Plato's Glaucon, who praised injustice, not seriously, but to goad Socrates to the praise of justice. Likewise, so that I may hear you defend eloquence I have attacked it rather violently, for a little while even over the protest of my feelings and natural disposition."[14] Pico does not completely agree with those who make such arguments as he has rehearsed, but his device enables him to draw attention to the error of valuing mere rhetoric over true philosophy, even when the latter fails to be eloquent. Pico's topic is not to address the union of philosophy and eloquence, though the ideal is implicit. Although Pico's views on the surface seem hostile to rhetoric, on second glance Pico is best seen as part of the Ciceronian tradition where eloquence is defined as "wisdom speaking copiously" (*De part. orat.* xxiii.79).

Pico's main concern is to respond to Barbaro who was, in his opinion, too harsh on the scholastics; for though they lack eloquence, they do possess much truth. Pico is criticizing Barbaro for too quickly dismissing philosophers who fail to be eloquent, and reminding him that rhetoric without truth is more dangerous than truth without rhetoric. In this primary aim of his letter, Pico is firmly within the Ciceronian tradition, with its roots in Plato and Aristotle.

Pico must have known that Barbaro meant to oppose to scholasticism the true eloquence of the Ciceronian tradition.[15] One could imagine Barbaro sending a short note back to Pico saying: you know I meant to contrast eloquence as "wisdom speaking," and not mere sophistry, to the scholastics who may give some wisdom but lack eloquence. Though Barbaro agrees that the ideal is both, he did leave himself open to the reminder from Pico that one should not prefer eloquence over the truth. Barbaro sees the irony of Pico's letter, and does not reply with a pedestrian plea to get the definition straight, resolving their verbal disagreement and revealing their common position. Instead Barbaro sees the jest and plays along.

Barbaro invents another character, one he says is real, not made up like Pico's, and this Paduan scholastic grudgingly points out the major lines of a Ciceronian response; that philosophy is not incompatible with rhetoric, that his critic's argument depends entirely on collapsing the distinction between an orator and a sophist.[16] The Paduan attributes such arguments to ill-will, since he knows a humanist like Pico knows better than he himself the tradition on this question. Of the rhetorical and topical books of Aristotle he says, "we ourselves do not care."[17] Speaking again of philosophers like himself, he says of the debate over rhetoric, "we keep away from this contest over Aristotle as from a precipice."[18] Barbaro enjoys making the Paduan search for *topoi* in defense of the connection between philosophy and eloquence that are at Pico's fingertips, having the Paduan say "nor can I find where Aristotle said it."[19]

In 1558, Melanchthon wrote another response to Pico's letter. He was dissatisfied with Barbaro's defense, perhaps because he did not see as clearly that Pico was being ironic and Barbaro was playing along. Even though Melanchthon seems to acknowledge that Pico's true position is not the same as his arguments against rhetoric, when going through the criticisms of rhetoric, he falls into attributing these views to Pico, to such an extent that he thinks Pico should write a palinode for eloquence.[20] For historians of philosophy Melanchthon provides the valuable service of making clear that the true orator of Plato's *Phaedrus* was read together with Aristotle's *Rhetoric*.[21] Since Pico does not directly mention Plato's dialogues on his theme, and Barbaro only alludes to the connection, it is useful that Melanchthon clearly locates the roots of the Ciceronian tradition in Plato and Aristotle. Melanchthon's reply is that Plato "in the *Phaedrus* sapiently and copiously argues about the nature of eloquence and how necessary it is for explication of things divine and human," but since he does "not know whether those barbarians of yours would give to Plato a place among the philosophers," he adds that "Aristotle writes the same things in his *Rhetoric*."[22] He concludes that "these princes among the philosophers therefore define eloquence as a power divinely bestowed on the human race, so that men may be able to teach each other correctly and clearly concerning great and necessary things."[23]

The identification of Aristotle's *Rhetoric* as an elaboration of Plato's ideal orator in the *Phaedrus* is what is most significant. Barbaro does not explicitly argue this point, though since we know that Pico encouraged Barbaro to read Plato, this would have been a good serious response, if Barbaro had not chosen to keep up the jest. Melanchthon is further to the orator's side of the debate than either Barbaro or Pico, but he gives the princes of philosophy, Plato and Aristotle, as examples of eloquence. He does think eloquence is a necessity, but he means speech that is truthful. Melanchthon qualifies that "I am really not so far out of my mind that I will make more of empty loquacity than wisdom. This is what I truly uphold, that eloquence is a necessity when it comes to clarifying great subjects."[24] In the end, Melanchthon is advocating the same ideal of joining wisdom and eloquence.

So we can say of Pico what Cicero said of Plato, that "it was when making fun of orators that he himself seemed to be the consummate orator" (De or. iii. 31. 122).[25] But this reconciliation of eloquence in the speech of the philosopher himself is not the same as Melanchthon's praise of the necessity of eloquence, when he claims that "clearly there is no use for wisdom unless we can communicate to others the things we have deliberated and thought upon."[26] As a philosopher, falling short of the ideal of "wisdom speaking" by failing to speak well is less serious than failing to speak the truth. This debate draws attention to the philosophical concern that eloquence should not be valued over wisdom, but instead eloquence must be seen as the perfection of wisdom.

Vico's Eloquence as the Flower of Wisdom

Pico's letter reminds us of the Renaissance debate over the relationship between philosophy and eloquence which was the stage for Vico's own thought on this question. Steeped in this debate, how might Vico have reconciled his first author, Plato, with his commitment to rhetoric? It is suggestive of the harmony Vico thought was possible between Plato and eloquence that he does not explicitly criticize or defend Plato's position on rhetoric. As a professor of Latin Eloquence, if Vico thought Plato was an enemy of all rhetoric, if he thought Plato cared nothing for speech or language, he would certainly have criticized him for this mistake. That Vico does not charge Plato with this error indicates that he does not see Plato as an enemy of eloquence. This argument from omission is supported by Vico's claims which echo Cicero, who does consider Plato to be eloquent (De or. i.11.47). When Vico defines eloquence as "wisdom speaking," he is locating himself in the Ciceronian tradition.

The evidence for the Ciceronian ideal of eloquence in Vico is extensive. In Vico's *Autobiography* he writes of himself that "he never discussed matters pertaining to eloquence apart from wisdom, but would say that eloquence is wisdom speaking" (*A* 199). The Ciceronian definition of eloquence is firmly appropriated, and it will be used again. In the seventh oration, which was revised and published as *On the Study Methods of our Times*, Vico contrasts the ancient ideal of eloquence with its neglect in modern times.

Vico notes that advocating eloquence may lead some who misunderstand to criticize him. Vico recalls that in ancient times eloquence and philosophy were allied; "there was an epoch when the 'fourfold philosophy' (i.e., logic, physics, metaphysics, and ethics) was handed down by its teachers in a manner fitted to foster eloquence: i.e., the attempt was made to fuse philosophy with eloquence. Demosthenes was a product of the Lyceum; Cicero, of the Academy: there is no doubt that they were the two foremost speakers of the two most splendid languages" (*SM* 37). In contrast, Vico observes that "today, those branches of philosophical theory are taught by such a method as to dry up every fount of convincing expression, of copious, penetrating, embellished, lucid, developed, psychologically effective, and impassionate utterance" (ibid). Because Vico's own approach to philosophy and eloquence accords with the ancient epoch, not his own modern one, he predicts the criticism that "some learned pundit might object that, in the conduct of life, I would have our young students become courtiers, and not philosophers; pay little attention to truth and follow not reality but appearances; cast down morality and put on a deceitful 'front' of virtue." (ibid.). In Ciceronian manner, Vico replies, "I have no such intention. Instead, I should like to have them act as philosophers, even at court; to care for truth that both is and has the appearance of truth, and to follow that which is morally good and which everybody approves" (*SM* 37–38). In this assessment, Vico succinctly locates himself in terms of the ancient acceptance and the modern rejection of the union of philosophy and eloquence.

In this speech, Vico reveals his awareness that the quarrel of the ancients and the moderns has further polarized the quarrel of philosophy and rhetoric. Eloquence has been reduced to mere sophistry by modern philosophers, such as Descartes and Locke, and as a result Vico must be more careful than Pico to articulate their shared ideal of eloquence. Only if one reads Vico from the point of view of modern philosophy, which rejects all rhetoric as sophistry, rather than within the Renaissance tradition, does

Vico appear to betray philosophy. This recognition of Vico's context is essential for assessing his philosophical worth.

In Vico's final philosophical work, he explicitly addresses the question of the relationship between philosophy and eloquence in the speech he gave to the Academy of Oziosi. Vico's brief commentary on the precepts of Horace on the proper use of language is a good summary of his ideal. Of the precept that "right thinking is the first principle and source of writing," Vico explains, "because there is no eloquence without truth and dignity, of these two parts wisdom is composed" (*PE* 89). Regarding the correct choice of subjects, Vico agrees with Horace that "the Socratic writings will direct you in the choice of subjects" (ibid.). Amplifying the third precept, "when the subject is well conceived, words will follow naturally," Vico says this is so "because of the natural bond by which we claim language and heart to be held fast together, for to every idea its proper voice stands naturally attached. Thus, eloquence is none other than wisdom speaking" (ibid.). Vico concludes his speech with a prayer for perfection of man in both mind and language (*SM* 90). In "On the Heroic Mind" Vico similarly says, "rhetoric exists to ensure that the tongue does not betray nor fail the mind, nor the mind its theme" (*HM* 235–36).

Adding these statements to the importance granted eloquence in the sixth oration (as the third cure for human corruption) makes clear that Vico finds no inherent conflict between philosophy and eloquence. Vico cannot remain a Platonic philosopher if he values appearances and probabilities over truth, as would some in the rhetorical tradition, but he can be Platonic philosopher and endorse eloquence as "wisdom speaking" in the Ciceronian sense. Vico does not directly criticize the kind of rhetoric which betrays philosophy as Pico did, but it is clear that Vico himself never separates rhetoric from wisdom. This connection is crucial for seeing how Pico and Vico agree about the nature of eloquence, and the relationship between philosophy and eloquence. Pico's exchange of letters with Barbaro, in which he criticizes rhetoric, illuminates this Platonic evaluation of rhetoric implicit in Vico. Whereas Pico explores the failure to achieve the ideal relationship between philosophy and eloquence and alludes to the ideal, Vico defends the ideal with allusions to its failure. Both are Platonists in valuing *res* over *verba* if there is a conflict, but both also see the ideal as the union of *res* and *verba*.[27] Vico would not praise the Renaissance for eloquence if he saw in it a conflict with the truth.

So far it is clear that Vico, like Pico, reconciles wisdom and eloquence on philosophy's terms. But what indication is there that Vico viewed Plato as eloquent? In other words, what evidence is there that Vico saw Plato as a source of the Ciceronian ideal? Vico writes in his *Autobiography* about his role as a professor of eloquence that "he never discussed matters pertaining to eloquence apart from wisdom, but would say that eloquence is wisdom speaking, that his chair was the one that should give direction to minds and make them universal; that others were concerned with the various parts of knowledge, but that his should teach it as an integral whole in which each of the parts accords with every other and gets the meaning from the whole" (*A* 199). Vico explains that the eloquence that he is trying to achieve through his role in the university is parallel to Plato's philosophy itself; "a Plato (to take a conspicuous example) among the ancients was the equivalent of an entire university of studies of our day, all harmonized in one system" (*A* 199). Plato is an example of an ancient who embodies eloquence because, for Vico, speaking about the whole is identified with eloquence. For Vico "the whole is really the flower of wisdom" (*SM* 77).

As Vico makes clear in the *Study Methods*, he makes a connection between eloquence and knowledge of the whole in his reflections on his professional duties. In the discussion of his task as a professor of eloquence, to inspire students with an annual inaugural oration, Vico says he must know all the arts and sciences (*SM* 78). As a modern, Vico must recapture the universal wisdom of the ancients, like Plato, through harmonizing the fragmented arts and sciences. Vico takes seriously his task to speak about all the fields of knowledge, and that his teaching must be the capstone of the university education (*SM* 78). Vico asks rhetorically, "what is eloquence, in effect, but wisdom, ornately and copiously delivered in words appropriate to the common opinion of mankind?" (ibid.). The definition of eloquence as "wisdom speaking copiously" is now used with the emphasis on "copiously." Vico states that the highest praise for a speech is to say that it is "comprehensive" (*SM* 15). At the end of his *Autobiography*, Vico identifies himself with Socrates; here we see him identify with Plato's comprehensive scope, with his eloquence.

So far I have considered primarily Vico's remarks on eloquence in his orations. No reading of Vico is complete, however, without exploring his philosophical as well as professional reasons for praising eloquence. Knowing from the orations that Vico understood eloquence as wisdom speaking, we can now ask the more complex question: what thematic role does eloquence play in Vico's *New Science*?

As in the orations Vico gave under his professional aegis, so in the *New Science*, human beings are defined not only by rationality but also by speech. Vico makes speech central when he states in summary that "man is properly

only mind, body, and speech, and speech stands as it were midway between mind and body" (*NS* 1045). Locating what is at the middle is to
think topically. Through connecting Vico's middle terms, we discover that
eloquence can be further understood as the embodiment of heroic mind.
Speech is midway between body and mind for Vico, and likewise the middle
realm is that of the heroes.[28] Through perfection of *logos*, in the dual meaning of *ratio* and *oratio*, human beings perfect themselves.[29] The whole is
"the flower of wisdom," and eloquence is the final fruit and goal of *paideia*.
Such wise speech is the highest human activity.

Lady Metaphysic also occupies this same middle realm on the frontispiece of the *New Science* (see illustration, page 212). So the intermediary
realm between human and divine is occupied by metaphysics, by *eros*, by
heroes, and now we see also by speech. Consider the significance of the
jewel on her breast. Speech is associated with the heart as well as the tongue,
and (in Cicero) eloquence is defined as the union of heart and tongue. The
heart of metaphysic is "clean and pure," so what metaphysic says will be
true, not deceptive (*NS* 5). Her rhetoric is not meant to deceive, but to
persuade us in the truth. The jewel is convex, not concave, which means it
is directed towards others, as speech always is (ibid.). Vico explains the image
of the jewel as revealing the social aspect of metaphysics: "it indicates that the
knowledge of God does not have its end in metaphysic taking private illumination from intellectual institutions and thence regulating merely her own
moral institutions, as hitherto the philosophers have done. For this would have
been signified by a flat jewel, whereas the jewel is convex, thus reflecting and
scattering the ray abroad, to show that metaphysic should know God's providence in public moral things or civil customs" (ibid.).

The most fully human act is passionately to speak the truth to others
about things divine and human. The goal is not only the perfection of
one's own knowledge, but also the instruction of others. To raise up weak
and fallen man is exactly Vico's purpose in the orations (axiom 5, *NS* 130).
It is so difficult to achieve this highest expression that Vico associated its
achievement with heroism, with transcending the human condition. Lady
Metaphysic is a Platonic philosopher such as is described in axiom 5 of the
New Science (ibid.). The aspect highlighted there is the political dimension
of Platonism as opposed to Stoicism and Epicureanism, which were considered solitary philosophies. Plato is not seen as opposed to speech, but as
one of the philosophers who has a "clean and pure heart"(*NS* 5).

Ironically, Vico lets us know that his *New Science* is really teaching us
how to be eloquent in the section called "Method." Vico's method is no
method that Descartes would recognize. Vico speaks directly to the reader,

in an enthusiastic style reminiscent of his inaugural orations: "Indeed, we make bold to affirm that he who meditates this Science narrates to himself this ideal eternal history as far as he himself makes it for himself by that proof 'it had, has, and will have to be.' . . . And history cannot be more certain than when he who creates the things also narrates them. . . . And this very fact is an argument, O reader, that these proofs are of a kind divine and should give thee a divine pleasure, since in God knowledge and creation are one and the same thing" (*NS* 349). As is well known, the maker's knowledge principle is crucial for understanding the *New Science*. Vico's method requires his readers to take the axioms and principles and make the proof that this is in fact human wisdom for themselves. The individual's role in discovering wisdom is an important feature of the ideal of eloquence; a human being is eloquent, and for every eloquent speech, there must be a speaker. Vico's method places the labor on the reader, for everyone must be his own Hercules.

Having sketched how speech plays a significant thematic role in the *New Science,* I now turn to the question of Vico's own eloquence: how is the *New Science* the flower of Vico's wisdom, that is, his knowledge of the whole of things divine and human? At first glance Pico's *Oration* (and the scholastic theses it was to preface) and Vico's *New Science* are very different kinds of philosophizing. Yet Donald Phillip Verene rightly makes the connection between the comprehensive projects of Pico and Vico, echoing Vico's own parallel in his *Autobiography.* Verene claims that "the *Scienza nuova* is not a treatise but an oration similar to the *Oratio de hominis dignitate* of Giovanni Pico della Mirandola."[30] What is similar about Pico's *Oration* and Vico's *New Science* when each is considered as a whole (as opposed to comparing isolated similar themes)? How do both embody the same ideal of eloquence as wisdom speaking?

Once again understanding Pico helps us see Vico in a new light, for both are charged with eclecticism when they are, in Renaissance terms, more correctly called copious. According to the theory and practice of Pico and Vico, eloquence is not achieved by restricting oneself to one school of thought. Recall that Pico was not content to rest with espousing the tradition of poetic theology, and claims to defend his own discoveries in the theses as well (*O* 245). Pico acknowledges the vanity of his own vast learning if none of it were his own: "what were it to have dealt with the opinions of others, no matter how many, if we are to come to a gathering of wise men with no contribution of our own and are supplying nothing from our own store, brought forth and worked out by our own genius?" (*O* 244). There could not be a clearer parallel than what we find in Vico's third oration, "let us bring something of our own to the common store of knowledge." (*IO* 3.13)

Vico also echoes the rest of the passage from Pico's *Oration*. "It is surely an ignoble part to be wise only from a notebook (as Seneca says) and, as if the discoveries of our predecessors had closed the way to our own industry and the power of nature were exhausted in us, to produce from ourselves nothing which, if it does not actually demonstrate the truth, at least imitates it from afar" (*O* 244). Compare Vico's thesis in the *Study Methods*. Vico generalizes this point, in a way that is only implicit in Pico, when he warns that imitation of great masterpieces can hinder "inventive genius." (*SM* 70). He reasons that "those who left us masterpieces of the arts, had before their eyes no model to imitate except the best that is in nature . . . to equal them is impossible, since imitators are not endowed with the force of imagination of their predecessors . . . Since imitators cannot surpass or even equal the innovators, they can only fall short of their achievement" (*SM* 71). In "On the Heroic Mind," Vico also echoes Pico's judgment against those who contribute nothing of their own, warning that "whatever you do, do not be taken in unawares by that opinion, springing either from envy or cowardice, which says that for this most blessed century of ours everything that could ever have been achieved in the world of learning has already reached its conclusion, its culmination, and perfection, so that nothing remains therein to be desired. It is a false opinion, stemming from scholars with petty minds. For this world is still young" (*HM* 242–42).

From the *Autobiography* we know that Vico does have four authors to whom he looks for inspiration. However, in accordance with his ideal of self-knowledge, his own imagination must take what is true from each and arrange it into an eloquent speech. Vico's attitude toward the study of authors is irenic not eristic (*IO* 3.7).[31] In this Vico is quite similar to Pico, whose *Oration* is truly the work of the Prince of Concord, whose philosophy was often associated with *pax philosophia*.[32] Ernst Cassirer makes this point explicitly: "The same universalistic attitude pervades the whole of Pico's work and gives it its characteristic stamp. . . . Pico does not wish to fight for the rights and the meaning and goal of any particular philosophical school: for him the real meaning and goal of philosophy lies not in fighting, but in peace. The *pax philosophia* is his real ideal."[33] This interpretation is also that of Cesare Vasoli "Pico saw himself as searching for the deepest common truth, where *sapientia* and its various temporal manifestations might reside, untroubled by doctrinal squabbles."[34]

The claims for the originality of the *New Science* indicate how Vico tried to be an innovator not merely an imitator. Calling what came before "a tissue of confused memories," Vico writes that "for the purposes of this inquiry, we must reckon as if there were no books in the world" (*NS* 330). Likewise, at the end of Book 5 of the *New Science*, Vico makes a bold assertion of his work's originality and comprehensive scope, claiming that "we could not refrain from giving this work the invidious title of a New Science, for it was too much to defraud it unjustly of the rightful claim it had over an argument so universal as that concerning the common nature of the nations" (*NS* 1096).[35] In "On Heroic Mind," Vico also states the newness of his theme; "I take it to be my task to bring before you a theme which is wholly new" (*HM* 229).

The eloquent orator finds wisdom wherever he can and is not a slave to one system or one school. The truth that must be spoken, if one has the virtue of eloquence, must be self-knowledge, not the opinions of others. Far from being in conflict with the Socratic ideal of self-knowledge, when understood as "wisdom speaking," eloquence is the Socratic ideal. The ideal of eloquence is inextricably intertwined with the ideal of self-knowledge. The wise speak from what is written on their souls (*Phdr.* 276a). This self-knowledge is the only wisdom which one can speak truly. There is a virtuosity or ingenuity that characterizes the philosopher who is eloquent. This ideal of eloquence as the expression of wisdom (as opposed to system and clarity) unites Pico and Vico as kindred thinkers perhaps more than any other single similarity. Strangely, this shared quality proves to be the biggest obstacle to acceptance of either as truly philosophical by modern critics. Beginning with Descartes's identification of truth with clarity, eloquence is so much forgotten, and rhetoric so much despised, that an eloquent philosopher is mistrusted not admired. The wisdom and eloquence of both Pico and Vico have been misunderstood and overlooked by later philosophers, who no longer strive for eloquence as the ideal expression of knowledge and virtue.

Ernst Cassirer raises the same question about Pico that Alasdair MacIntyre raises about Vico.[36] What value is found in eclectic philosophers who defy systematization? Both answer that one must sift through the chaos to find the philosophical insights hidden there. This attitude has led historians of philosophy to skip over the whole Renaissance as unphilosophical, because of its unsystematic character, and Vico as "the owl of Minerva of Renaissance Humanism" is guilty by association.[37] In this way MacIntyre says that "Vico's new science . . . is recognizably one more of these strange tapestries, out of which can be separated various illuminating strands of thought."[38] When Cassirer asked whether there could be in Pico a "wise eclecticism" or if that were just an "oxymoron," it was not surprising that his answer was that, unless some systematic quality could be found in Pico, he was not really a philosopher. Studying Pico and Vico together reveals that Cassirer was struggling to define a quality called "eloquence" when he asked whether "wise eclecticism" were possible.

Cassirer comes closest to seeing Pico's eloquence when he writes "What is characteristic for Pico is hence not the way in which he *increases* the store of philosophic truth, but the way in which he made it *manifest.*"[39] Cassirer introduces his best insights with the phrase "it is as though" Pico was thinking this or that, since Cassirer himself did not think this way. For example, "it is as though Pico's ambition was to assemble the positions he desired to treat and defend from every region of '*globus intellectualis*'"[40] Notice that in the following formulation Cassirer touches on the heart of the Renaissance ideal to make wisdom speak, to render ideas "vocal:" "It is as though he had made it his goal to render vocal at the same time *all* the intellectual forces which had heretofore cooperated in establishing religious, philosophical, and scientific knowledge. None of them is to be merely attacked or rejected; each of them is granted a definite positive share in the totality of philosophic knowledge and truth. There is no longer for Pico any limitation or dogmatic restriction."[41]

Cartesian and Kantian assumptions color Cassirer's evaluation of Pico, which bears an uncanny resemblance to many current criticisms of Vico. Cassirer seems to grasp the comprehensive project of Pico, yet his assumptions about the systematic, purely rational character of philosophy make it impossible to appreciate Pico on his own terms. Cassirer asks: "can the goal Pico set himself be formulated and justified from a systematic and philosophic point of view?"[42] Cassirer answers that "If we measure Pico's thought by strictly philosophical standards, we often get the impression that we are here dealing less with a fixed *doctrine* of definite form and clear outline, than with a kind of intellectual alchemy."[43] Instead of system, Cassirer is incredulous to find that "it is as though Pico never tired of assembling all the positions he encountered, uniting them all with each other, mixing and combining them, in order to see what kind of product would arise from this treatment. He loves to seek out just the most diverse and curious doctrines, in order to throw them all into the crucible of his thought and to submit them there to a process of purification and clarification."[44]

Cassirer points out that "this objection has been directed against Pico from the very beginning, and it has determined the traditional estimate of his philosophy. His many-sidedness and comprehensiveness have been admired, but in the same breath his thought has been denied any philosophic value. For men saw in it for the most part nothing but an expression of eclecticism and syncretism."[45] Eclecticism and syncretism are pejorative terms used by modern philosophers to categorize unsystematic treatments of traditionally philosophical subjects.

Cassirer mentions that scholars, such as Eugenio Garin, have tried to defend Pico from the negative epithet of syncretism or eclecticism. The mistake of such advocates was to allow the narrow definition of philosophy. If philosophy is merely about clear and distinct ideas (Cartesian adjectives Cassirer uses in stating the ideal for philosophy in contrast to what he finds in Pico), then the Renaissance will remain outside of the canonical history of philosophy; and so will Vico. This conceit of scholars is so pervasive that even Cassirer, who deserves enormous credit for reviving the philosophical study of the Renaissance, commits it. Cassirer reports of an early French scholar, that "Renan speaks of a 'wise eclecticism' which Pico sought to preserve in his philosophy."[46] Cassirer dismisses this as meaningless, "but is there any clear and distinct meaning to be associated with such a phrase? Or is not this oxymoron rather but the expression of the embarrassment into which we fall, when instead of judging Pico's thought by purely historical standards we approach it with genuinely systematic claims? A 'wise' eclecticism seems indeed no other and no better than a wooden piece of iron."[47] Contrary to Cassirer's response, "wise eclecticism" is a noble attempt to reinvent the idea of eloquence in a time when it has been utterly lost.

Cassirer's defense of Pico (by finding an "inner form" to his philosophy) also reads his own philosophical ideas back into Pico. When one sees that Pico sought to be wisdom speaking, one does not have to force Pico into a later ideal for philosophy. Before Descartes it was possible, as Cassirer asserts it is now impossible, to attribute philosophical significance to a figure who "takes no definite *stand* on the great antitheses of metaphysics, epistemology, and ethics; which poses no definite problems and which maintains or rejects no definite solutions."[48] Cicero was nothing if not a gatherer of various ideas from different schools of thought, and Petrarch honored him as the "father of Roman eloquence."[49] As the father of Renaissance humanism himself, Petrarch was much more concerned with truth than certainty, seeking continually for a more complete account of the things divine and human. Likewise, the "eclecticism" of Pico and Vico is not arbitrary as the term suggests; rather it is eloquence in the sense of a wise and copious speech.

Both Pico and Vico are independent thinkers who make original contributions as well as find what is good in the thought of others. Both seek to be wisdom speaking, and since wisdom for human beings is essentially self-knowledge, instead of the empty maxims of the schools, they bring their entire experience as human beings to their thought. This passion to stretch the limits of one's knowledge is the intellectual manifestation of courage. Heroic mind is difficult to achieve, but Vico shares with Pico the courage to attempt it. This achievement could lead to pride in one's own dignity, unless it is balanced with piety, as it was for both of them. But without some sense of human ability, we would never explore the angelic side of our nature and would lack the *eros* for truth that makes us human.

Vico surely admired Pico's daring proposal to make public what he had learned in order to test himself, and tell others what he found. Circumstances prevented Pico from giving a heroic speech. Yet Pico was revered by many contemporaries as "a phoenix, a miracle of nature, a hero, the marvel of the age."[50] Pico's friend Angelo Poliziano wrote of him: "Nature seemed to have showered on this man, or hero, all her gifts. He was tall and finely moulded; from his face something of divinity shone forth. Acute, gifted with a prodigious memory, in his studies he was indefatigable, in his style perspicuous and eloquent. You could not say whether his talents or his moral qualities conferred on him the greater lustre. Familiar with all branches of philosophy, and the master of many languages, he stood high above the reach of praise."[51] Such was the man who is often not counted among the philosophers, because he seems to lack clear and distinct ideas. Unlike Pico, Vico was able (though at great personal expense) to give his speech in the *New Science*. But Vico never had the audience of great thinkers which he desired, and never had contemporaries who recognized his talents. By the eighteenth century, eloquence was such a dim memory, that of an eloquent Vico all that was said was that "he was obscure or eccentric and had odd ideas" (*A* 200).

PART TWO

THE PIETY OF AUGUSTINE

this Science carries inseparably with it the study of piety . . .
he who is not pious cannot be truly wise.

Vico, *New Science*

Introduction

Vico's "Particular Protector"

Vico signs his "Corrections, Ameliorations, and Additions" to the 1730 edition of the *New Science*, by noting that he is finishing it on the eve of Saint Augustine's day, and by making the intriguing remark that Augustine is his "particular protector" (*mio particolare prottetore*).[1] Vico also wrote a poem in honor of Augustine, for the saint's day in 1735.[2] In his closing prayer at the end of his oration to the Academy of Oziosi, Vico again shows his affinity for Augustine. He selects "the great Father Augustine" from among the saints who protect that Academy, as the one who dictates the formula for his "thought of highest reverence" (*PE* 90). The uniquely Vichian prayer opens by humbly asking to be heard not by "fabulous Minerva" but by "Eternal Wisdom," and closes by dedicating the reopening of the Academy to the glory of God, that it might achieve the humanistic goal of perfecting intelligence by wisdom, "because wisdom, which is mind and language, is the perfecter of man in his properly being man" (ibid.). This prayer reveals the tension between Vico's admiration for the Christian theologian Augustine and his philosophical commitment to *paideia* and human wisdom.

There is no simple answer to the precise relationship between Augustine and Vico.[3] There are many direct citations of influence and indirect echoes of Augustine in Vico, and I will explore them in turn, but the number of references can mask the genuine complexity (and some say impossibility) of fully answering this question.[4]

In this study, I am remaking the *New Science* for myself from the philosophical angle, and only indirectly commenting on either the Hebrews or Christianity.[5] With Frederick R. Marcus, I think that to understand Vico one must see his work in relationship to the Hebrews, philosophy, and Christianity, and in that order. All three angles are necessary for a complete reading of the *New Science*, and Vico's unique perspective may be that he is to some extent an outsider to all three traditions, and yet influenced by each. Inspired by Peter Gimpel's *The Carnevalis of Eusebius Asch*, Frederick R. Marcus makes the persuasive speculation that Vico's interest in the Hebrews may be that of a Converso, a hidden Jew, or a descendent of hidden Jews.[6] If Vico were a Converso, his familial memory of Judaism might explain his unusually philo-semitic philosophy.

Further, Vico's explicit defense that his philosophy is "consonant with Christian piety" (*AW* 109) may be a response to the atmosphere of Inquisition.[7] Augustine may be Vico's "particular protector" because the genuine parallels between their work could conceal the disanalogies from those judging whether his writings were acceptable to the Catholic Church. That these are *genuine* parallels is very important, because often contextualizing Vico as living during the Inquisition opens a Pandora's box of suspicion that leads to Vico being read as disingenuous and deceptive whenever he discusses religion, divine providence, and piety. This reaction confuses more than it clarifies. If Vico only wanted protection, any Christian writer would have been sufficient to pretend a connection, but Augustine offered "particular" protection.

Where Vico places Christianity in the *New Science* is difficult to ascertain, but some suggestions may be helpful by way of introduction. To be eloquent Vico must encompass all things divine and human, and that means sacred as well as gentile history must be included in his speech, even as a silent pointing. Vico includes sacred history as the standard for the ideal eternal history of the gentile nations, but the standard is outside of the work itself. The separation of the Hebrews from the gentiles, and their exemption from the conceit of scholars that corrupts all gentile chronologies, is an axiom of Vico's Science.[8] In the context of the unique eternal status given to the Hebrews, the fact that Vico discusses Christianity within the *New Science* as definitive of the *ricorso*, weakens its designation as revealed theology, since only insofar as it is poetic, civil, or natural theology can it be discussed within the *New Science*.

Vico considers Christianity as a mixture of his types of theology, and as the starting-point for the *ricorso*, the returned age of the gods (*NS* 366). For Vico, Dante is the summary poet of the initial ages of Christian Europe as Homer was for pagan Greece. Dante is the summary poet of the *ricorso* divine and heroic times, just as Homer is the summary poet for the *corso* divine and heroic times. Vico says we must search for the true Dante as for the true Homer.[9] With the Renaissance Platonists, Dante thought that the connection between Pseudo-Dionysius and the theology of the *Timaeus* was genuine, so he is part of that fruitful illusion of poetic theology connecting Neoplatonism and Christianity, as explored in chapter 1.

Pico, like Augustine, ultimately considers Christian theology superior to Platonic philosophy. The poetic wisdom of the *ricorso* has an image for this belief: in *The Divine Comedy*, Dante leaves behind Virgil, his guide in the liberal arts and philosophy, who can only take him part way, and follows Beatrice, who can teach him the mysteries of divine grace, of revealed theology.

In this study's descent through the family of Plato, with Augustine we descend from returned human times of the *ricorso* to the returned divine times. Dante is, like the Renaissance Platonists, closer to Augustine than to Vico, who lived in the age of humans of the *ricorso*. Vico is perhaps the only one of the members of the *ricorso* generation of the family of Plato who does not leave philosophy behind for Christian theology. Vico stands to Dante as Plato stood to Homer, as philosopher to poet. At this point, the reader realizes that Vico is quite far from Augustine, even further than the Italian Platonists were.

In writings other than the *New Science* there is also mixed evidence of Vico's attitude toward Christianity, such that one can find in the sixth oration a strong endorsement of revealed theology as the apex of humanistic education (*IO* 6.13), and yet in the fourth oration Vico reverses the usual commonplace and makes theology one of the handmaids of the liberal arts (*IO* 4.10). In the *Autobiography* Vico says that the best philosophy is "that of Plato subordinated to the Christian faith" (*A* 155). This passage is where Vico sounds the most compatible with Augustine, but an examination of the *New Science* reveals that Vico remains a philosopher and does not subordinate his Platonism "to the Christian faith." Vico does make clear at the end of the *New Science* that "this Science carries inseparably with it the study of piety" and that " he who is not pious cannot be truly wise" (*NS* 1112), but Vico does not have to be Augustinian to be pious. Vico has a different solution to the challenge of the proper relationship of philosophy and religion, of wisdom and piety, than any of his predecessors.

Now with an introduction like this one, why devote a third of a book on Vico and Plato to Augustine? The answer is that even though Vico is not recreating Augustine's project, Vico's *New Science* is heavily indebted to Augustine, and in particular as a mediator for Platonism.[10] A few illustrations will make this debt clear. Vico's most significant allusion to Augustine is the metaphor the "great city of the human race" (*NS* 342; cf. *NS* 1107, *A* 141).[11] Augustine's metaphor of the two cities profoundly influenced the way Vico conceived history in the *New Science*. Although Vico is concerned primarily with Augustine's earthly city, he does not ignore that this image implies the contrast to the City of God.

The most important debt to Augustine is in Vico's metaphysics, specifically, the nature of providence. Most accounts of Vico's metaphysics explain the connection between making and knowing, and how God's making and knowing is the standard for human making and knowing. Such an
emphasis is important for countering the charges of historicism, but it is
incomplete for describing Vico's metaphysics. In addition to knowing and
making, there is also governing, at the divine and human levels.[12] Divine
providence or divine governing is as central an image in Vico's *New Science*
as in Augustine's *City of God*.[13]

Making is the middle term that connects knowing and governing. To
know is to make; to make is to govern; therefore, to know is to govern.
This syllogism applies at the divine level as well as the human. We know
what we make, and in consequence we can govern ourselves, or make ourselves in light of that knowledge. Self-knowledge, as knowledge of divine
and human things, is a moral guide, so Vichian metaphysics begins in
knowing and ends in governing, with making as the middle term. Self-
governing is virtue, which is the goal of *paideia*. The idea of *paideia* as self-
governing has already become evident from comparing Vico's inaugural
orations and Pico's *Oration*. When one reads Vico with Augustine, providence emerges as the divine governing that makes our human self-governing possible. For Vico as for Pico, the human being is a "maker and molder
of thyself" (*O* 225). Vico is more optimistic than Augustine about the
extent to which self-governing is possible through our own efforts, but the
nature of providence is similar nevertheless. The acknowledgment of human reliance on divine providence adds humility and piety to Vico's
humanism.

Given the many levels of correspondence, from Roman history to jurisprudence to moral philosophy, answering the question of the relationship
of Vico and Augustine could lead far beyond the importance of Augustine
as a mediator of Platonism. Yet that is the context within which I will
address their relationship. Augustine's reading of the Platonists is fundamental for understanding how Vico himself sees Plato and Platonism. Perhaps ironically for my study, Augustine's critique of Platonism is as important as his praise. Augustine is the single most important figure for
understanding why Vico seeks to make his metaphysics "compatible with
human frailty" and consonant with "Christian piety" (*AW* 109). Vico's
Science, his new combination of philosophy and philology, is not Augustinian, because unlike Augustine's mature writings, it is not dogmatic Christian theology or polemical philosophy. Nevertheless, Augustine's thought
greatly shaped Vico's *New Science*, including how he looked at the Platonists.

Chapter 4

Rational Civil Theology

Vico defines the first aspect of the *New Science* as "a rational civil theology of divine providence" (*NS* 2, 342). On the surface, this claim seems to support thinking of Vico as simply another Augustine, who combines pagan philosophy and Christian theology, subordinating the former to the latter. If Vico is not undertaking a project analogous to Augustine's work in this way, then what light does Augustine shed on Vico's "rational civil theology of divine providence"? If declaring that the first aspect of his Science is "a rational civil theology" does not make Vico a theologian, what kind of philosopher is he?

Vico is a philosopher, not a theologian in the usual sense of that discipline, yet wisdom for Vico is the knowledge of things divine as well as human, and the knowledge of the divine directs the human (*NS* 364). Vico says that he thinks Varro took this humanist definition for the plan of his *Antiquities of Divine and Human Institutions*, and, as for other important references to Varro, Vico's source is Augustine's *City of God* (*CG* 6.3, 230). Vico makes plain that he intends his *New Science* to treat of the same divine and human things as did Varro (*NS* 364). In a philosophical tradition which holds that wisdom must be "knowledge of things divine and human" (Cicero, *Tusc. Disp.* V. 3. 7), speaking of God does not make one a theologian. As Vico reports, Cicero refused to discuss law with an Epicurean until he had granted the existence of divine providence (*Leg.* 1.7.21; *NS* 335). In this way, the first aspect does not have to be interpreted as "an article of faith," just because it speaks of divine things (*NS* F6).

Once one understands what Vico means by "theology" in his ascription of the aspect of "rational civil theology" to his *New Science*, how Vico can reconcile his piety and his philosophy without ceasing to be a philosopher becomes much less mysterious. When Vico's kinds of theology are appropriately distinguished, there is no need to minimize the role of providence to preserve Vico's identity as a philosopher. Since figuring out what Vico means by "rational civil theology" is difficult, I will begin with Augustine's report of Varro's division of theology and Augustine's critique of these distinctions. These are the acknowledged immediate origins of Vico's types of theology, though for the *archai* of theology itself one must descend to the divination of the theological poets (*NS* 739). Since Vico builds on distinctions made by Varro and Augustine, articulating the nature of Vico's appropriation of the types of theology in Varro and Augustine will make it easier to distinguish what types of theology Vico recognizes, and most importantly to see how he defines his *New Science* relative to these types.

Augustine and Varro on Types of Theology

Augustine always praises Marcus Terentius Varro as the most learned of the Romans, saying of him that he read so much that one wondered that he had any time to write, and wrote so much that one marveled that he had any time to read (*CG* 6. 2, 230). Vico agrees with Augustine's estimate of Varro (*NS* 6, 196, 284, 364, 735, 1045, 1046), and also uses him as an authority. Augustine respects Varro, but ultimately thinks he does not go nearly far enough in his critique of the depiction of the pagan gods (e.g., *CG* 3.4, 92). Varro's erudition makes him an important interlocutor in Part One of Augustine's *City of God*, since Augustine is arguing against the most learned of the Romans and is not merely defeating a straw man.

The purpose of the first half of the *City of God* is to discredit the pagan gods in order to answer the charge that the Christian prohibition of worshiping these gods led to the fall of Rome. Augustine's argument is that these gods were so fickle, immoral, and powerless that they did not help their believers when they did worship them, so the prohibition against worship could not cause the fall of Rome. Augustine's polemical purpose is to convince his educated pagan readers, who are earlier versions of himself before his conversion, that Christianity is superior in every way to paganism.[1] Even in the fall of Rome the name of the Christian God protected the Romans as no pagan god did (*CG* 2.2, 49). Exposing the stories about the pagan gods as "a mass of lies and delusions" undermines the credibility of the attempts to reconcile philosophical wisdom and these depictions of the gods (*CG* 6.9, 247).

Augustine summarizes and responds to Varro's types of theologies in greatest detail in Book 6. Prior to this book Augustine introduces Varro's opinions on the gods and alludes to his division of theology. In Book 2, after criticizing the depictions of the gods as immoral (citing the stories about the gods committing adultery, theft, and other acts for which humans would be judged immoral), he anticipates the objection that these things are not taught by the temple rites but only in the fables of the poets (*CG* 2.8, 56). Augustine will collapse this distinction which Varro makes between poetic and civil theology. For Augustine, the moral critique of poetic fiction about the gods applies to the civic religion as well.

Augustine credits Plato with anticipating the Christian conclusion ("'such gods are in no way to be worshipped'") (*CG* 2.13, 62), by preferring truth over such poetic fictions and civil rites. Augustine goes so far as to suggest "how much better and more honourable would it be to have a temple to Plato where his books were read" (*CG* 2.7, 55); how much better to worship as a god the humanity of Plato, even though he is only a man than to encourage imitation of immoral behavior by worshiping such false divinities (*CG* 2.14–15, 63–65). The strong moral criticism of poetic and civil theology in Plato's *Republic* is the initial standard against which Augustine can measure Varro's reluctance to condemn the falsehood of the pagan depiction of the gods.

In the first mention of Varro, Augustine says "Varro, the most learned of the Romans, almost admits their falsity, though timidly and diffidently" (*CG* 3.4, 92). Varro argues that fictions, such as those that brave men are sons of gods, are useful insofar as they inspire confidence. To this Augustine asks us to notice "what a wide field it offers to falsehood" (ibid.). In the opening of Book 4, Augustine regrets that Varro classifies theatrical performances under "divine things," since the plays are not worthy of the esteem such a classification gives. Augustine adds in Varro's defense that he was following tradition in this classification. Varro's own view was that there was one god, Jupiter, which should be worshipped without an idol (*CG* 4.9, 146; 4.31, 174–75).

Augustine further anticipates the main discussion of Varro's division of theology in Book 6 when he reports the distinctions between poetic, natural, and civil theology from the work of the jurisconsult Q. T. Scaevola. Vico will link Scaevola and Varro as well (*NS* 284). Scaevola distinguishes three strains in the Roman theological tradition: that of the poets, the philosophers, and the statesmen (*CG* 4.27, 168). Scaevola prefers the theology of the statesmen, since he dismisses the first as "trivial nonsense, a collection of discreditable fictions about the gods" and holds that the second has "no value for the commonwealth, in that it introduced much that was irrelevant, and also much that was harmful for the people in general to know" (ibid.). Scaevola and Varro are in agreement on the usefulness of the lie that Hercules and others were gods, though both do think such divinization of men is untrue. Both accept the teaching of Euhemerus, the fourth century B. C. E. Sicilian thinker, that the gods were deified human beings (CG 4.27, 169, n. 97).[2] Euhemerism is true, but not useful for the many to know. Euhemerism plays a significant role in Augustine's description of the errors of poetic theology (CG 6.7, 239–40; 7.18, 276; 7.28, 290; 8.5, 306; 18.8, 769–70). The discussion of Scaevola here emphasizes further that the critique of the poetic tradition is a moral one, since good men are better than such gods, which is absurd, because by definition gods are superior beings (CG 4.27, 169). We are not given a sense of what the third option of civil theology would involve for Scaevola.

The distance between what Varro thinks is true and what he allows as acceptable for the people is reinforced by Scaevola's comments. In the next discussion of Varro, Augustine holds that while Varro himself rejected popular superstition and held that one god should be worshipped, he fell short of the worship of the true God, and still sanctioned the corrupted pagan rites. Varro judges Roman custom as it is; if Roman custom were what it ought to be, then the customs would reflect the nature of the gods. However, because Varro is not founding a city, but living in an already old one, he asserts that he is bound to maintain the traditional stories and names of the gods as they have been passed down to him (CG 4.31, 174). In this way Varro makes the argument for a toleration of falsehood in civic religion.

Augustine suspects that Varro "is not revealing all that he knows" (ibid.); and he supports this claim by referring to another place where Varro does say concerning religious rites "that there are many truths which it is not expedient for the general public to know, and, further, many falsehoods which it is good for the people to believe true" (ibid.). Varro reveals the extent to which he judges the current religious rites as corrupted by saying that once the ancient Romans worshipped the gods without images, as the Jews worship their God (CG 4.31, 175). This statement may be a significant parallel to Vico's claim that there is a true Homer, the true and severe narrations of the first Greeks, hidden behind the corrupted versions of the stories collected in the *Iliad* and *Odyssey* (NS Book 3). For Augustine's exposition of Varro, this claim serves to support his reading that Varro philosophically approached an understanding of what the appropriate nature of the worship of the true God would be, but for civic reasons did not follow through on his critique of pagan religion.

In Book 6 Augustine reintroduces Varro with extended praise of his learning, and asks what we are to make of such an intelligent scholar's tenacious concern about the preservation of at least the memory of the religious rites that he acknowledges are composed of falsehoods. Here the reader finds the most detailed exposition of Varro's types of theology. Augustine's summary of Varro's *Antiquities* makes the reader regret as greatly as Vico did the "injustice of time" that deprives us of his learning (*NS* 364).

In the course of the description of Varro's *Antiquities*, there is much that Vico would have found analogous to his own project (ibid.). For example, Varro treats of the human matters before the divine matters because "human communities first came into existence and divine institutions are afterwards established by them" (*CG* 6.4, 232). Augustine takes this priority as the essence of the religion of the earthly city, and firmly contrasts the City of God which was established by true religion rather than any earthly community (ibid.). Augustine's point, in drawing the distinction between the two cities in this context, is that by placing the pagan religious rites and poetic theology under human affairs, Varro is signaling that he is not considering the divine from the point of view of the truth about the divine nature (*CG* 6.4, 233). Augustine has already made clear in the earlier books mentioned above, that Varro distinguished the philosophical truth about the gods from the customs of Rome, despite their falsehood, for civil reasons.

Now with much of the groundwork laid, Augustine presents Varro's division of theology: mythical, physical, and civil. Augustine adopts Latin names for the first two; "fabulous" from the translation of "*mythos*"which means "fable" and "natural" from the translation of "*physis*"which is Greek for "nature." Varro himself uses the Latin "civil," and one could add for symmetry that Varro could have called it "political," since "*polis*" is Greek for "city" and corresponds to the Latin "*civitas*." Augustine preserves Varro's own words in describing the types: "'The name 'mythical' applies to the theology chiefly used by the poets, 'physical' to that of the philosophers, 'civil' to that of the general public. The first type contains a great deal of fiction which is in conflict with the dignity and nature of the immortals'" (*CG* 6.5, 234). Augustine continues to quote Varro's descriptions of the three types. First, about poetic theology, Varro makes the point, which is now familiar to Augustine's reader, that the gods are depicted as adulterers and thieves and are described not only as like men, but even worse (ibid.). Augustine explains that Varro is candid about the injustice done to the gods by these false fables because he feels free to criticize the poetic theology in contrast to his restraint about the civil theology.

The description of natural theology resembles Scaevola's remark that, from the point of view of a jurisconsult, it was a matter of indifference, and thus harmless. Varro is perhaps less sure that having philosophers in the marketplace is a matter of indifference, saying that the philosophical questions about the gods are matters "'which men's ears can more readily tolerate within the walls of a lecture-room than in the marketplace outside'" (*CG* 6.5, 235). Augustine glosses this passage positively, saying Varro did not find fault with physical theology, yet notes that even so Varro removes the subject from the marketplace and shuts it up in the lecture-room. Varro's care to protect the public from hearing such truths which might cause them to doubt their false beliefs seems ludicrous to Augustine. The answer to why a Platonist like Varro (as he considers the Platonists the best sect of philosophers in "On Philosophy," *CG* 19.1–3, 843–51) would make such a decision must lie in the value he places on civil theology. The exposition of Varro, however, turns into criticism, so that we do not hear further why Varro defends civil theology.

In the course of his description of Varro's civil theology, Augustine raises excellent questions: "If 'natural' theology is really natural, what is found wrong with it, to cause its exclusion from the city? While if so-called 'civil' theology is not natural, what merit has it to cause its admission?" (*CG* 6.5, 235) How could Varro answer the charge that "to wish to separate natural theology from civil, is surely tantamount to an admission that civil theology itself is false" (ibid.)? Again Augustine's point is that if both mythical and civil theology contain falsehood in contrast with the philosophical, then Varro is maintaining a distinction without a difference between them. If there is a real distinction, then it will be discovered in the civil purpose which the civil serves and the mythical does not; and thus, on the grounds of utility not truth, the civil is higher than the fabulous.

Augustine takes the standpoint of truth and ignores the appeal to utility as irrelevant. Thus in his estimate, Varro's situation is the following: "you desire to worship 'natural' gods; you are compelled to worship the 'gods of the city.' You have found other gods, those of the fables, and you can be less reserved in loosing off your feelings about *them*. But, whether you like it or not, some of your shots land on the 'civil' gods as well" (*CG* 6.6, 236–37). Augustine does not explain why Varro is wrong in his concern to distinguish the degree of truth acceptable in the city as opposed to the academy or theatre. Varro does admit the falsehood and the corruption of the religious rites of the city. Augustine then continues by quoting a statement from Varro that may suggest an answer to the question about the relationship between the civil and natural which Augustine raised (*CG*, 6.5, 235). Varro finds poetic theology an inadequate guide for the people to follow, and philosophy too difficult for them to follow. Civil theology is described as a mixture of these two forms. The mixture of natural and poetic theology in civil theology explains why civil theology occupies a place higher than the poetic and yet is still lower than the natural in Varro's hierarchy of theology. There is then a real reason for Varro to distinguish all three types, if it is true that the civil theology contains truths from natural theology in addition to the falsehoods from poetic theology. The mixture arises from the fact that the people *are* more inclined to believe the poets, and yet they *ought* to cultivate the society of the philosophers more.

Augustine concludes from this discussion only that the poetic is an integral part of the civil, and thus that the civil theology is thoroughly contaminated by falsehood (*CG* 6.7, 239). Nevertheless, Augustine reopens the question of the presence of natural theology in the civil when he considers the naturalistic explanations of the gods (*CG* 6.8, 242–43). Augustine barely raises the idea before he rejects it, however, saying that, if such interpretations of the gods as symbolic of physical phenomena can justify the civil distortions of the divine nature, why not extend this and excuse the poets as well? (ibid.). I will return to Varro's and Augustine's suggestions for interpreting the myths in relation to Vico's own explanations of poetic wisdom, which they resemble more than the allegorical or esoteric interpretations that Vico associates with the conceit of scholars.

To reinforce his conclusion that "poetry and priestcraft are allied in a fellowship of deception" (*CG* 6.6, 237) and "the whole of this 'theology' is a mass of lies and delusions" (*CG* 6.9, 247), Augustine appeals to another Roman authority. Seneca attacks pagan civil religion as boldly and directly as Varro and Scaevola attacked the poets (*CG* 6.10, 248–51). Augustine agrees with Seneca that poetic and civil theology—that of poets in theatre and priests in temples—is all of one piece.

Augustine says that there may be more divisions, but he has shown that the theology of the city and the theatre, united by falsehood and indecency, belong to the same division, that of civil theology (*CG* 6.9, 247). Although this summation sounds like Augustine's conclusion, his discussion of Varro or naturalistic explanations of the gods is not completed. Augustine knows that he is trying to root out a deep error when he urges the reader to reject pagan civil theology (*CG* 6.12, 253), and he wishes to cover all the possible lines of defense.

In Book 7, Augustine raises the question of allegorical interpretation again, in particular its use to defend the pantheon and the other gods that make up the twenty select gods Varro names (*CG* 7.2, 255). Varro appeals to allegorical interpretation to explain how natural theology might inform civil theology, at least in part. Varro is accused of forgetting his earlier claim that the ancient Romans did better when they worshipped the gods without images (*CG* 7.5, 261). Varro here follows other pagans in finding an esoteric meaning in the images of the gods. Varro says these images were invented so that initiates of the mysteries could use the images to see with their minds the true gods which, resembling the Neoplatonic philosophy, are understood as the World-Soul and its manifestations (*CG* 7.5, 262).

Augustine asks that if Varro succeeds in bringing the civil theology under the natural through such explanations, then why did Varro make so much of the distinction between the natural and the civil? (ibid.). This argument assumes that it is not possible for the types to be mixed, as Varro thinks the civil is a mixture. If the civil is taken as a mixture, the natural elements might keep civil theology from complete falsehood, without being identical to natural theology itself. Augustine continues to hold that Varro was not "guided by the actual truth," but was writing "under the pressure of tradition" (*CG* 7.17, 275). Varro is quoted comparing himself to Xenophanes who, even earlier than Euhemerus, attacked polytheism and anthropomorphism in the sixth century B.C. E., and most likely influenced Plato (ibid.). I will return to the discussion of Varro's esoteric interpretations in regard to Vico's understanding of the nature of poetic and civil theology.

Augustine respects Varro's belief in providence (*CG* 7.17, 275), but regrets his errors in defending anything other than the best pagan natural theology. He considers Varro's attempts to save civil theology as a failure in a misguided and impossible project (*CG* 7.28, 289). His ultimate judgment on Varro is that he was inconsistent in theology (ibid.). The reason for the apparent inconsistency is that sometimes Augustine is arguing with "Varro the politician," as he once calls him (*CG* 7.23, 281), in contrast to Varro the philosopher who, in Augustine's judgment, should let nothing distract him from the search for the truth about the divine.

Augustine's discussion of natural theology is straightforward in contrast to the preceding, rambling exposition and criticism of the poetic and civil theology. Despite the criticisms Augustine will make of natural theology, he does consider fabulous or civil theology a different matter; "in discussing 'natural' theology we shall have to cross swords not with the man in the street, but with philosophers; and that name means that they profess to be lovers of wisdom" (*CG* 8.1, 298). Augustine limits his scope to those philosophers whose opinions pertain to theology, and then he restricts this even further, confining himself to a certain sort of Platonism. The Platonism he wishes to engage is superior to the natural theology of Varro, which can conceive as the highest Being only the World-Soul, whereas these other followers of Plato "acknowledge a God who transcends any kind of soul" (*CG* 8.1, 298–99). The description of God as a maker can be traced to the *Timaeus* and to the Neoplatonic theological interpretations of that dialogue of Plato's. Interestingly, Augustine does not note that here.

After a brief and excellent summary of the early history of Greek philosophy, from the Ionians and the Italians to Socrates and Plato, Augustine returns to the explanation of why "theological questions are to be discussed with the Platonists rather than with any other philosophers, whose opinions must be counted inferior" (*CG* 8.5, 304–5). For the purposes of understanding the types of theology, what is interesting is that Augustine ranks Platonic philosophy over fabulous and civil theology as the highest form of natural theology. Augustine writes that "Platonism must take pride of place over 'fabulous' theology, with its titillation of impious minds by rehearsing the scandals of the gods, and over 'civil' theology, where unclean demons, posing as gods, have seduced the crowds who are wedded to earthly joys, and have desired to make human errors serve as divine honours for themselves . . ." (*CG* 8.5, 305).

What does Augustine think distinguishes the natural theology of the Platonists from inferior versions of natural theology? The primary distinction is exactly what in the *Confessions* Augustine praised the Platonists for helping him to see: the immateriality of God (*CG* 8.6, 307).[3] Varro's natural theology fails to move beyond seeing Jupiter as World-Soul, the allegorical interpretation of Virgil's adaptation of the Homeric phrase "all things are full of Jupiter" (*CG* 7.9, 267; 7.13, 271). Varro does not see that God is the maker of souls, not a great soul Himself; whereas, in contrast the Platonists praised by Augustine understand that no material object can be God (*CG* 8.6, 307). Acknowledging an immaterial and immutable God who governs the world is the highest achievement possible for natural theology.

The rest of Augustine's discussion of the nature of philosophy, especially the divisions into natural or speculative, rational, and moral, while in itself interesting, sheds little additional light on the division of theology originating from Varro and informing Vico. Likewise, the specific discussions of Apuleius, Porphyry, and Hermes Trismegistus, do not directly bear on the question of the nature of theology. Augustine is, of course, at pains to show how the Platonic falls short of the Christian theology—its failure to discover the path of universal salvation because of pride, and other important errors—but as far as the division of theology is concerned, he concludes firmly that in the hierarchy even the best of philosophy is a distant second best to Christianity. Even with the claim of Paul that "what can be known of God has been revealed among them" (*Rom.* 1. 19), Augustine takes seriously the reproach that accompanies this praise, that "though having some acquaintance with God, they have not glorified him as God, nor have they given thanks to him; but they have dwindled into futility in their thinking and their stupid heart is shrouded in darkness" (*Rom.* 1. 21).

Revealed theology serves as a standard by which all the other types of theology are measured. Augustine says "there are none who come nearer to us than the Platonists" (*CG* 8.5, 304). There is a definite hierarchy, and the highest form of the pagan theology, that of the Platonists, is not nearly so high as the faith of a Christian uneducated man (*CG* 2.14, 64). Such pagan philosophy may prepare the way for revealed religion, but the gap between the two is immense. What ultimately matters to Augustine is that all religion is false if pagan, and true only if Christian; you are either part of the City of God or the earthly city, and though it is hard to discern in this life the exact citizenship of each, at the final judgment this will be clear.

Augustine's hierarchy is an amendment to Varro's, though he does not explicitly tell us he is adding another type of theology as the apex of the scale. Varro made the natural theology of the philosophers the highest, the poetic the lowest, and the civil a mixture in between. For Augustine the highest theology is revealed Christian theology, and the other types are ordered by how closely they approximate it. From this point of view, the natural theology of the Neoplatonists, like that of Plotinus and Porphyry (judged superior to Varro's own Platonism, which is considered too naturalistic), is the second best, and the falsehood of the civil and the poetic give them the lowest ranking together.

Therefore, Augustine restricts Varro's types of theology to varying degrees of falsehood. Augustine does not extend Varro's types of theology beyond paganism any more than he does the sects of philosophy. Augustine opposes Christian revelation to all sects of philosophy as well as to all the pagan theologies. As a result, Augustine does not locate his own work within Varro's distinctions or combinations of types. Unlike Vico, Augustine does not apply Varro's distinctions to Christian theology, so he would not describe Christian theology as poetic, civil, or natural. For example, Augustine is not interested in Varro's defense of civil religion in principle, such that Augustine might think of the applications of this account for the Christian religion in its role as civil religion. Despite the extensive use of the metaphor of the two cities, Augustine does not call his own theology a mixture of civil and revealed theology.

Augustine's judgment of natural theology in Books 8–10 as inadequate compared to the true religion of Christianity makes evident why he had so little patience with a watered down version of so-called pagan truth in civil theology, as Varro defended it. The Platonic natural theology, the highest of the forms of theology Varro acknowledged, falls so short of the truth of the City of God that Augustine cannot see any sense in defending civil theology, if it is not identical to natural theology (and it is not), since even the natural falls short of the truth. Even the best of the earthly city's wisdom is folly from the perspective of the City of God. The reader can discern here and elsewhere a prideful, inquisitorial tone in Augustine's rigid, sweeping judgments that makes one wonder if Vico is not more humble and pious than his "protector."

Vico's Division of Theology

Vico states that in the *New Science* he will "distinguish more truly than Varro" the types of theology (*NS* 366). He draws on Augustine as his source for Varro, and is won over by Augustine's collapsing of the distinction between pagan poetic and civil theology. Nevertheless, Vico agrees with Varro that poetic or civil theology plays an important role. For Vico, this role exists not as a strictly civil one, in the sense Varro meant, but as the historical origin of the development of wisdom in "this great city of the human race" (*NS* 342). Human beings are by nature social (*NS* 2), and thus their wisdom will have a communal origin.

The longest book of the *New Science* is dedicated to a new understanding of poetic wisdom. After the introduction to this second book of the *New Science*, "Poetic Wisdom," in a section called "Wisdom in General" (*NS* 364), Vico collects the commonplaces that undergird the search for wisdom in his *New Science*. I have already mentioned his definition of wisdom as "the perfecter of man" from Plato's *Alcibiades* in connection with Pico in chapter 2 (*Alc. I* 124e). In this chapter I will delve more deeply into this section of the *New Science*, as its divisions of theology provide the best commentary on why Vico would define the first aspect of the *New Science* as "a rational civil theology of divine providence" (*NS* 2, 342).

In addition to the humanistic definitions of wisdom (the perfecter of man, the knowledge of things divine and human, the ordering faculty of all the disciplines), Vico makes his own fundamental distinction. Wisdom must be either poetic and vulgar (*sapienza poetica*) or philosophical and esoteric (*sapienza riposta*).[4] Vico opposes the conceit of scholars which collapses this distinction. Such thinkers read their own way of thinking into poetry, rather than seeing poetic wisdom as the civil wisdom of the childhood of the human race. Using several contrasting pairs of terms (poetic, civil, and vulgar against philosophical, natural, and esoteric), Vico indicates that the distinction between poetic and philosophical wisdom is essential to understanding his exposition of the nature of poetic wisdom. This division of poetic from philosophical wisdom permeates Book 2 of the *New Science*; "throughout this book it will be shown that as much as the poets had first sensed in the way of vulgar wisdom, the philosophers later understood in the way of esoteric wisdom; so that the former may be said to be have been the sense and the latter the intellect of the human race" (*NS* 363; cf. 779).

Two main questions emerge from comparing this basic division, the three types of theology, and Vico's claims about the nature of his own Science, that is, his way of knowing the things divine and human. Where does Vico locate his own *New Science* relative to poetic and philosophical wisdom and in terms of the types of theology he acknowledges? Further, how can human wisdom find expression in two types (poetic and philosophical), and yet Vico distinguishes three types of theology (poetic or civil, natural or philosophical, and Christian theology, a mixture of the other forms with revealed theology)?

After the general remarks about wisdom, Vico gives a condensed summary of the development of wisdom in gentile as well as sacred history (*NS* 365). This account of poetic wisdom requires a new division of the types of theology. As described here, wisdom begins among the gentiles with the Muse, and is defined by Homer as the "knowledge of good and evil," which Vico adds was later called "divination" (*NS* 365). Vico contrasts this poetic religion with the true religion of the Hebrews which prohibited divination, and from which the Christian religion arose.

Returning to the initial poetic wisdom, Vico says that the Muse must mean the science of divining by auspices, which is the vulgar wisdom of all nations. The theological poets are the founders of the humanity of Greece, and thus provide the link between poetic and civil theology. The theology of the poets is the civil theology. There is a progression of sages from astrologers, to statesmen, to metaphysicians. Each marks a stage in the unfolding of the *corso* beginning in the poetic and civil wisdom of the age of gods and heroes and culminating with metaphysics or divine science (the knowledge of "natural divine things") in the age of humans.

Instead of then tracing the *ricorso* of wisdom, Vico abruptly ends the development he has described by implying that the final manifestation of wisdom is revealed theology. Vico concludes that "finally among the Hebrews and thence among us Christians, wisdom was called the science of eternal things revealed by God; a science which, among the Tuscans, considered as knowledge of the true good and true evil, perhaps owed to that fact the first name they gave it, 'science in divinity'" (*NS* 365). Nevertheless, in the description of *The Course the Nations Run* and the *Recourse of the Nations*, the Christian revelation itself serves as a new starting-point for a *ricorso*. Vico considers pagan divination and revealed theology together in the first of the three types of reason, divine reason, and likewise in other triads (Book 4). In this way he anticipates how the *ricorso* will unfold, which is significant since the description of the *ricorso* is quite abbreviated (Book 5).

Vico alludes to the parallelism of the two divine times by echoing the opening definition of divination as "knowledge of good and evil," noting that the Tuscans called revealed theology "scienza in divinitá," meaning "knowledge of the true good and true evil" (*NS* 365).[5] As knowledge of good and evil, even though separated by the degree of truthfulness, the wisdom of the pagan poetic theology and Christian theology are closely linked as the beginning points of the *corso* and *ricorso* respectively, though Vico does not point out this fact explicitly here.

What Vico summarizes is the nature of wisdom in the three ages of the *corso* (exemplifying the types poetic or civil theology and natural theology) and the first of the *ricorso* ("the science of eternal things revealed by God"). He does not explore what wisdom means for the returned heroic and human ages, nor does he identify the revealed theology as a return of the divine times in his double cycle of ideal eternal history. The status of Hebrew wisdom relative to the Christian in the *ricorso* remains unclear, and it is hard to find an answer that does not contradict the special status clearly granted to the Hebrews. Vico does not show us where the wisdom of the Renaissance of philosophy belongs, much less where that of the *New Science* itself belongs. Philosophy, such as Pico's, is best understood as the *ricorso* of the metaphysics that developed among the gentiles, culminating with Plato, described here for the *corso*, but these later times of the *ricorso* are precisely what is overlooked. To say that Vico minimizes the cyclic nature of his view of the development of wisdom would be an understatement.

With this omission in mind, the three-fold division of theology that follows also can be seen as an oversimplification of the development of wisdom and theology as described in the *New Science* as a whole. The more complete (still not explicit) accounts in Books 4 and 5 will show us that Vico does not hold a simple progression from (a) gentile poetic or civil theology to (b) metaphysics to (c) revealed Christian theology, as a beginning, middle, and end, as Augustine and other Christian theologians might see it. This progression is a linear account of the development of wisdom. For Vico this account can be only a partial truth, for his own discovery is the cyclic nature of history. The mixture of sacred and gentile histories alone ought to warn against too simplistic an interpretation, since elsewhere Vico carefully separates these histories. If the passage is not read as an exhaustive scale of types of theology in the *New Science*, then it can be useful for understanding why Vico names the first aspect of his Science "a rational civil theology of divine providence." The primary reason not to see the division of theology as exhaustive is that Vico's own theology is not among them. Trying to make Vico's "rational civil theology" fit into one of three divisions would miss the unique philosophical synthesis Vico achieves in the *New Science*.

Compared to Augustine's lengthy exposition and criticism of Varro's types of theology, Vico's discussion is extremely compressed. I will use what Augustine summarized and criticized of Varro to assist in elaborating Vico's claims. The analogies and disanalogies will shed light on the significance of Vico's revision of the types of theology.

Vico concludes his brief survey of the development of wisdom, especially poetic wisdom, with the following division of theology, on which the remainder of this chapter will be a commentary: "We must therefore distinguish more truly than Varro did the three kinds of theology. First, poetic theology, that of the theological poets, which was the civil theology of all the gentile nations. Second, natural theology, that of the metaphysicians. Third, our Christian theology, a mixture of civil and natural with the loftiest revealed theology; all three united in the contemplation of divine providence. (Our third kind takes the place of Varro's poetic theology, which among the gentiles was the same as civil theology, though he distinguished it from both civil and natural theology because, sharing the vulgar common error that the fables contained high mysteries of sublime philosophy, he believed it to be a mixture of the two)" (*NS* 366).[6]

It is paramount not to overlook that Vico offers the division as a conclusion. Vico must modify the divisions of theology to include his discovery of the nature of poetic wisdom, briefly summarized in the preceding passage (*NS* 365). Collapsing the distinction between the poetic and civil theology leaves only two of Varro's three types of theology, the civil or poetic (for clarity I will continue to call Vico's first type by both names) and the natural. These two map on to the distinction between *sapienza poetica* and *sapienza riposta*.

Vico blurs the layers of Renaissance and earlier ideas of poetic wisdom which I am separating now. In chapter 1, I showed how Vico's poetic wisdom is best understood as a response to the Renaissance esoteric interpretations of poetic theology. I noted there that Vico overgeneralizes from the Renaissance commonplace and then attributes this view, the conceit that Homer contains esoteric wisdom, to Plato and all the other philosophers (*NS* 780). The *Republic* stands as a strong moral critique of poetry and as a counter-example to the conceit of scholars within Platonism itself. Unlike Pico, who promised to write a work on *Poetic Theology*, showing the philosophical truths hidden in Homer, Augustine extended Plato's moral critique of Homer to the Roman poetic and civil theology. Ironically, Petrarch acknowledged Augustine as the source for Renaissance ideas of poetic theology, since it was Augustine who preserved the critique of such allegorization as merely excusing the immorality of the pagan poetry.

Varro is influenced by both attempts (the allegorical revision and the moral critique) to resolve the quarrel of philosophy and poetry. While he agrees that philosophy not poetry teaches the truth about the gods, since poetic theology distorts the gods by depicting them engaged in immoral acts, Varro borrows the trope of allegory to defend civil theology. Vico overlooks the complexity of Varro's position, when he accuses him of "sharing the vulgar common error that the fables contained high mysteries of sublime philosophy."[7] In fact, one can learn as much about Vico's poetic wisdom through a comparison with Varro's ideas as from the contrast Vico sets up against the Renaissance's conceit.

Vico agrees with Augustine that Varro's distinction between poetic and civil theology should be collapsed. Vico acknowledges Augustine's moral critique of the poets, but seems to think Augustine understates the case, or if he recalls the extent of Augustine's critique, he is being ironic. In an explicit reference to Augustine's critique in the *City of God*, Vico explains how the fables about Orpheus provide a model for immoral behavior, even though Plato and Bacon both think they contain esoteric wisdom (*NS* 80). "In view of these things," Vico says, "it is a very slight reproof that Saint Augustine makes of the gods of the gentiles in his *City of God*" when one of Terence's characters is led to violate a slave girl after seeing a painting of Jove with Danae (*NS* 80; *CG* 2.7). Given the extensive and harsh critique in the *City of God*, unless Vico's memory was failing him, Vico's comment must be understood as an ironic statement of the strongest condemnation that these fables deserve.

Notably, Vico himself does not collapse the distinction between the two theologies on these moral grounds. Unlike Augustine, Vico does not want to dismiss the poetic and civil theology as mere falsehood. Vico discovers that the first histories were poetic (*NS* 813). Reinterpreted in this way, poetic wisdom forms an essential foundation for philosophy, as the "embryos or matrices" in which the "outlines" of philosophical wisdom can be found (*NS* 779). Given Vico's own defense of the significance of poetic or civil theology as he reconceives it, is Vico right to accuse Varro of the conceit of scholars for the way he reinterprets it? On the surface at least, Vico has misunderstood Varro's claims, because there is more common ground between Vico and Varro than Vico thinks.

First, Vico thinks Varro said *poetic* theology was a mixture of poetic and natural theology, when in fact, according to Augustine, Varro said *civil* theology was a mixture of the other two. Varro agrees that there is no way to save the poetic theology by philosophical interpretation, but he does think that naturalistic explanations reveal a kernel of truth in civil theology (which is a mixture of the lowest form, the poetic, and the highest, the philosophical). This observation leads us to the second point. Vico's memory of Augustine's report of Varro's allegorical interpretations is imprecise as well. Varro did not give the usual esoteric interpretations. Instead of simply reading philosophical explanations into the poetic theology, as Vico implies, Varro does admit the poetry is false. Vico is putting Varro together with the Renaissance Platonists, thinking his explanations also commit the error of the conceit of scholars.

The mistakes about Varro in this compressed passage of Vico's (that is, in the parenthetical comment, *NS* 366) make the comparison between Varro's and Vico's ideas not so much a question of influence, since Vico does not seem to remember it, as an interesting resonance. Perhaps if Vico had had access to Varro's *Antiquities*, he would have seen in Varro's work a genuine precedent for his search for the exoteric truth of the poetic or civil theology. At any rate, both Varro and Vico accept the moral critique of poetry, but offer another way, a temporal way, to think about how the ancient stories became false. We do not know how far Varro developed the idea of a true ancient wisdom corrupted over time, but what Augustine does tell us is suggestive.

Varro, unlike Augustine, thinks that the Romans originally had true stories, but these were corrupted, as I have said above. Varro believes that there is a residue of the true meanings of the ancient Roman religion in civil theology. Vico's search for the true Homer is motivated by exactly the same intuition. Vico also thinks that the first stories about the gods would not contain such falsehoods. Since the first humans are incapable of creating poetic veils for hiding esoteric teachings in immoral stories, then the stories must be a degenerated form of the initial *vero e severo* narrations (*NS* 814). Vico makes the same point about Homer and the Greeks as Varro makes for the ancient Romans.

Varro's idea that the ancient Romans had true accounts of the gods before these were corrupted is extended by Vico to the childhood of all the gentile nations. Vico's example is the discovery of the true Homer. Vico proposes that "the fables, which at their birth had come forth direct and proper, reached Homer distorted and perverted. As may be seen throughout the Poetic Wisdom above set forth, they were all at first true histories, which were gradually altered and corrupted, and in their corrupt form finally came down to Homer" (*NS* 808). Vico's discovery that the first humans thought in imaginative not intelligible universals, since they were stronger in imagination that intellect, led him to this discovery (*NS* 787).

Varro explores possible naturalistic explanations for the Roman pantheon in order to give a rational justification for why the founders (who worshipped without images) invented these gods. For example, Varro explained that Saturn "had a hook on account of agriculture;" and similarly, in an even more resonant passage to Vico's own description of Saturn, "Varro says that Saturn was called *Chronos*, a Greek word meaning 'time'; for 'without the passage of time,' he says, 'the seed cannot be productive'" (*CG* 7.19, 277). The parallel to Vico's explanations in "Poetic Wisdom" is striking. In "Poetic Chronology," Vico explains that "Saturn, who was so called by the Latins from *sati*, sown, and who was called Chronos, or Time, by the Greeks, gives us to understand that the first nations (all composed of farmers) began to count their years by their harvests of grain (the sole or at least the chief thing for which the peasants labored all year)" (*NS* 732; cf. *NS* 3, 73, 549, 730).

What Varro discovers is only in part the philosophical ideas he reads into the myths, such as Jupiter as World-Soul (*CG* 7.13, 271). His description of Saturn is a different type of explanation. If the former were that all Varro suggests, then Vico would be right to dismiss his attempt as another in the series of errors generated by philosophers trying to justify the immoralities of the gods in the inherited stories. But the naturalistic explanations, such as of Saturn, do not commit the conceit, but acknowledge a different way of thinking about the world, one very like Vico's own philological interpretations of poetic or civil theology. Varro does attribute more intellect to the founders than he should, from a Vichian point of view, but the explanations are still vulgar and common, not esoteric and for the few. So Varro is not unambiguously reading *sapienza riposta* into *sapienza poetica* as Vico's parenthetical comment implies (*NS* 366). Instead Vico's grounds for identifying the civil and poetic are similar to the naturalistic explanations Varro gives to hold civil theology superior to poetic. Augustine thinks these are dangerous explanations because they might be used to excuse the immorality of the poetic theology as well. Augustine judges that "this attempt is impossible," saying "the gods wriggle out of his clutch" (*CG* 7.28, 289). But do the gods wriggle out of Vico's clutches? Vico's greater self-consciousness about the difference between a philosophical and philological explanation allows him to make a strong case for the type of naturalistic explanation Varro suggests.

Although Augustine has little patience for exploring the details of false theology, he accepts the teaching of Euhemerus that the gods emerged from the divinization of men; in this respect, he agrees with Varro and Vico (*NS* 889), for this is a naturalistic explanation, not an esoteric one. What is more surprising is that Augustine has a sense of development of human faculties that could inform Vico's own, though Augustine sees the first stage as a childhood to be left behind. Perhaps Augustine is thinking of Paul, who said "when I was a child, I used to speak as a child, think as a child, reason as a child; when I became a man, I did away with childish things" (1 *Cor.* 13:11). In this way Augustine compares the life of human beings in general, or at least God's chosen people, to the experience of individual human beings. Augustine writes that "there is a process of education, through the epochs of a people's history, as through the successive stages of a man's life, designed to raise them from the temporal and the visible to an apprehension of the eternal and the invisible" (*CG* 10.14, 392; cf. 10.32, 423–24; 16.24, 683; 16.43, 710). There is a providential unfolding to human history just as there is in a human life, though Augustine is not unequivocally extending this pattern to all the nations as Vico does. Vico thinks that providence also guides the development of the gentiles, but through cycles, historical cycles which Augustine argues against (*CG* 12.18, 494–96). Cyclical history does not have its goal in the final stage as does linear history. In contrast to Augustine, Vico does not see divine providence exclusively working toward the Christian revelation.

Even so, Augustine sometimes seems to acknowledge a sense of natural development among the pagans. For example, Augustine refers to Cicero's observation that the later Romans made Romulus a god as surprising since by that time most people were learned ("it grew up in times of enlightenment, when false fables did not meet a ready reception"), unlike when the initial divinization of humans occurred (*CG* 22.6, 1029–30). Augustine is aware, from this passage which he quotes from Cicero at least, of the idea that earlier humans were more primitive in thinking (cf. *CG* 3.14, 104). Insofar as Augustine senses the distinction, intelligible universals are clearly superior and in no way dependent on the imaginative ones. Augustine thinks the pagans foolish for worshiping so many different gods to ensure temporal happiness, when if that is what they wish, they should simply worship Felicity (*CG* 4.23, 116). Augustine is perplexed that they do not think logically as he does, and frequently calls pagan theology and the attempts to defend it "nonsense" (*CG* 18.8, 769). From a Vichian point of view, Augustine is enacting the way the imaginative universal appears to the intelligible universal. But Augustine does acknowledge more than one might expect the developmental differences Vico makes central. Vico focuses on this aspect of poetic and civil theology in a way neither Augustine nor Varro fully explore, but there are adumbrations in the *City of God* of the idea that poetic wisdom is a different way of thinking, characteristic of the childhood of the human race.

Vico's second type, natural theology, is the only one on which Varro, Augustine, and Vico are in agreement. Natural theology is identified with that of the metaphysicians (*NS* 366). All three even agree that the best natural theology is the Platonic. In the previous paragraph tracing the development of wisdom, Vico makes Plato the example of the apex of wisdom in the *corso* because he discovers providence (*NS* 365). In Augustine's summary of Varro's *On Philosophy* the Platonists are the best sect since they not only understand what the highest good is, but also are concerned with finding happiness for others (*CG* 19.1–3, 843–51). Augustine agrees with Varro that the Platonists are the best of the pagan philosophers, because they are the closest to Christianity. Vico may be drawing on Varro's division of philosophers into social and solitary (one of the many differentiae for defining the two hundred and eighty-eight sects) when he excludes the Stoics and Epicureans and embraces the Platonists and other political philosophers (*NS* 130; *CG* 19.1, 845). The combination of knowledge of providence and social orientation makes the Platonic the best sect of philosophers for Varro, Augustine, and Vico.

The *New Science* is recognizably Platonic, with divine providence and the social realm as its foci. To specify his own *New Science*, Vico makes a further division of natural theology. In contrast to natural theology or metaphysics as practiced up until now, Vico's Lady Metaphysic looks for divine providence in the civil world not in the natural world (*NS* 2). Vico is deepening the commitment to the social, as defined by Varro, by making it the subject matter of metaphysics; so his is a unique form of natural theology, a "rational civil theology." The origin of Vico's reorientation of metaphysics is the principle that "the true is the same as the made" (*verum esse ipsum factum*), first articulated in the *Ancient Wisdom* (*AW* 45; cf. *NS* 331, 332, 349, 350). The previous metaphysicians tried to know the objects of God's knowledge, such as nature itself, rather than the civil world, which is a proper object of human knowledge, since we cooperate in making it. As Cicero said of Socrates, Vico is bringing philosophy down from the heavens to live in the cities (*Tusc.* iii.1). This social orientation does not mean that Vico destroys philosophy by reducing it to politics or history any more than Socrates did; Vico continues to engage in philosophy when it "undertakes to examine philology" (*NS* 7). Because modern metaphysics had lost the civil dimension that Socrates had had, Vico has to make explicit what for Varro and Augustine was a intrinsic part of philosophy, that speculation would return to practice, as the philosopher in Plato's *Republic* to the Cave (*CG* 8.4, 303; *R.* 519c–20d).

"Rational civil theology" is a combination of Vico's first two types, the civil or poetic theology and the natural theology. In his *Autobiography* he calls it "metaphysics of the human race . . . a natural theology of all nations" (*A* 167). Since either "natural civil theology" or "civil natural theology" would be an oxymoron, given the usual meaning of metaphysics as knowledge of the natural as opposed to the civil, Vico substitutes "rational" for "natural" to signify "philosophical." It is "civil," since he defines poetic theology as civil theology, and collapses the distinction into the civil theology, and it is "rational" because that is the philosophical element.

In a new way Vico unites poetic wisdom and philosophical wisdom, *sapienza poetica* and *sapienza riposta*. By combining the sense and the intellect of the human race, Vico discovers ideal eternal history, the action of providence, through philosophical contemplation of the human civil world. This type, a hybrid of the first two types, is also united to the others in its contemplation of divine providence.

In chapter 5, when I turn to the nature of divine providence in the *New Science*, I will consider how Vico captures in the phrase "rational civil theology" the intertwined aspects of certainty and truth. Only then will my argument be complete that Vico's "rational civil theology of divine providence" is best understood as a revision of the natural theology of the metaphysicians. A rival possibility is that Vico's own type is the third one he presents, Christian theology as revealed theology mixed with natural and civil, to which I now turn in order to complete my commentary on this compressed passage (*NS* 366).

Understanding what the third type, Christian theology, means is so complex that the reader is tempted to claim, with Max Fisch, that Vico is violating his own separation of sacred history as outside his *New Science*, and leave it at that (*NS* F7). There must be an explanation on which the reader is not forced to accept Fisch's conclusion that "the distinction [between Hebrew and gentile] loses importance" (ibid.). Recall how Vico defines his third type of theology: "our Christian theology, a mixture of civil and natural with the loftiest revealed theology" (*NS* 366). The combination of the natural and civil in this theology makes it look like the hybrid nature of Vico's "rational civil theology." The final assertion of the passage indicates, however, that he is thinking of the third type as primarily revealed theology based on faith, and the other elements are thus subordinated. Vico's final claim is as follows: "divine providence has so conducted human institutions that, starting from the poetic theology which regulated them by certain sensible signs believed to be divine counsels sent to man by the gods, and by means of the natural theology which demonstrates providence by eternal reasons which do not fall under the senses, the nations were disposed to receive revealed theology in virtue of a supernatural faith, superior not only to the senses, but to human reason itself" (*NS* 366).

The difficulty is that, like the summary of the development of wisdom (*NS* 365), this account of the guidance of divine providence leaves out the heroic and the human times of the *ricorso*. Granted, these build upon the revealed theology of the age of gods of the *ricorso*, but they build on it as Plato built upon Homer. Vico may tell us where Augustine is in the *ricorso* with this third type, but he does not tell us where he himself is. If the reader does not see this omission, Christian theology could be taken as Vico's standard for the other types, just as Augustine made it. I do not see how one could reconcile the overall cyclic nature of ideal eternal history, the central insight of the *New Science*, with such a linear scale. The whole structure of the *New Science* would collapse.

How can this apparently linear progression be reconciled with the explanation of wisdom as either poetic, the sense, or philosophic, the intellect, of the human race? From the cyclic point of view, the third type is best understood as the poetic wisdom of the *ricorso*. Interpreted in light of the summary progression, the revealed dimension is primary in the third type, not the mixture of civil and natural theology, as Vico has elsewhere given us reason to see is the nature and scope of his *New Science*. Both Vico's special type of natural theology (rational civil theology) and Christian theology share a mixed nature, that includes the civil or poetic as well as the natural. The Christian theology is essentially revealed (or what is called poetic wisdom in the corresponding phase of the *corso*), whereas Vico's is essentially *philosophical*. Christian theology as religion is primarily poetic and civil; Vico's rational civil theology as philosophy builds on the poetic wisdom of the *ricorso*, which is the Christian religion in his case, but it is still philosophy.

The fact that Vico calls the third type "our Christian theology" might make the reader assume that this is Vico's meaning for his "theology" in the *New Science*. As a member of a Christian commonwealth, Vico as a citizen would call it "our Christian theology," but, as philosopher, Vico would not limit himself to this type of theology (cf. *AW* 122).

Augustine would make this final type of revealed theology the standard for all the other types, and he certainly would not think it was mixed with any of the other types. Instead of singling out the truth of the Christian theology, as Augustine would, Vico emphasizes here that "all three types [are] united in contemplation of divine providence," thus accentuating the commonality, not the differences, among the three types (*NS* 366). Again it is instructive to compare this claim to that of *The Course that Nations Run*. There Vico says that the triads, of reason, judgment, authority, and the others, are "all embraced by one general unity," that of divine providence (*NS* 915). If Vico's were a simple linear hierarchy, then it would make more sense to note the differences than the similarities of the three types.

The questions raised by the third type of theology lead into the complex question of the nature of divine providence in the *New Science*, which is the topic of chapter 5. Like theology, the idea of providence has more than one level in Vico. A study of Vico's references to divine providence will contribute to answering the question of a third way of knowing God (a *logos* of *theos*) beyond the sense of the poetic-civil theologians and the intellect of the philosophers. If there is such a way of knowing beyond sense and intellect, it is not part of the Science itself, but is included to make the science complete by defining its boundaries.

Chapter 5

Divine Providence: Certain and True

The *subject* of Vico's "rational civil theology," his metaphysics and his unique type of theology, is "divine providence" (*NS* 2, 342). In this chapter, I will treat the nature of divine providence in the *New Science* in its multiple levels of complexity. Given the indebtedness and differences already evident between Vico and Augustine, the question arises naturally: how Augustinian is divine providence in the *New Science*, and how does Vico's idea of it differ from Augustine's? Answering this question will confirm, as suggested in chapter 4, that Vico's "rational civil theology of divine providence" is better understood as a revision of Vico's second type of theology, the natural theology of the metaphysicians, in particular the Platonists, rather than as an example of his third type, Christian theology (*NS* 366). Vico makes room for the latter in the *New Science*, but that is not his own perspective as it is Augustine's.

Recall that in the first positive axiom, after the conceits, Vico's alternative to a metaphysics of Stoic fate or Epicurean chance is a metaphysics of Platonic providence. Vico "dismisses from the school of our Science the Stoics, who seek to mortify the senses, and the Epicureans, who make them the criterion. For both deny providence, the former chaining themselves to fate, the latter abandoning themselves to chance" (*NS* 130). When Vico admits the Platonists, he is taking up their providential metaphysics as his own. In fact, Vico thinks perhaps it was for the demonstration of providence that Plato deserved to be called "divine" (*NS* 365). In order to see what of Vico's idea of providence comes from the pagan Platonists, it is first necessary to ascertain how much of it comes from Augustine. Augustine is a key mediator on this question. Skipping over Augustine and attempting to compare Vico directly with Plato on divine providence, the reader would not grasp the whole truth.

Augustinian Providence in the *City of God* and the *New Science*

Vico teaches us that "doctrines must take their beginning from that of the matters of which they treat," so acknowledging that the roots of Augustinian providence are biblical is important (*NS* 314). Augustine continually draws upon biblical authority, and in this way, certain aspects of Vico's idea of providence are ultimately derived from the Bible. Augustine follows the Bible closely on the nature of providence, so I will take him as a proximate authority for biblical providence. Augustine himself cites biblical authority when he opens Part Two by stating: "the City of God of which we are treating is vouched for by those Scriptures whose supremacy over every product of human genius does not depend on the chance impulses of the minds of men, but is manifestly due to the guiding power of God's supreme providence, and exercises sovereign authority over the literature of all mankind" (*CG* 11.1, 429).

Throughout the *City of God*, Augustine holds as axiomatic that "all tend, in God's plan, to that end which is included in the whole design for the government of the universe" (*CG* 12.4, 476). Since Augustine is more orator than logician, providence is not so much an axiom as the *topos* in terms of which everything is understood. In a specific reference to his commonplace's origin in the Bible, Augustine quotes Paul, who taught that "we know that God makes all things co-operate for good for those who love him" (*Rom.* 8:28; *CG* 1.10, 17). Just as confession permeates Augustine's *Confessions*, so the idea of God as a good governor, both of the City of God and the earthly city, is inscribed in every page of the *City of God*.[1]

The most prominent Augustinian element in Vichian providence is the biblical idea that providence cooperates with us to bring good out of evil. Vico, like Augustine, holds that: "God turns evil choices to good use" (*CG* 11.17, 449; cf., 22.2, 1023). This act does not mean that God causes the evil choices for the sake of the good which could be brought out of them. According to Augustine, God is not a tyrant who takes away the human "power of free choice," but a good governor who can even turn the evil choices to good ends, "judging it an act of greater power and greater goodness to bring good even out of evil than to exclude the existence of all evil" (*CG* 22.1, 1022).

This idea is further articulated in terms of the Plotinian idea of evil as privation (*Enn.* 3.2.5). Plotinus's idea of evil as privation remains central to Augustine the Christian, and Vico agrees with the idea that human beings are evil or unjust because they are fallen, which is to say they are evil by privation and not by nature (*NS* 310). Everything that God made is good, and only by free choice can evil appear as a privation of that good. Evil results from turning away from the goodness God intended for that creature. The creature's error does not compromise the overall goodness of God's creation though, since God can turn that evil to good use. For example, Augustine writes that "it follows that the actions of sinners, whether angels or men, cannot obstruct the 'great works of God, carefully designed to fulfil all his decision,' since in his providence and omnipotence he assigns to each his own gifts and knows how to turn to good account the good and the evil alike" (*Ps.* 111:2; *CG* 14.26, 592). About the first fallen angel, the devil, Augustine explains that though he was created good, by his foreknowledge God knew he would choose evil, and "laid plans for making good use of him even in his evil state" (*CG* 11.18, 449; cf. 14.11, 568–69). God would not have created an angel or a human being knowing his future evil state if he had not also known how he would put them to good use, "and thus enrich the course of world history by the kind of antithesis which gives beauty to a poem" (*CG* 11.18, 449; cf. 17.12, 740).

Vico's metaphysics discovers a pattern that is imperfectly realized in the civil world (which we participate in making), but is uniform enough to point to a superhuman governor. Vico's God (in the *New Science*) is more in the spirit of the likely story of the Demiurge in Plato's *Timaeus*, who is Reason persuading Necessity, than Augustine's Creator *ex nihilo*. Vico does not tell us how the universe as a whole appears to God, since that would be to engage in a type of theology or metaphysics that tries to know something he had no part in making. Vico consistently maintains that we cannot know what we did not make, and that is true above all for knowledge of who created us; yet we can know in natural theology that there is providence.

The idea of God bringing good from evil is mapped onto the history of the human race differently by Vico and Augustine, since Vico is primarily concerned with natural providence and Augustine with supernatural providence (*NS* 136). Nevertheless, the similarities between the way providence is described by Augustine and Vico are considerable. Vico's idea of God as a good and a just governor who brings good from evil without undermining human freedom has its strongest precedent in Augustine's *City of God*. Vico makes comparable claims about how God as providence turns evil to good within the civil world, and in our own lives. The pervasive references to providence bringing good from evil in the *City of God*, and the application of this idea to history, likely influenced Vico to emphasize this same quality of providence, as he does throughout the *New Science*.

Vico concurs that "often against the designs of men, providence has ordered this great city of the human race"(*NS* 342; cf. 629). Through providence the civil world is "directed to a good always superior to that which men have proposed to themselves" (*NS* 343). God takes the narrow ends at which human beings aim, and makes them wider (*NS* 1108). Vico makes this Augustinian idea the subject of his metaphysics, that characteristic which distinguishes it from others. Until now philosophers considered providence in the natural not the civil world, and the purpose of Vico's metaphysics is "to show His providence in the world of human spirits, which is the civil world or world of nations" (*NS* 2). The philosophers have not contemplated God's providence in making human beings social, the principal property of human nature. Providence is described as making human beings social through their own actions, "while intending almost always to do something quite different and often quite the contrary" (*NS* 2).

The best summary statement of Augustinian providence, whether embodied in the *City of God* or in the *New Science*, was written by Shakespeare: "there's a divinity that shapes our ends, rough hew them how we will" (*Ham.* V. ii. 10–11). This idea of God bringing good from evil is as fundamental in the religion of the *ricorso* as "all things are full of Jove" was in the *corso*. There is a philological dimension to Shakespeare's metaphor that Vico would appreciate. The image portrays the cooperation needed, for example, between two men trimming a hedge. The first "rough hews" the hard branches, and the other follows behind him, "to shape the ends."[2] The image makes plain that unless the first acts, neither can the second. Like the workmen trimming their hedges, human beings chop away at the decisions of their lives, and the divine intervenes to bring about the good.

Vico also follows Augustine in emphasizing how providence is a cooperation between human action and divine intervention. Vico shares Augustine's enthusiasm, when upon seeing the action of providence as cooperative, he exclaims, "events on earth, but directed from heaven! The actions of men, but the operation of God!" (*CG* 16.37, 701). This insight into the goodness of God's providence is what makes Lady Metaphysic tremble with love for God (*NS* 2). The most striking metaphor for providence in the *New Science* occurs when Vico compares providence to a queen as opposed to a tyrant. Vico writes that "such were the institutions that providence established for the state of the families, not like a tyrant laying down laws but like a queen it is of human affairs working though customs" (*NS* 525). Vico makes Dio Chrysostom's original formulation of this same idea, that "custom is like a king and law like a tyrant," an axiom of his

Science (*NS* 308) Vico points to the naturalness, order, and end, of the civil institutions as the philosophical or divine proofs of providence's guidance (*NS* 343). Only an omnipotent God could institute such uniform institutions so far apart from each other and with such ease; only eternal wisdom could give them such beauty and order; only eternal goodness could make the institutions so well suited to human needs (*NS* 344).

Vico holds that the civil world is too well ordered not to have a superhuman governor (*NS* 362), especially given the weakness of the reason of the first humans. Yet God's governing is not absolute in a way that makes us merely puppets. If so, that would be Stoic fate, which is as antithetical to Platonic providence as is Epicurean chance. Both Augustine and Vico are careful to distinguish providence from both fate and chance. Human beings have been given genuine freedom of choice. If we forget that we have a real role to play in first hacking out what God will shape, then we might think our actions do not matter, and that God's plan is something to observe passively as it occurs, not something in which we are partners.

Augustine steers a way between the Skylla of fate and the Charybdis of chance and argues that "without the slightest doubt, the kingdoms of men are established by divine providence" (*CG* 5.1, 179). Chance is a denial that there is a governor who orders events (*CG* 9.13, 358). The opponent here is the Epicurean who thinks events "have no cause, or at least no cause which depends on any rational principle"(*CG* 5.1, 179). The assertion that events are not left to chance may seem to err in the other direction, that of fate, where events happen in "an inevitable sequence, independent of the will of God or man"(*CG* 5.1, 179). Augustine counters this error by explaining that, though God governs events, "yet God is not bound in subjection to this order of events; he is himself in control, as the master of events, and arranges the order of things as a governor" (*CG* 4.33, 176). Vico shows a strong family resemblance to Augustine when he likewise advocates providence as opposed to the rival philosophies of Stoicism and Epicureanism. Vico locates providence between fate and chance on several occasions (*NS* 130; 335; 342; 345; 387; 630; 1101). For example, about ideal eternal history he says "that which did all this was mind, for men did it with intelligence; it was not fate, for they did it by choice; not chance, for the results of their always so acting are perpetually the same" (*NS* 1108). The choices human beings freely make are guided by providence into a pattern which then points to providence itself.

Augustine and Vico diverge somewhat, though it is not clear, from the *City of God*, how much, on the question of the extent we can know the pattern of providence in the civil world. The solution may simply be that

Vico draws a firmer distinction between natural and supernatural providence. Vico is motivated to do so because he is arguing for the independence of knowledge of the former from the revelation of the latter, and so the distinction matters more for his purposes than for Augustine's. In Augustine, the adjective "inscrutable" often accompanies a discussion of the plan of providence. Augustine thinks of providence as what is hidden from us, "an order completely hidden from us, but perfectly known to God himself" (*CG* 4.33, 176), "the inscrutable providence of the true God" (*CG* 7.35, 297). Again Augustine draws on biblical authority to answer the difficult question of the reason behind evil events. If asked about why evil events are allowed, Augustine says that "we must answer that the providence of the Creator and Governor of the universe is a profound mystery, and 'his judgments are inscrutable, and his ways cannot be traced'" (*Rom.* 11:33; *CG* 1.28, 39; cf. *CG* 5.21, 216). Also, Augustine claims that "no event is to no purpose under the all-embracing government of God's providence, even if the reason for it is hidden from us" (*CG* 12.28, 508).[3]

Vico agrees that providence as *pro-videre* involves something hidden from us as the future is, just as divinity is linked to *divinari* (*NS* 342). Then Vico adds that providence is also sometimes something "hidden in us" (ibid.). Unlike Augustine, who holds that providence has a "deep design which no human being can discover"(*CG* 12.15, 49; *Ps.* 12:8), Vico holds that human beings can know the pattern of God's providence at least in the civil world (cf. *NS* 345). This statement would seem to stand in clear opposition to Augustine, who says God's design is "inscrutable to natural human understanding" (*CG* 10. 32, 422). Nevertheless, Augustine does appear to leave open the possibility that we might by great effort be able to discern the purpose, and ascribes a purpose to the difficulty of discovering it.

Augustine holds that "divine providence thus warns us not to indulge in silly complaints about the state of affairs, but to take pains to inquire what useful purposes are served by things. And *when* we fail to find the answer, either through deficiency of insight or of staying power, we should believe that the purpose is hidden from us, as it was in many cases where we had great difficulty in discovering it. There is a useful purpose in the obscurity of the purpose; it may serve to exercise our humility or to undermine our pride" (*CG* 11.22, 453–54, emphasis added). Here Augustine allows for humble inquiry, and does not rule out the idea that we can sometimes discover the providential, useful purpose in an experience. This possibility makes intelligible the fact that Augustine does describe certain events in his own life and in history as providential. Still there is a tension in Augustine between absolute statements that we cannot know God's ways and a limited sense in which we can.

On occasion Vico uses the adjective "inscrutable," to refer to "the inscrutable counsels hidden in the abyss of divine providence" (NS 949). Why would Vico in this instance restrict our knowledge, as Augustine usually does? The solution to this usage is the distinction between natural divine providence which we can know, and the supernatural providence or divine grace which we cannot know (NS 136). Vico agrees with Augustine that "the manner of its making is as hidden from man and as incomprehensible to man as is he who made it" (CG 10.12, 390), if the reference is to divine grace and its miracles, and not to natural providence. Vico also agrees that insofar as we are not sole makers of ourselves or our histories, we cannot know either fully (A 127). Now this does not mean that we cannot see the repetition of the cycles of history which confirms that such a divine governor exists. Vico thinks we can understand natural providence through philosophical memory, in addition to believing it by supernatural faith.

Vico does not locate himself or Augustine as occupying an extreme in the matter of grace. In his Autobiography, Vico explicitly links his own view to those of Augustine on grace, which is supernatural providence. Vico says that after studying canon law and dogmatic theology, "he found himself in the very middle of Catholic doctrine in the matter of grace" (A 199). Reading the theologian Richardus convinced him that Augustine too occupied a middle ground; "St. Augustine is midway between the two extremes of Calvin and Pelagius, and equidistant likewise from the other opinions that approach these two extremes" (A 119). The interpreter of Vico does not have to look only to his earlier writing to find Vico supporting Augustinian ideas of the Fall, grace, and free will. In the New Science Vico derives "the first principle of the Christian religion" and "the Catholic principles of grace" (NS 310) from axiom 104 that custom is like a king not a tyrant, taken with axiom 8 and its corollaries. Axiom 8 is "things do not settle or endure out of their natural state" (NS 134). Vico claims that "this same axiom, together with 7 and its corollary, proves that man has free choice however weak, to make virtues of his passions; but that he is aided by God, naturally by divine providence and supernaturally by divine grace" (NS 136). Unlike Augustine, Vico claims that in regard to the way God aids human beings naturally by providence, "the Christian religion is in accord with all others" (NS 310). From Augustine's point of view, the extent of overlap between Christianity and other religions is at best preparatory and at worst misleading and irrelevant. From the point of view of the *New Science*, which strives for eloquence about divine and human things, the guidance of all of the nations is important, and the overall unity is especially so.

In striving for eloquence human beings imitate God. As Augustine so beautifully states, God's providence is "a kind of eloquence in events, instead of words" (*CG* 11.18, 449). In Vico's oration "On the Heroic Mind" he calls God the divine orator (*HM* 237). For both Augustine and Vico the pattern of history is the arrangement of God's speech. Vico focuses on discovering God's speech to the gentiles, but he also acknowledges the special speech given to the chosen people. In Book 4, Vico says that God reveals himself "to the Hebrews first and then to the Christians, this has been by internal speech to their minds as the proper expression of a God all mind; but by external speech through the prophets and through Jesus Christ to the Apostles, by whom it was declared to the Church. To the gentiles it has been through the auspices . . . supposed to come from the gods . . . it permitted them to fall into the error of following in place of reason the authority of the auspices, and to govern themselves by what they believed to be the divine counsels . . ." (*NS* 948). In this way, Vico acknowledges the special status of the Hebrews and of the Christians, while describing how God is communicating with all the nations.

Augustine in contrast makes central sacred history, with its linear story of Creation, Fall, Redemption, and Judgment. For Augustine the gentile pattern is irrelevant unless it leads to the story of the incarnation. Augustine states, "but in the end the Mediator himself came in flesh, and he and his blessed apostles now revealed the grace of the new covenant and disclosed openly what in previous ages had been indicated by veiled allusions, when hints were given in accordance with the stages of mankind's development, following the plan decided upon by God, in his wisdom" (*CG* 10.32, 423–24). So for Augustine the providential significance of pagan history is ultimately defined solely in terms of how it prepares for the truth, not how it achieves its own truth. As a result history becomes the subject of careful study as the confirmation of the Hebrew prophecies, beginning with the identification of Jesus as the Christ. In this sense, Augustine's linear sacred history, which is the vision that permeates the *City of God*, is located outside the narrative of the *New Science*. Vico finds that divine providence is not only a speech given to the few, but a speech given in so many different ways, and written in such large letters, that it is a wonder than anyone fails to recognize the truth that God governs the universe.

Vichian Providence: Poetic and Philosophical

Having established the resonance of Vico's general claims about providence with Augustinian providence, I now turn to how Vichian providence is innovative. Vico adapts the Augustinian commonplace that God governs the civil world, bringing good from evil, to the particular scope of his inquiry. Even in describing the similarities, the differences began to emerge. Vico focuses primarily on the natural instead of the supernatural aspects of divine providence. Natural providence in the *New Science* is discovered on two levels by human beings, one characteristic of the childhood of the human race and the other of the adulthood (e.g., *NS* 209). Vico's rational civil theology of divine providence encompasses both the certain and the true, the poetic and the philosophical, the *coscienza* of God through the senses and the *scienza* of God through the intellect (*NS* 137). In addition to providence's role as the subject of the first aspect of the New Science, religion and providence together are the dual first principle of humanity. Platonic division is followed by collection (*Phdr.* 265d–66b), and so Vico collects the divisions of theology and providence to arrive at the definition of his study of providence, a rational civil theology of divine providence.

As made evident in the preceding summary of wisdom, divine providence guides the process in which it is discovered (*NS* 366). Vico's division repeats itself here for the levels of providence; providence works through sense, intellect, and faith. So just as before, there are three ways to look at providence's guidance correlative to the types of theology. In both cases, there are two natural types and one supernatural. In addition to the division of natural providence and supernatural grace, there is a subdivision of Vichian natural providence. First, I will consider the natural, with its subdivision into poetic and philosophical, and then return to the questions about faith and supernatural providence. Faith is better understood as being governed not by natural providence as the others, but by divine grace, and as such is outside the scope of Vico's rational civil theology of divine providence.

What are the axioms and principles which led Vico to such complex accounts of theology and providence? I have already referred to axiom 5 several times to demonstrate that Vico prefers Platonism to Stoicism and Epicureanism. The grounds on which he does so are relevant here. The Platonists agree with the lawgivers on three basic points: "that there is divine providence, that human passions should be moderated and made into human virtues, and that human souls are immortal. Thus from this axiom are derived the three principles of this Science" (*NS* 130). The philosophers consider human beings as they ought to be and lawgivers consider them as they are (axiom 6 and 7); but they concur on the three principles of humanity. The principles of humanity illustrate the dual nature of Vico's *New Science*. Vico introduces these principles here, though properly they belong in the "Principles" (*NS* 333 ff.). The axioms which follow the introduction of the principles of humanity are also essential to understanding how these principles are both certain and true.

Axiom 9 draws the most fundamental epistemological division of the *New Science*: "men who do not know what is true of things take care to hold fast to what is certain, so that, if they cannot satisfy their intellects by knowledge (*scienza*), their wills at least may rest on consciousness (*coscienza*)" (*NS* 137).[4] This fact about human nature, that human beings rely on awareness of what is certain when ignorant of the true, is the origin of the division of human wisdom into two poles, that of the certain and the true. Other pairs of terms amplify this one: poetic or philosophical wisdom; philology or philosophy; *coscienza* or *scienza*; the sense or the intellect of the human race. Each of these pairs could be taken as the central distinction out of which the others flow, but the distinction between certainty and truth is generally the one Vico employs to explain the others. For instance, in axiom 10 Vico makes explicit the division between philosophy and philology using the technical distinction between the certain and the true: "philosophy contemplates reason, whence comes knowledge of the true, philology observes that of which human choice is the author, whence comes consciousness of the certain" (*NS* 138).

Philosophy and philology have distinct spheres of concern, and the errors of both can be found in not understanding the interdependence of the sources of certainty and of truth. For Vico "the philosophers failed by half in not giving certainty to their reasonings by appeal to the authority of the philologians, and likewise how the latter failed by half in not taking care to give their authority the sanction of truth by appeal to the reasoning of the philosophers. If they had done so they would have been more useful to their commonwealths and they would have anticipated us in conceiving this Science" (*NS* 140). Vico underscores how essential this division is for his New Science by summarizing the general axioms according to the distinction of the true and the certain. The first four axioms provide the basis for refuting all previous mistaken opinions about the principles of humanity; axioms 5–15 "which give us the foundations of the true, will serve for considering this world of nations in its eternal idea, by that property of every science, noted by Aristotle, that science has to do with what is universal and eternal (*scientia debet esse de universalibus et aeternis*)" (*NS* 163);

and axioms 16–22 "will give us the foundations of the certain" (*NS* 163) and instruct us to follow Bacon's method of philosophizing, which Vico later refers to as "think [and] see" (*NS* 359).[5]

In the *New Science* the certainty of the poets (the sense of the human race) and the truth of the philosophers (the intellect of the human race) are joined. Since "the certain is part of the true," Vico has extended at the macrocosmic level the truth of Aristotle's maxim that there is nothing in the intellect that is not first in the senses (*NS* 363; *De An.* 432a7).[6] The developmental insight informs how Vico sees the unfolding of ideas such as providence. The rational civil theology of divine providence "began in the vulgar wisdom of the lawgivers, who founded the nations by contemplating God under the attribute of providence, and which is completed by the esoteric wisdom of the philosophers, who give a rational demonstration of it in their natural theology" (*NS* 385). This claim about providence involves the application of some of the most innovative and fundamental axioms and principles of Vico's New Science.

In axiom 5 Vico stated in philosophical form the principles of humanity, which are held by all Platonists, including Vico himself.[7] The most concise summary of the dual nature of the principles occurs in the section on *Method*: "from all that has been set forth in general concerning the establishment of the principles of this Science, we conclude that, since its principles are (1) divine providence (2) marriage and therewith moderation of the passions, and (3) burial and therewith immortality of human souls; and since the criterion it uses is that what is felt to be just by all men or by the majority must be the rule of social life (and on these principles and this criterion there is agreement between the vulgar wisdom of all lawgivers and the esoteric wisdom of the philosophers of greatest repute)— these must be the bounds of human reason. And let him who would transgress them beware lest he transgress all humanity" (*NS* 360). Vico omits the pairing of the certainty of religion and the truth of divine providence in this formulation; but that he intends the three philosophical principles (divine providence, moderation of the passions, and immortality of human souls) as correlatives of the three poetic principles (religion, marriage, and burial) is clear elsewhere (*NS* 130).

Now it is evident how the philosophical versions of the principles are linked to the certainty of the common sense of the human race (axioms 11–13). The philosophical truths of divine providence, moderation of the passions into virtues, and the immortality of the soul, are contained in embryo in the poetic wisdom of the lawmakers as religion, marriage, and burial, respectively (*NS* 360, 779). In the section on *Principles* Vico states that "we observe that all nations, barbarous as well as civilized, though separately founded because remote from each other in time and space, keep these three human customs: all have some religion [cf. *NS* 334–35], all contract solemn marriages [cf. *NS* 336], all bury their dead [cf. *NS* 337]. And in no nation, however savage and crude, are any human actions performed with more elaborate ceremonies and more sacred solemnity than the rites of religion, marriage, and burial" (*NS* 333).

Vico concludes from the universal presence of these customs that they are true; "for, by the axiom that 'uniform ideas, born among peoples unknown to each other, must have a common ground of truth,' it must have been dictated to all nations that from these three institutions humanity began among them all, and therefore they must be most devoutly guarded by them all, so that the world should not again become a bestial wilderness. For this reason we have taken these three eternal and universal customs as three first principles of this Science" (*NS* 333). The three Platonic philosophical principles are not less true for being grounded in certainty. Vico speaks sincerely when he says the immortality of the soul was "later proved true by Plato" (*NS* 12). The duality of certain and true holds for all three principles of humanity.

The best answer to the puzzle of providence in the *New Science* is found in the distinction between the certain and the true. The reconciliation of the two becomes possible when one sees that for Vico "the certain is part of the true."[8] This insight that "the certain is part of the true" which enables Vico to see the dual nature of the principles of humanity has its origin in his jurisprudential work. The unique application beyond law makes the *New Science* innovative.[9] Vico also calls the *New Science* the "jurisprudence of human race" because it links the particular and the universal.[10] Vico is not choosing authority over philosophy, but asserting the interconnection of the two, and the dependence of philosophy on authority, on the common sense of the human race. The entire development of wisdom is guided by divine providence, so truth is clearly primarily transcendent and by imitation human, as is authority. As for Plato, for Vico the divine is always the measure for the human, not the Protagorean inversion. Only when one sees the equal duality of the certain and the true, the lawgiver-poets and the philosophers, the sense and the intellect of the human race, does the *New Science* reveal its strength and its breadth. Vico unites these opposites as no one else has; that is what makes it a New Science, in which one can find what one is seeking (*NS* 1096).

Providence acts through both levels, making us human through revealing itself to the senses (*coscienza*) and then to the intellect (*scienza*). In each of the three principles of humanity, the certain precedes and contains within it the true. For the first principle of divine providence this means that the truth of a philosophical idea has its roots in the certainty of the religions of all the nations. Now I will focus in more detail on the poetic and philosophical levels of providence separately, but remaining mindful of the new vision of the relationship between philosophy and philology in Vico's unique reconciliation of the two. I will consider the first principle of humanity, religion or providence, though the arguments involve all three principles of humanity.

The Certainty of Poetic Providence

How is providence "sensed" by the first humans? It cannot be "sensed" in the way modern empiricists, such as John Locke, mean by sensory impressions. Vico discovers that the first humans invented the world through an imagination (*fantasia*) that can only be understood with great difficulty (*NS* 34). To understand the origin of the idea of providence the reader of the *New Science* has to descend to a time before the "idea" was an idea in the mind of a rational human being. The first humans sensed providence with a degree of certainty we can hardly understand. Providence was an "idea" in the literal Greek sense of "something seen."[11] It is this certainty of the imaginative universal of providence that makes the rational idea of providence possible.

Vico draws upon the axioms discussed above to explain how authority preceded rational theology. Vico states that "by the definitions of the true and certain proposed above, men were for a long period incapable of truth and of reason, which is the fount of that inner justice by which the intellect is satisfied . . . In the meantime the nations were governed by the certainty of authority, that is . . . the common sense of the human race, on which the consciences of all the nations repose" (*NS* 350). In this way, Vico's distinction between the certain and the true leads from the first aspect of rational civil theology of divine providence to the second aspect of the New Science, that it is a "philosophy of authority" (*NS* 386; 350).[12] Vico writes that "this philosophy of authority follows the rational civil theology of providence because, by means of the former's theological proofs, the latter with its philosophical ones makes clear and distinct the philological ones; and with reference to the institutions of the most obscure antiquity of the nations it reduces to certainty human choice, which by its nature is most uncertain—which is as much as to say that it reduces philology to the form of a science" (*NS* 390). This aspect explains what Vico meant when he said philosophy must "undertake to examine philology" (*NS* 7).

Philosophy must consider as its past not only the great philosophers, but also the lawgivers; for the authority of the human race precedes the authority of the learned (*NS* 350).[13] As an example of "the history of philosophy told philosophically," Vico traces Socratic self-knowledge back to the lawgiver Solon's maxim "know thyself" (*gnothi seauton*) which was inscribed on the Temple at Delphi (*NS* 1043; cf. 416, 424, 426). This part of the story about Socrates is a commonplace, but Vico means it much more strongly: that the lawgivers made philosophy possible in Athens. In Plato's *Crito*, Socrates acknowledges a debt to the Laws of Athens which he was willing to die honoring (*Crit.* 50a–54e). What is most significant in this context is that the philosophical ideas in the third age of humans have certain counterparts in the poetic theologians and lawgivers of the first two ages (the ages of gods and of heroes).

So "a history of human ideas," the third aspect of the New Science (*NS* 391; 347), must descend further than the first rational formulation of an idea into the origin in poetic wisdom, which is the vulgar wisdom of the lawgivers. The Vichian history of the idea of providence involves the entire history of human ideas. Vico summarizes that "our new Science must therefore be a demonstration, so to speak, of what providence has wrought in history, for it must be a history of the institutions by which, without human discernment or counsel, and often against the designs of men, providence has ordered this great city of the human race. For though this world has been created in time and particular, the institutions established therein by providence are universal and eternal" (*NS* 342). Vico's New Science is a Science of origins. Providence is the first principle of humanity and first aspect of the Science because it is the origin of humanity and of the possibility of a Science of investigating origins.

Vico's philosophical idea of providence resembles Augustine's, as seen above. To see the poetic level, the origin of the philosophical, we must descend further than the lawgiver Solon to the first human act of imagining Jove. How does providence reveal itself before human beings are capable of reason, before they are even human beings? Answering this question involves what is new about the *New Science* more than any other aspect. The conceit of nations renders all the philologians and the conceit of scholars all the philosophers of no use in discovering the principles of this inquiry (*NS* 330). What everyone missed, Vico teaches us, was that before there were intelligible universals, there were imaginative universals.[14] Before human beings could reflect on the world, first the human world had to be invented. Since knowledge requires making something true for oneself (because *verum esse ipsum factum*), providence guided the human making of the civil world (*NS* 331).[15] The first imaginative universal is the origin of the idea of divine providence itself. In the imaginative universal we find the answer to the question of how providence is sensed.

As stated above, the descent from our refined natures to the primitive creatures who first began to think humanly is an extremely difficult one (*NS* 338). The beginning of providence is found in a sense of God suited to the savagery of the cyclops or the giants. Vico holds that these creatures desire something superior to themselves to save them from nature, and "something superior to nature is God" (*NS* 339). The passions of these first humans were violent, but the fear of God transformed these bestial passions into human ones (*NS* 340). Vico concludes, "thus it was fear which created gods in the world; not fear awakened in men by other men, but fear awakened in men by themselves" (*NS* 382). Vico discovers how "the fear of the Lord is the beginning of wisdom" (*HM* 231; *Ps.* 111:10).

The way in which the giants formulated the imaginative universal of Jove is described in "Poetic Metaphysics." The giants on the mountain tops when the flood waters dried out were frightened by the thunder and lightning, and imagined that the sky was "a great animated body, which in that aspect they called Jove" (*NS* 377). Vico is insistent throughout that the reader does not confuse the strong, bodily imagination (*fantasia*) of the first humans with our own refined, spiritualized imagination (*imaginazione*) (*NS* 338, 375, 378). Pointing to a cloud that looks like a rabbit when you know it is just water vapor is much more refined and weak than the formulation of the imaginative universal of Jove by the pointing and the shaking of the first humans. There is no transference of meaning as in metaphor; rather there is an identification or naming that constitutes the being of the named, because the meaning is univocal not analogical (*NS* 403). The thundering sky *is* Jove. Vico describes how "Jove was born naturally in poetry as a divine character or imaginative universal, to which everything having to do with the auspices was referred by all the ancient gentile nations, which must therefore have been poetic by nature. Their poetic wisdom began with this poetic metaphysics, which contemplated God by the attribute of his providence, and they were called theological poets, or sages who understood the language of the gods expressed in the auspices of Jove; and were properly called divine in the sense of diviners, from *divinari*, to divine or predict" (*NS* 381). How far we have descended from the poetic theologians of the Renaissance.

The first humans took thunder as signs from Jove, and these signs are the origin of divination, "the science of the language of the gods" (*NS* 379). This divination is the first wisdom of the gentiles, as discussed above (cf. *NS* 366). Vico concludes that this moment is the origin of the idea of God: "thus Jove acquired the fearful kingdom of men and gods; and he acquired the two titles, that of the best (*optimus*) in the sense of strongest (*fortissimus*) (as by a reverse process *fortis* meant in early Latin what *bonus* did in late), and that of greatest (*maximus*) from his vast body, the sky itself. From the first benefit he conferred on mankind by not destroying it with his bolts, he received the title *Soter*, or savior (This is the first of the three principles we have taken for our Science)" (*NS* 379). As Vico states elsewhere, "every nation had its Jove" (*NS* 193).

The first humans founded religion by their imaginative universal of a governor of the world, who is to be praised for saving them and feared for his greatness and strength. Vico summarizes the discovery as follows: "from what has been said up to this point it is concluded that divine providence apprehended by such human sense as could have been possessed by rough, wild, and savage men who in despair of nature's succors desired something superior to nature to save them (which is the first principle on which we have established the method of this Science), permitted them to be deceived into fearing the false divinity of Jove because he could strike them with lightning. Thus, through the thick clouds of those first tempests, intermittently lit by those flashes, they made out this great truth: that divine providence watched over the welfare of all mankind" (*NS* 385). The idea of God is not certain because a philosopher like Descartes discovers it by introspection of the contents of his mind. It is certain because the first humans saw it. Divine providence was discovered by our frightened ancestors when "out of the flash of thunderbolts, in which this true light of God shone forth for them: that he governs mankind" (*NS* 1098). The poetic dimension of divine providence requires us to understand poetic in the broad sense of *poiesis*, the making of the imaginative universal of Jove, from which all other knowledge flows. The crude, poetic metaphysics summarized above is the trunk of the poetic tree of knowledge (*NS* 367).

Witnessing Jove is the origin of all governing as well as knowing in the human world. The middle term that makes these possible is making, the making of *fantasia*. Divine providence and law are twins (*NS* 398). The certainty of the imaginative universals leads to certain customs, which were perpetuated by authority. Religion, marriage, and burial, were carefully guarded customs since they were the means by which the feral became the human (*NS* 333). The birth of Jove marks the beginning of the taking of the auspices which is the first divine institution by which human institutions were governed (*NS* 398). Vico says that the treatment of law must begin with providence, since they have the same origin (*NS* 398, 336).

Law is what Cicero refuses to discuss with the Epicurean until he "granted the existence of divine providence" (*Leg.* 1.7.21, *NS* 335).

How exactly does providence work through the authority of law to establish the certainty of providence? Divine providence, as a good governor, considers human beings as they *are* (*NS* 132). Even with the fear of God, the first humans still acted out of self-love, so that justice emerged only through providence (*NS* 341). Now the significance of axiom 7 is clearer. Axiom 7 states that "legislation considers man as he is in order to turn him to good uses in human society. Out of ferocity, avarice, and ambition, the three vices which run throughout the human race, it creates the military, merchant, and governing classes, and thus the strength, riches, and wisdom of commonwealths. Out of these three great vices, which could certainly destroy all mankind on the face of the earth, it makes civil happiness" (*NS* 132). Nevertheless, this "legislation" capable of turning the three great vices into civil happiness is not created by human beings alone, as modern jurisprudential scholars thought (*NS* 135; 310). The corollary to axiom 7, which Vico refers to in making his case for free choice and providence, is a statement of the nature of divine providence acting in the civil world. Vico states that "this axiom proves that there is divine providence and further that it is a divine legislative mind. For out of the passions of men each bent on his private advantage, for the sake of which they would live like wild beasts in the wilderness, it has made the civil institutions by which they may live in human society" (*NS* 133).

Vico's most innovative application of Augustinian providence as bringing good from evil is found in how providence turns the selfish actions of the first humans into the institutions of the civil world. Vico agrees with Augustine that self-love is definitive of the city of this world (*CG* 14.13, 573; 14.28, 593), or what Vico calls "the great city of the human race" (*NS* 342). Vico holds that "men, because of their corrupted nature, are under the tyranny of self-love, which compels them to make private utility their chief guide. Seeking everything useful for themselves and nothing for their companions, they cannot bring their passions under control to direct them toward justice" (*NS* 341). From the fallen state of human beings, which was introduced on the first page of the *New Science* (*NS* 2), Vico concludes that, even after having begun to live civilly, each still desires his own utility. Providence takes this self-love and founds the city of the human race.

There is an echo of Thomas Hobbes throughout this description of the state of nature and of how self-interest remains within the social realm.[16] Vico's quarrel with modern jurisprudence is exactly on this issue of how governing emerges from self-interest. Hobbes, for instance, believes a rational far-sighted calculus of self-interest persuades the self-interested individual to submit to law.[17] Vico holds instead that it must be the guidance of providence, because the first humans are not capable of the sort of reasoning the modern jurisconsults attribute to them. Thus, modern jurisprudence commits the conceit of scholars when it reads its own level of reasoning into the origin of human cities. Vico concludes: "therefore it is only by divine providence that he can be held within these institutions to practice justice as a member of the society of the family, of the city, and finally of mankind. . . . That which regulates all human justice is therefore divine justice, which is administered by divine providence to preserve human society" (*NS* 341). As quoted above, the civil world is ordered not by human counsel but by divine providence (*NS* 342). As further evidence of divine guidance, Vico points to the fact that law emerges the same everywhere though the peoples are remote from each other (*NS* 146). Since God is not a tyrant, "but like a queen working though customs" (*NS* 525), human beings retain their freedom, but their free choices, often quite contrary to their own designs, are turned to good use. The uniformity of customs (especially religion, marriage, and burial) reveals that nations do not arise by chance, and the degree of variance between nations shows that it is not fate, but providence that orders the civil world (*NS* 133).

The Truth of Philosophical Providence

Vico agrees with Augustine that the history of humanity can be understood as an individual writ large. Poetic theology or myth is characteristic of the childhood of the human race and philosophy of its adulthood. Providence reveals itself by working naturally through both; first to establish the reality of providence as certain and then as true. If philosophy discovers the "truth" about providence, why does Vico retain the earlier "certain" discoveries and give them such importance? In other words, if philosophy is a superior source for truth, why must philosophy examine philology (*NS* 7)? Whereas Augustine agrees with Paul, that as adults we should put away childish things, Vico gives the childhood of the human race a much more important role, as I have explored above. Because the discovery of the imaginative universal comprises the most original element of the *New Science*, one might overlook that Vico does think that reason completes the imagination (e.g., *NS* 498; 1045). I explained in detail how Vico emphasizes the balance and the interdependence of philosophy and philology, the sense and the intellect, in the axioms and principles of the *New Science*. Now I can turn to what this means for philosophy and its knowledge of providence.

In the *Study Methods*, Vico argues persuasively that education should follow the natural development of human faculties, in which imagination is stronger in childhood as reason is in adulthood (*SM* 13–14). *Ars topica* should be cultivated first, and only later be disciplined by the *ars critica*. Vico applies his insight into the education of individuals to the education of the human race. The argument about *ars topica* and *ars critica* in the *Study Methods* becomes even more significant as one of "the final corollaries of the logic of the learned" in the *New Science*: "providence gave good guidance to human affairs when it aroused human minds first to topics rather than to criticism, for acquaintance with things must come before judgment of them. Topics has the function of making minds inventive, as criticism has that of making them exact. And in those first times all things necessary to human life had to be invented . . . Thus the first peoples, who were the children of the human race, founded first the world of the arts; then the philosophers, who came a long time afterward and so may be regarded as the old men of the nations, founded the world of the sciences, thereby making humanity complete" (*NS* 498). God is not only a divine legislator, but also a divine teacher. Providence appears to the senses in the childhood of the human race, and to the intellect in the adulthood. But the truth of the idea of providence in the adulthood of humanity depends on the certainty of making the imaginative universal of Jove in the childhood of humanity.

Human beings are not complete as children, but neither are they complete if as adults they expunge any trace of child-like powers of imagination in favor of an abstract reason. Philosophy, like reason itself, is an inherently dependent, not originary, aspect of humanity. Philosophy has to examine philology not to find the truth about wisdom, but to discover certain starting-points for its reasoning. This dependence is why Vico retains a more significant role for the childhood of the human race. He views providence working through the imagination of the first humans to establish the *sensus communis*. Vico does not choose philosophy over poetry, but finds a way to unite the authority of the poets with the reason of the philosophers. As discussed above, either alone is incomplete according to Vico.

The *New Science* confirms authority with reason and grounds reason with authority. Vico concludes that "with the help of the preceding philosophical proofs, the philological proofs both confirm their own authority by reason and at the same time confirm reason by their authority" (*NS* 359). Philosophy can correct the moral errors of poetry, and poetry can assuage the doubts of untethered reason by bringing it back to the *sensus communis.* Philosophy goes wrong if it attempts to provide its own start-ing-point, as something apart from the certainty of common sense. The certain starting-point for reason is not found within reason itself; *ars critica* cannot make an argument without drawing on *ars topica* for its premises. Philosophy's esoteric wisdom completes the vulgar wisdom of the poets, but philosophy cannot begin in esoteric wisdom any more than one can skip being a child and commence human life as an adult.

Augustine would see Vico's attention to the earlier approximations of the truth about providence as misguided. Augustine is not alone in want-ing to dismiss poetic theology, indeed all theology before his own, as false. Recall how Varro and Augustine followed Euhemerus in explaining the historical origins of the gods as human beings who were divinized. This interpretation of myth resembles Vico's poetic wisdom because it views fables as true histories, and usually rejects allegorical interpretations. That is where the similarity ends. Merely to state that Vico is advocating a ver-sion of Euhemerism is misleading.[18] The reason this parallel is misleading is that Euhemerism does not adequately acknowledge how differently the first humans thought. It is not just that their thought was an inferior ver-sion of our own, but that its strength is our weakness and vice versa. We cannot create an imaginative universal such as Jove any more than one of the giants could have proved a geometric theorem. Once one sees the edu-cation of humanity in terms of *ars topica* and *ars critica*, as strong in child-hood and adulthood respectively, the mistake is evident (*NS* 185, 186, 211, 212; *SM* 13–14). The mistaken adult thinker assumes that the child has the same faculties, but is simply misusing them. The assumption is that the first humans perceived the world in basically the same way as the philosophical. This assumption is manifested in the two conceits which Vico holds responsible for all the errors in philosophy and philology prior to his New Science (*NS* 330).

Despite some insight into the different stages of the development of humanity, Augustine sees the earlier stages as inferior versions of the later, such that once one has the later form, the earlier one is discarded. From the point of view of the *New Science* Augustine was wrong to dismiss the poetic theology as mere falsehood of no further purpose, when he judged it for its weakness of reason instead of seeing its strength of imagination (*fantasia*). For Vico the stages have a more organic interrelationship. Vico admits the falsehood of the pagan poetic theology (or at least of the cor-rupted versions of the stories that have come down to us), but he sees providence's hand in it, though not in the way the Renaissance or August-ine did. Providence works through the false but certain fables giving rise to philosophy, by which a true understanding of divine providence will be possible (*NS* 362). Augustine did think pagan learning contributed to the preparation for Christianity, but he did not see the earlier stages as making us human and making ideas themselves possible.

For Vico the discovery of the philosophical idea of providence depends on the certainty of the imaginative universal Jove. Augustine correctly criticizes the falsehood of the fables, but he (like all other philosophers) fails to see how the emergence of the idea of God is first founded in this way and given certainty, despite the errors surrounding its initial expression. Like a root of a tree, once lost, certainty cannot be regained. To put it more positively, the roots are not the goal of the tree, but without the roots it cannot grow into a tree. Such is the Vichian tree of life and wisdom.

Augustine does not cut himself off from wisdom by severing the ties to the authority of the pagan poetic theology in the same way as modern philosophers do. Augustine is not paralyzed as later modern philosophers because he draws on another authority, not the pagan poetic wisdom of the *corso*, but the poetic wisdom of the *ricorso*, the Christian scriptures. Augustine still has an authority besides that of the learned (*NS* 350), and in this Vico resembles him closely. Christian theology, as explored in chapter 4, is a mixed form which includes a poetic or civil dimension (*NS* 366). Augustine avoids skepticism because he has another source for certainty. So Augustine is a much more complex case because he does not privilege philosophy over the authority of religion, as many modern philosophers will.

Vico's criticism of Polybius illustrates how he envisions the interdependence of philosophy and religion. Recall that the first principle of humanity has two aspects: religion and divine providence. Religion begins with the fear of God, and out of that piety develops the idea of divine providence. The certain is part of the true, and the true cannot be generated without the poetic origin. Polybius claimed that there could be a society of philosophers, and it would be morally superior (*NS* 179, 334, 1043, 1110). Vico responds that on the contrary: "if there had not been religions and hence commonwealths, there would have been no philosophers in the world, and if human institutions had not been thus conducted by divine providence, there would have been no idea of either science or virtue" (*NS* 1043). The principles of humanity are the bounds of human reason because they are the condition for its possibility (*NS* 360).

In modern philosophy, once the authority of poets and lawgivers of the *corso* and the revelation of the *ricorso* are rejected, then philosophy cannot get out of skepticism, if it is consistent. Everything important ends up a matter of opinion or a prejudice or a presupposition and not knowledge. Compare Immanuel Kant's practical postulates to Vico's principles of humanity. They are almost identical. For Kant they are the existence of God, human freedom, and the immortality of the soul.[19] Human freedom and God together lead to an idea of providence, since if God were fate, human freedom would be compromised. If one ignores the roots of these ideas in the common sense of the human race, one ends up thinking (in accordance with Kant's postulates) that one cannot know as much as one can. Vico claims that his "metaphysics compatible with human frailty" does not deny human beings all truths, but only some (AW 109). Vico allows knowledge of all three principles that Kant thinks we cannot know but can only act "as if" they were true. In terms of the New Science, Kant has it backwards. The philosopher's task is not to discover what "Religion within the Bounds of Reason" is, but what reason is within the bounds of religion.[20] The principles of humanity provide the boundaries of human reason, not the other way around (NS 360). Kant's error is emblematic of the Enlightenment error of thinking that philosophers could produce a better society by rooting out superstition, by simply being more rational. The problem is that when one roots out all imaginative origins, the tree of knowledge is killed. When reason is detached from the sensus communis, it cannot generate its own starting-points. When reason attempts to create its own foundations, it builds systems that are not connected to the human world and do not contribute to self-knowledge.[21]

Modern philosophy's quest for certainty excluded from consideration precisely the certainty upon which not only philosophy but the consciences of commonwealths rest. By eliminating philology (history, law, languages, poetry) as uncertain and unworthy of philosophical study, the Cartesians led modern philosophy away from the very poetic grounds that would end the skeptical doubt of ungrounded reason.[22] The conceit of scholars kept modern philosophers from seeing that human beings were not always rational agents like themselves. Epistemological foundationalists will never find foundations for reason as long as they only look to reason itself.

Many contemporary thinkers have realized this error, but they retain the skepticism, and the prejudices against religion and rhetoric. They do not rediscover the piety lost by the modern philosophical turn. They do not go back to the origin, but are merely reacting to the previous mistake. What must occur to revive philosophy is a descent to the fear of God from which wisdom originated. It was there that Vico found the golden bough of the imaginative universal, which allowed him to return to the human world with a new understanding.[23] The master key is not only fantasia, but the fear of God that accompanies its discovery. This discovery is why the *New Science* concludes that "this Science carries inseparably with it the study of piety, and that he who is not pious cannot be truly wise" (*NS* 1112).

Vico's unique Platonism is evident from the way that he argues for divine providence, and analogously for the moderation of the passions and the immortality of the soul. All of these are recognizably Platonic ideas. When he says in axiom 5 that "this axiom admits to our school the political philosophers, and first of all the Platonists, who agree with all the lawgivers on these three main points," he does not say all philosophers agree with the lawgivers, with the common sense of the human race. This link to the lawgivers gives a certainty to Platonism not shared by Stoicism and Epicureanism, including their modern equivalents.[24] This certainty is naturally derived from human nature (guided by natural providence) and not from logic or revealed authority, so Vico's Platonism avoids both skepticism and fideism.

The importance of reviving this kind of self-understanding of philosophy is that providence has a special role for philosophy in the third age, the age of humans. In this age philosophy must remember its religious origins to guard human beings from slipping back into bestiality and to find the certainty to speak wisely about things divine and human once again. The urgency rises when religion begins to lose its ability to make human beings virtuous through the fear of God (*NS* 1101). Philosophy must make known the idea of virtue once religious sentiments no longer prompt the practice of virtuous actions (*NS* 1110). The duality of religion and philosophy is most evident here, since in both cases the goal is cleansing the heart of human beings to love properly. Education into virtue or *paideia* is truly the heart of philosophy so understood. Vico clearly shares this family resemblance with Augustine who eloquently defines virtue as "rightly ordered love" (*CG* 15.22, 637).

But if philosophers fail to see that philosophy needs to remember its roots, then they will not perform the task of moral education, that of purifying the heart of humanity. Philosophy is essentially memory, and a forgetful memory is no memory at all.[25] Vico is clear that philosophy must become eloquent to take up religion's humanizing function (*NS* 1101). As I pointed out in the introduction to part 1 on Pico, unlike the Renaissance philosophers who inspired Vico, Descartes rejects rhetoric, along with poetry and history. Once memory and eloquence are rejected, then philosophy cannot perform its cooperative role in helping providence as moral teacher. This role for philosophy demonstrates how much closer Vico is to the Renaissance philosophers who embraced eloquence and history than to the modern philosophers of his own day. A philosophy without memory cannot find the certainty needed to discover the truth. A philosophy without eloquence cannot persuade others of the truth that it finds.

To most contemporary philosophers, the idea of placing reason within the bounds of religion especially, but the other principles of humanity as well, will sound like shackling reason. But Vico would have us ask, what growth would be stunted by pruning a tree of knowledge that is already dead from being cut off from its roots? In fact, philosophy is not reduced or destroyed but enlivened by the reconnection with the common sense of the human race, the certains that ground all the truths that develop out of poetic wisdom. Poetic wisdom contains esoteric wisdom in embryo, or serves as its matrix, and philosophy completes the development. The errors of poetic wisdom are used by philosophers to help them begin to think abstractly, in terms of intelligible universals. But without the initial invention of the world through imaginative universals and the three universal customs of religion, marriage, and burial, there would be no notion of art or science and no humanity to ask such questions (*NS* 1043).

Vico's rational civil theology enables the reader to glimpse the pattern of providence and to join authority and reason. Vico's "method" instructs his reader to narrate this Science to himself (*NS* 349). As a human being, the reader inherits the making of the first humans, which enables the reader to know the civil world through the convertibility of *verum* and *factum*. Since in God authority and reason are one (*NS* 948), the reader will feel a "divine pleasure" in imitating that coincidence of the certain and the true. God knows eternally what human beings have to work out sequentially, beginning with the certainty of authority and moving to the truth of reason. Vico's *New Science* enables us to see certainty and truth together as they are in God. We imitate God in discovering through time, which Plato defines as "the moving image of eternity," that which is united in God (*Ti.* 37d). Ideal eternal history is guided by divine providence, and in the course of it human beings discover divine providence first imaginatively in the thundering sky as Jove, and then philosophically as the idea of divine providence. Providence finally guides human beings to realize that the certain is part of the true, and that both point to a divine governor of the civil world.

I have shown that Vico does believe we can know the pattern of natural providence in the civil world—developing from the poetic to philosophical—because we cooperate in making it. Vico leaves room for supernatural guidance that we cannot know, since it is not a shaping of our own efforts. Recall that in an early axiom Vico states that human beings are "aided by God naturally by divine providence and supernaturally by divine grace"

(*NS* 136; cf. 1046). Strictly speaking Vico calls this type of providence, this supernatural guidance from God, divine grace, so providence in the *New Science* is natural providence, either poetic or philosophical. This formulation supports my suggestion that Vico's own type of theology is better understood as revision of natural theology than revealed, the second instead of third type he delineates by adapting Varro (*NS* 366). Thus, divine governing is subdivided into divine providence and divine grace. Divine providence is a natural governing, which is common to all human beings, and begins as the poetic and the certain and develops into the philosophical and the true. Divine grace, on the other hand, is supernatural governing, and is only given to a few, and is outside of Vico's rational civil theology of divine providence. Vico does not undermine the philosophical integrity of his account of natural providence by allowing for supernatural providence or grace which is known by faith rather than sense or intellect. In Aristotelian fashion, Vico completes his definition by saying what providence in the *New Science* is not.

Chapter 6

Educating the Fallen Image of God

I have explained, in chapters 4 and 5, how Vico's *New Science* is a type of metaphysics or natural theology, specifically a rational civil theology of divine providence (*NS* 2, 342). But the question remains, how is this metaphysics made "compatible with human frailty" (*AW* 109)? Augustine's critique of Platonism reveals how hard a task Vico has undertaken, and how significant the results if Vico succeeds. Vico wishes to humble philosophy and yet preserve its ability to speak eloquently about things divine and human and to guide human beings in wisdom and virtue. From Augustine's point of view, Vico does not go far enough in limiting the ability of philosophy to cure corruption and "raise and direct weak and fallen man" (*NS* 129). For Augustine, only God can do what Vico says philosophy must if it is to be useful to the human race (ibid.).

Now I return to the questions of human nature and education raised in chapter 2, when I compared Pico's "Oration on the Dignity of Man" and Vico's inaugural orations. Not surprisingly, as a philosopher, Vico responds differently to the idea of the Fall than Augustine as a Christian theologian does, but Vico does respond to it. Vico's humanism is evident in the sixth oration where he lists the cures for human corruption as wisdom, virtue, and eloquence (*IO* 6.5), as explored in chapters 2 and 3. Now this line of inquiry must turn to the *New Science* for Vico's mature answer to the question of the role which philosophy plays in curing the corruption of human beings, and whether philosophy can raise up human beings to become again the image of God. The answer involves discovering nothing less than the nature and place of philosophy in human affairs. First I will consider Augustine's critique, which makes even the best philosophy a distant second best to faith in the Christian religion; then I will show how Vico humbles philosophy in a manner which preserves it as a way to educate fallen man.

Augustinian Humility and Platonic Pride

In the *City of God* Augustine praises the Platonists as the best of the philosophers, and therefore as the only ones he must engage. For example, he asks, "if Plato says that the wise man is the man who imitates, knows and loves this God, and that participation in this God brings man happiness, what need is there to examine the other philosophers? There are none who come nearer to us than the Platonists" (*CG* 8. 5, 304; cf. 8.10, 313; 8.12, 315; 9.1, 343). To the Christians who are wary of philosophy because of Paul's warnings, Augustine points out that Paul does say that some of the philosophers have "some acquaintance with God" (*Rom.* 1: 21ff; *CG* 8.10, 312), and adds that they are acquainted even with the idea that in God we live, and move, and have our being, "as some of your own writers have also said" (*Acts* 17:28; *CG* 8.10, 312). Augustine eloquently summarizes Varro's *On Philosophy* which delineates the various philosophical sects, and agrees with his choice of Platonism as the best (*CG* 19. 1–3, 842–851).

Augustine does not stop with the best of the philosophers, as Varro does; rather he places Christianity as superior to the best type of philosophy (*CG* 19.4, 852). Despite his repeated claims that the Platonists are above the other philosophers, the *City of God* makes clear that the Platonists are a great distance from the truth. Augustine sums up this evaluation well, when he says that "those Platonist philosophers excel all others in reputation and authority, just because they are nearer to the truth than the rest, even though they are a long way off from it" (*CG* 11.5, 434). Augustine's praise of the Platonists must be put in the context of his ultimate critique of philosophy's pride.

This one word, "pride," sums up Augustine's critique of the Platonists. But what does Augustine mean by pride? Pride is far from a minor sin; in fact, it is the root of all sin: "the beginning of all sin is pride" (*Ecclus.* 10:13; *CG* 12.6, 477). According to Augustine's definition, "pride is a perverted imitation of God" (*CG* 19.12, 868). The Platonists are right to try to imitate God, but wrong to think they can do so through their own efforts. Tracing all the references to pride and humility in the *City of God* would be comparable to tracing the imagery of stars or light in Dante's *Divine Comedy*. What is central in this context is the meaning of the critique of Platonism which turns on his distinction between pride and humility. In *Confessions* Book 7 Augustine emphasizes the difference between confession and presumption; in the critique of the Platonists in the *City of God* humility and pride are most often paired.[1] Most of Augustine's points against pride and in favor of humility are explicitly supported by the Bible. The Fall is caused by pride. Pride is the most fundamental error about divine things, because the proud fail to see the proper relationship between God and themselves. The recurrent metaphor for pride is something swollen, inflated, or puffed up; for example, "the power of humility is unknown to men whose souls are inflated with the impurity of inflated pride" (*CG* 9.20, 366). Love builds up, whereas pride merely inflates (I *Cor.* 8:1; *CG* 9. 20, 366).

From the very first page of the *City of God*, Augustine draws a firm division between the proud and the humble: "I know how great is the effort needed to convince the proud of the power and excellence of humility" (*James* 4.6; *CG* 1.1, 5). Augustine is writing for the proud in order to persuade them to humble themselves and accept the Christian religion. The philosophers are guilty of the most inveterate sickness, infecting the heart as well as the mind (*CG* 1.1, 7). Divine providence allowed the Platonists to discover some truths, but they fell short because they did not understand the way of humility (*CG* 2.7, 54–55). The pride of the philosophers is the reason why the Platonists reject the Christian religion despite its similarities to their own views in other respects (CG 10.28, 413; 10.29, 416).

The Neoplatonist Porphyry is made an example to help others like him who admire humanistic learning. Porphyry's error is a moral as well as an intellectual one.[2] In the chapter entitled "The blindness of Porphyry to the true wisdom, which is Christ," Augustine says that if Porphyry were a true lover of wisdom, he would have acknowledged Christ "instead of shying away from his saving humility, inflated with the swollen pride of useless learning" (*CG* 10.28, 412). In the following chapter, Augustine reveals that his intended audience is the learned who admire Porphyry. In a moment, which reveals that Augustine is engaged in the education of souls, not polemics, he pauses to reflect on his own critique: "if only you had been able to see his incarnation . . . But what can I do? I know it is to no avail that I speak to a dead man, to no avail, that is, as far as you are concerned. But there are people who hold you in high regard, who are attached to you by reason of some kind of love of wisdom, or a superstitious interest in those magic arts which you should never have studied, and they are the audience to whom my colloquy with you is really directed, and it may be that for them it is not in vain" (*CG* 10.29, 414). Porphyry is even closer than Plato to Christian doctrine (*CG* 10.30, 417), yet he too is kept from the truth by his pride. Augustine knows his task is difficult since "humility was the necessary condition for submission to this truth; and it is no easy task to persuade the proud necks of you philosophers to accept this yoke" (*CG* 10.29, 415; cf.*CG* 10.24, 404–05).

For Augustine, this pride is the source of a fundamental mistake about happiness and virtue. The mistake is thinking that the intellect can know the truth and order the soul by its own efforts, without divine grace. God alone makes human beings righteous, but the proud think that they achieve it by themselves; "arrogant as they are, they think that by their own righteousness, not God's, they can please God" (*CG* 17.4, 718). All the philosophers err in this way from the Christian point of view; "all these philosophers have wished, with amazing folly, to be happy here on earth and to achieve this bliss by their own efforts" (*CG* 19.4, 852). The Christian answer to the supreme good which defines its view of happiness is eternal life. To escape eternal death and have eternal life does not depend upon human effort; "for we do not yet see our good, and hence we have to seek it by believing; and it is not in our power to live rightly, unless while we believe and pray we receive help from him who has given us the faith to believe that we must be helped by him" (*CG* 19.4, 852). Augustine here reminds the reader of Paul's warning that "'the Lord knows that the thoughts of wise men are foolish'" (*CG* 19.4, 852; 1 *Cor* 3: 20).

Human weakness and misery is such that in this life "our righteousness itself, too, though genuine, is nevertheless only such as to consist in forgiveness of sins rather than the perfection of virtues" (*CG* 19.27, 892). In this life we cannot achieve a state where there is no vice in us and where the struggle ceases (*CG* 19.4, 854). Augustine incorporates the Platonic *topos* of the fool at war with himself, but believes that victory cannot be achieved in this life: "God forbid, then, that, so long as we are engaged in this internal strife, we should believe ourselves to have already attained that happiness, the end we desire to reach by our victory. And who has reached such a height of wisdom as to have no struggle to maintain against his lusts?" (*CG* 19.4, 854; cf. *IO* 2). As T. S. Eliot eloquently states, this condition is the lot of most of us "who are only undefeated/ Because we have gone on trying."[3]

The so-called virtues attained through liberal education are not virtues at all, but vices, since they express pride. Virtue is proper governing of the soul, and Augustine admits that "the soul may appear to rule the body and the reason to govern the vicious elements in the most praiseworthy fashion," but unless the soul is in right relation to God this rule is in appearance only (*CG* 19.26, 891). Augustine concludes, "thus the virtues which the mind imagines it possesses, by means of which it rules the body and the vicious elements, are themselves vices rather than virtues, if the mind does not bring them into relation with God in order to achieve anything whatsoever and to maintain that achievement" (ibid.). Pride is the culprit, masking vices as virtues; "for although the virtues are reckoned by some people to be genuine and honourable when they are related only to themselves and are sought for no other end, even then they are puffed up and proud, and so are to be accounted vices rather than virtues"(ibid.).

Again quoting Paul, Augustine states that "'he who thinks himself to be something important, when he is nothing, is fooling himself' (*Gal.* 6:3; *CG* 17.4, 718). Augustine interprets this judgment in terms of his primary metaphor of the two cities; "these words are directed to the adversaries of the City of God, who belong to Babylonia, who presume on their own strength, and glory in themselves, instead of in God" (ibid.). Self-reliance is a vice not a virtue because it refuses to acknowledge human dependence on God for goodness. For Augustine, pride is a manifestation of self-love, which defines the earthly city. Self-love is how philosophers, even Platonists, are citizens of the earthly city instead of the City of God, which is characterized by the love of God (*CG* 14.13, 573). The love of self manifested as pride keeps the Platonists from genuine love of God, which would issue in humility. Virtue is defined as "rightly ordered love," and for Augustine unless this love is truly directed to God and not tainted with the self-love of pride, then one is not virtuous (*CG* 15.22, 637).

The true cure requires the recognition that the philosopher's cure is another disease and, based on a profound sense of human weakness, submission to God's authority (*CG* 10.31, 420). To achieve happiness the philosopher must convert to the Christian religion. Liberal arts *paideia* must yield to Christian conversion. In his own life, after his conversion, Augustine quit working on a program of liberal education and teaching the rhetorical tradition.[4] Conversion is the only path to virtue, for Augustine firmly states that without true religion true virtue is impossible (*CG* 19.26, 891). The Christian religion is the only cure (*CG* 2.1, 480), and pride stands in the way (*CG* 10.29, 417; cf 2.1, 48). Augustine frames the choice as a stark dilemma: one must choose philosophy with its vice of pride or the Christian religion with its virtue of humility. Vico's *New Science* will endeavor to demonstrate that this is a false dilemma.

Augustine believes that the consequences of the Fall are more enduring than the ignorance which the philosophers believe education can overcome, so Augustine's cure is more radical. Only by belief in God's unique mediator can one be cured; so "a man's life cannot be right without right belief about God" (*CG* 5.10, 195). The cure is only effected when one sacrifices oneself, offering "on the altar of the heart, the sacrifice of humility and praise, and the flame on the altar is the burning fire of charity" (*CG* 10.3, 375). If a human being makes this sacrifice, it will lead to true virtue. The good for human beings "is nothing else but to cleave to him whose spiritual embrace, if one may so express it, fills the intellectual soul and makes it fertile with true virtues"(*CG* 10.3, 376). Augustine concludes, "thus, if a man knows how to love himself, the commandment to love his neighbor bids him to do all he can to bring his neighbor to love God. This is the worship of God; this is true religion; this is the right kind of devotion; this is the service which is owed to God alone"(*CG* 10.3, 376). This love of God motivated Augustine to write the *City of God*, to help others come to see what he saw.

What happens to the human dignity Pico praised? Human dignity resides in the perfection of the creation in the image of God, but after the Fall actualization of this dignity depends upon divine grace. For Augustine human dignity does not consist in the ability to actualize this original potential. The last book of the *City of God* makes clear that the capacity for good still visible in human beings reflects the way the mind was created to be; but only by grace can human beings actualize this capacity after the Fall. This account is very different from the idea of self-making encountered in the Renaissance, and the dignity of man whom Pico called "maker and molder of thyself" (*O* 225). Augustine is not advocating the destruction of the intellect, but its proper subordination to God whereby it is truly good. Even if misused, the intellect is "chief ornament of this mortal life without reference to the faith or to the way of truth by which man attains to the life eternal" (*CG* 22.24, 1073).

Augustine does not hesitate to admit the marvelous inventions of human industry, which are made possible by the mind that God gives to man. This mind is "capable of knowledge and learning, ready for the perception of truth, and able to love the good. This capacity enables the mind to absorb wisdom, to acquire the virtues of prudence, fortitude, temperance, and justice, to equip man for the struggle against error . . . So that he may overcome them because his heart is set only on that Supreme and Unchanging Good" (*CG* 22.24, 1072). But, as is more often the case, "man may indeed fail in this; yet, even so, what a great and marvelous good is this capacity for such good, a capacity divinely implanted in a rational nature!" (ibid.). Like all created things, the human mind is made good, but is fallen and tarnished by misuse. Through grace the mind can be brought into proper relationship with God, and achieve the virtues that the proud philosophers seek in vain without such faith.

When aligned with God, human beings do have a great dignity. Ironically, it is humility that exalts: "there is something in humility to exalt the mind, and something in exaltation to abase it. It certainly appears some-what paradoxical that exaltation abases and humility exalts. But devout humility makes the mind subject to what is superior. Nothing is superior to God; and that is why humility exalts the mind by making it subject to God. Exaltation, in contrast, derives from a fault in character, and spurns subjection for that very reason. Hence it falls away from him who has no superior, and falls lower in consequence" (*CG* 14.13, 572). It is not the divinity of the mind, as Pico thought and Vico in his orations also charac-terized it, that exalts human beings according to Augustine. Human be-ings are sublime to Augustine when their hearts are set on God in humil-ity, which acknowledges the distance between the divine and human.

It is well known that Augustine gives his reading the books of the Platonists a pivotal role in his conversion to Christianity (*Conf.* 7). Never-theless, it must be stressed that Augustine converts twice: first to philoso-phy and then to Christianity. The extent of Augustine's Platonism can be easily exaggerated if one does remember that, for Augustine the Christian, Platonism is a distant second best to faith in the true God.

Given the centrality of the critique of Platonism in the *City of God*, the common category of the history of ideas "Christian Platonism" is an oxy-moron not to be attributed to Augustine's thought. To Augustine, this would be comparable to saying "proud humility" or "humble pride." These two cannot coexist, and the Platonist (as lover of wisdom) must choose between the highest form of the earthly city, and remain a Platonist, or convert to Christianity, and become subject to the governor of the City of God. Dante must leave Virgil behind for Beatrice's guidance and ultimately submit to the authority of the Bible. The initial humanistic education's influence is still felt, but in terms of virtues, it must be left behind. Augus-tine would say of lovers of wisdom who think they can have it both ways are self-deceived.

For Augustine, Platonism with its pride is counterproductive of wis-dom. Savanarola also charged the Platonists with pride, but not with im-piety as he did the Aristotelians.[5] Augustine will not allow that the Platonists have piety, since for Augustine piety is defined in terms of worship of the true God. Augustine holds that "no one can have true virtue without true piety, that is without the true worship of the true God; and that virtue which is employed in the service of human glory is not true virtue; still, those who are not citizens of the Eternal City—which the holy Scriptures call the City of God—are of more service to the earthly city when they possess even that sort of virtue than if they were without it" (*CG* 5.19, 213). Since God can use anything for good purposes, Platonism often can lead pilgrims to the harbor of the land of desire or the City of God. Though as Augustine makes clear, the Platonists themselves, those who do not move beyond Platonism to Christianity, fail to reach the harbor toward which they often direct others.[6] Platonists are not citizens of the City of God. It remains to be seen whether Savanarola was more correct than Augustine when he does not charge the Platonists with impiety as well as pride.

Vico's Pious Humanism

Recall Vico's emphasis on philosophy's ability to cure corruption through wisdom, virtue, and eloquence (chapter 2), and to discover providence naturally, quite apart from supernatural guidance or divine grace (chapter 5). Augustine's charges against philosophy's pride would seem to make Augustine Vico's accuser rather than his protector. Vico seems on the surface guilty of precisely the pride from which Augustine would most wish to protect him. But this same Vico concludes his *New Science* with the claim that "he who is not pious cannot be truly wise" (*NS* 1112). Augustine would have Vico ask himself: how can philosophy make human beings virtuous and wise, if philosophy itself is based on presumption, which is the source of all vice (that is, the source of the very corruption it wishes to cure)? How would Vico defend his philosophy from the Augustinian charge of pride? How is the heart of Lady Metaphysic "not dirty or befouled with pride of spirit"? (*NS* 5) The answers lie in discovering how Vico finds a way to correct for pride and foster piety *within* philosophy by considering its place in ideal eternal history. This innovative humbling of philosophy is what the *New Science* as "a metaphysics compatible with human frailty" and "consonant with Christian piety" offers (*AW* 109). This correction of philosophy with the intention of preserving it in a humbled yet intact form is not a project Augustine undertook or foresaw.

Despite initial appearances, especially from the inaugural orations on human dignity and education, Augustine does protect Vico from the excesses of philosophy, and even those of the ones they both consider the best of the philosophers, the Platonists. It is with respect to human frailty or the fallen nature of man that Augustine, above all the other members of the family of Plato, undertakes to guide Vico, though Vico does not completely follow his guidance. I grant that Vico's philosophy would not be humble enough for Augustine; Vico is not an Augustinian theologian. If Vico is still susceptible to the Augustinian critique of pride, he is not nearly so much as other philosophers. That difference is what I want to emphasize now. What emerges, once one takes a step back from Augustine's absolute judgments, is that Vico is a more humble and pious philosopher than any Augustine encountered. Porphyry was not attempting "a metaphysics compatible with human frailty" and "consonant with Christian piety" which "does not set up human knowledge as the rule of divine knowledge, but divine science as the rule for human knowledge" (*AW* 109), so the critique of that Platonist does not automatically extend to the new Platonism of Vico.

There are several axioms which reveal how Vico undercuts philosophical pride. In the most general terms, Vico criticizes philosophers as a whole because they fail by half (*NS* 140) since they consider man only as "he ought to be" and not "as he is" (*NS* 131, 132). This criticism of previous philosophers is why the *New Science* must found a "new critical art" in which philosophy examines philology (*NS* 7). In his *Autobiography* Vico says of his first two authors that Plato considers man as he *ought* to be and Tacitus as he *is* (*A* 138). This is also why Vico says Plato was ignorant of the Fall of man (*A* 122). Vico is clear that philosophy has to examine the human world which some philosophers have held beneath them. About this human realm Vico says "because of the deplorable obscurity of causes and almost infinite variety of effects, philosophy has almost a horror of treating" it (*NS* 7). Being ashamed to be part of the human world is a symptom of pride, and Vico's transformation of philosophy overcomes that flaw.

Axiom 5 connects the utility of philosophy, and with it metaphysics, to the recognition and amelioration of the human condition as fallen: "To be useful to the human race, philosophy must raise and direct weak and fallen man, not rend his nature or abandon him in his corruption" (*NS* 129). This statement is Augustinian in the way it portrays the human condition, but not in the role it gives philosophy in curing it. That philosophy must not rend man's nature in saving him is very suggestive. Perhaps that is how Vico would reject the more Calvinistic elements of Christianity. Recall that Vico said he found himself with Augustine, in between the extremes of Pelagius and Calvin on divine grace, and hence human freedom (*A* 119). From this axiom, one must place Vico closer than Augustine to the pole of Pelagius.

Vico takes seriously that the idea of a Fall implies an initial state of perfection. Axiom 104, that "custom is like a king and law like a tyrant," draws together the essential axioms about the Fall and the possibility of virtue (*NS* 310). Building on axiom 8, Vico writes that "things do not settle or endure out of their natural state" (*NS* 134) and states that "man has free choice, however weak, to make virtues of his passions; but that he is aided by God, naturally by divine providence and supernaturally by divine grace" (*NS* 136). The conclusion Vico draws from these axioms together is that: "this axiom [*NS* 133], with 8 [*NS* 134] its corollary [*NS* 135 or 136], shows that man is not unjust by nature in the absolute sense, but by nature fallen and weak. Consequently, it demonstrates the first principle of the Christian religion, which is Adam before the fall, in the ideal perfection in which he must have been created by God" (*NS* 310). The establishment of human nature as fallen and weak, in the sense of privation, not negation, is reminiscent of Augustine's incorporation of Plotinus on evil as privation. Vico emphasizes the previous perfect state, the creation in the image of God, more than Augustine does, though Augustine, of course, acknowledges this part of the *Genesis* story as well. Vico does not discuss how grace makes man perfect again, but how wisdom, virtue, and eloquence can cure corruption. There is no mention of the divinity of the human mind in the *New Science*, as there was in the orations, though when the reader narrates the truth of ideal eternal history, he is said to feel a "divine pleasure," which comes from imitation of God in whom knowing and making are the same (*NS* 349).

Vico specifically states that the metaphysics of the *New Science* is not proud any more than it is solitary. Axiom 5 defines the opposite of solitary as social or political, but what is the opposite of proud for Vico? The answer is found in the description of Lady Metaphysic. The convex jewel which "adorns the breast of metaphysic denotes the clean and pure heart which metaphysic must have, not dirty or befouled with pride of spirit or vileness of bodily pleasures" (*NS* 5). The jewel is convex to direct the rays outward toward the human realm as a symbol for the social dimension of this metaphysics. That the heart is pure and clean shows it is the opposite of pride. The Christian beatitude that "blessed are the pure of heart, for they will see God" informs Vico's vision of metaphysics (*Matt.* 5:1–12). For Augustine "purity is a virtue of the mind" (*CG* 1.18, 27). Purity of heart for Vico as for Augustine must involve piety. The heart is cleansed with morality, which is first poetic and then philosophical (*NS* 502), and neither exists without piety and the humility that it implies.

Just as there are many ways see providence, on the natural and supernatural levels (as enumerated in chapter 5), so there are many ways to cure human corruption. It is as important to distinguish between the types of self-governing as it was for divine governing in chapter 5. Unlike Augustine, Vico does not focus on the supernatural cure for corruption, that is, the redemption accomplished in sacred history from the Fall to the Judgment. Vico does not humble philosophy in the same way as Augustine, by subordination to the authority of the Bible. Vico stays on the natural level in his consideration of education as providence, and as a result his way does not require faith to see that pride must be curbed. Vico humbles philosophy by showing its bestial roots. As explained in chapter 5, providence was first known as certain in the fear of Jove, and then later proved true by the philosophers; so too in virtue, the first morals are certain and only later are made true. The importance of poetic wisdom has already been treated for poetic metaphysics, and now I will turn to poetic morals.

"Poetic morals," the third section of "Poetic Wisdom," describes the way providence first makes humans virtuous. Vico explains the origin of virtues in religion and piety. Most philosophers never ask the question how virtues emerge in the human world. Vico answers that it was not through philosophical reasoning, but through the emotions of the first humans guided by providence. The question is how providence makes the giants into human beings. Philosophy forgets that wisdom and piety are inseparable unless it remembers the origin of philosophy in poetic wisdom.

Vico begins with the giants warring against the heavens. The thunder frightens these giants, and the experience of the thundering sky as Jove is the origin of their morals, for at that moment they became god-fearing (*NS* 502). Providence ordained that the giants "should, at the first thunderclaps after the universal flood, take refuge in the caves of the mountains, subject themselves to a higher power which they imagined as Jove, and, all amazement as they were all pride and cruelty, humble themselves before a divinity" (cf. *NS* 377–79). Notice the prominence Vico gives to overcoming pride with humility. Vico underscores the strong link between religion and morals. Vico states, "religion alone has the power to make us practice virtue, as philosophy is fit rather for discussing it. And piety sprang from religion which properly is fear of divinity" (*NS* 503). I will return to the question of philosophy broached here. Vico continues to describe the origins of prudence, justice, temperance, and magnanimity (*NS* 14, 516). Prudence and justice derive from the interpretation of how to live in light of the auspices (*NS* 14, 516), temperance from marriage (*NS* 14, 513, 514, 516), and magnanimity from the protection of the weak by the strong (*NS* 516, 1099). In the heroic times the magnanimous "cast down the proud and defended the weak," much in the way that God first humbled the giants through thunder (*NS* 1099). These poetic virtues are elaborations of the poetic aspect of the principles of humanity discussed in chapter 5.

Vico concludes "Poetic Morals" by presenting his thoughts on pagan religion in contrast to Plutarch. Vico has shown that the childhood of humanity was far from innocent as many scholars thought, and in fact was characterized by savagery, pride, and cruelty, which are tamed by a fierce religion and the piety and humility it engenders (*NS* 518). Plutarch wonders whether it is better to worship no god at all than to worship in this way. Vico answers that Plutarch is not weighing the consequences of cruel religion against atheism. For providence brings all the nations out of such frightful worship, but from atheism no nation has ever arisen (ibid.).

In ideal eternal history, philosophy has a parallel role to the role religion serves. Education unites religion and philosophy as the end ordained by providence for both. Poetic morals make the philosophical morals possible by making the nations possible. Vico explains that "these commonwealths gave birth to philosophy. By their very form they inspired it to form the hero, and for that purpose to interest itself in truth. All this was ordained by providence to the end that, since virtuous actions were no longer prompted by religious sentiments as formerly, philosophy should make the virtues understood in their idea, and by dint of reflection thereon, if men were without virtue they should at least be ashamed of their vices. Only so can people prone to ill-doing be held to their duty" (*NS* 1101). Although it is true that religion is what first makes human beings moral, once the influence of religion wanes in the luxurious phase of civilization, then philosophy is given the role of moral education, so at least virtue will be praised and vice condemned in such a way that might stir up feelings of shame and piety again.

In order for philosophy to persuade, eloquence is necessary. Vico adds that "from the philosophies providence permitted eloquence to arise and, from the very form of these popular commonwealths in which good laws are commanded, to become impassioned for justice, and from these ideas of virtue to inflame the people to command good laws" (ibid.). Now in the third age, the age of humans, nations are disintegrating, and "as the popular states became corrupt, so also did the philosophies. They descended to skepticism. Learned fools fell to calumniating the truth. Thence arose a false eloquence, ready to uphold either of the opposed sides of a case indifferently" (*NS* 1102).

This corrupt time is the "barbarism of reflection" which is worse than the prehuman "barbarism of sense," because at least the barbarians of sense were honest (*NS* 1106).[7] Vico holds that the mind can be corrupt, and this assessment of reason places Vico much closer to Augustine than to the books of the Platonists he read.[8] When there is no ruler from within or without to save such a nation, then the extreme remedy of providence is required. Vico describes that "for such people, like so many beasts, have fallen into the custom of each man thinking only of his own private interests and have reached the extreme of delicacy, or better of pride, in which like wild animals they bristle and lash out at the slightest displeasure" (*NS* 1106). By the final cure of providence, the survivors, "returning to the primitive simplicity of the first world of peoples, are again religious, truthful, and faithful. Thus providence brings back among them the piety, faith, and truth which are the natural foundations of justice as well as the graces and beauties of the eternal order of God" (ibid.). The main theme of the conclusion of the *New Science* is piety. Religion is the origin of piety, and when it is lost, "they have nothing left to enable them to live in society" (*NS* 1109). This is a strong statement, only somewhat mitigated by the role given eloquent philosophy to kindle the moral feelings again (*NS* 1110). What humbles philosophy is to admit that religion does a better job of making us human, since that is the goal of philosophical *paideia*. Philosophy can only remake us human with great difficulty.

The *New Science* teaches how to become human and stay that way, and to remember it even when religion is a fading influence. Wisdom is the goal of humanistic education in the most basic sense of humanizing. First, education should involve religion, and then philosophy, but to a lesser extent. Philosophy also leads people astray, when it misunderstands human limits, as it often does. Providence is essentially about educating the human race, as was also clear from Augustine's *City of God*. We cooperate with providence by using our free will. Self-governing is a way to imitate God, as long as one does not impiously put oneself in the place of God. Vico humbles philosophy without giving up philosophical education as a way to virtue, and yet Vico's humanism is not a secular but a pious one.

Throughout the *New Science* Vico argues against atheistic philosophy, citing Polybius and Bayle for their erroneous idea that a society of philosophers is not only possible but desirable (*NS* 1110). Vico is clear that without religion, which is the origin of poetic wisdom, the arts and sciences would not develop, as a tree cannot stand without its trunk (*NS* 367, 1043). Philosophy is a dependent activity growing out of poetic wisdom in an organic way which cannot discard its origin. Its metaphysics depends on poetic metaphysics, its morals on poetic morals. If philosophy is not pious, then it is rejecting that origin. Wisdom must be pious, whether in religion or philosophy. Any philosophy which is not pious is excluded by Vico from his Science.

The pride that philosophy has to overcome to be pure of heart, as Lady Metaphysic must be, repeats the pride the giants had to defeat. Religion gives birth to the piety which humbles the giants. This piety must be rekindled to humble the arrogance of the philosophers. For the battle between the giants and the gods continues to be waged within human souls. The gods did not destroy the giants, as the myth is handed down to us, but buried them under mountains, which became volcanoes. This is why the battle between the giants and the gods is one that is always going on (*Sph.* 246a–e). The human spirit is volatile like the molten lava, and will occasionally erupt in arrogance and impiety. To be human, one must choose to be humble before God instead of arrogant; "for atheists become giants in spirit"(*NS* 502). This choice is why in any age of the world, "he who is not pious is not truly wise" (*NS* 1112).

So far, religion and philosophy have been considered as allies in their common goal of education as ordained by providence, but there is a quarrel between philosophy and religion in the *ricorso*, which is the *ricorso* of the ancient quarrel between poetry and philosophy. As with Homer and Plato, the question is who educates, that is, who teaches virtue and wisdom to cure human corruption. At the level of abstract thought, there is no satisfactory solution to the rival absolute claims to wisdom, but when one meditates and narrates the *New Science* for oneself, a solution emerges.

As a philosopher, the claims of religion will be outside of one's thought, but as a citizen of a particular nation, the religion into which one is born or converted will provide a certain apprehension of providence and virtue which is correlative, if not complementary, to the philosophical providence and *paideia*. As a philosopher, Vico speaks of religion in general as the certain foundation of the truth about things divine and human. He acknowledges the poetic or civil wisdom out of which philosophical wisdom grows. As a human being, however, Vico participates in the religion of his nation, and enacts the principles of humanity as certain in worship (religion), marriage, and burial, in the Catholic church into which he was born and baptized as a child.

From the point of view of the religion itself, there is no distinction between certain and true. Augustine makes no such distinction. The Christian religion for Augustine is true and certain, and the pagan religions are false and uncertain. That is the way all other religions look from inside any particular religion. Vico gives us a clue that such particularity cannot be completely factored out of a genuine Science of the human world, since the writer would know he has his own place in a nation also. In the fifth oration Vico maintains "man has a dual citizenship, one of which has been given to him by nature, the other by the conditions of his birth" (*IO* 5. 7). I suggest that a recognition of the conditions of his own birth is the reason Vico calls his work "*The New Science of Giambattista Vico* . . . ." The particular starting-point does not prevent but makes possible a genuine understanding of the universal pattern of the human world. Heraclitus is right; "the path up and down is one and the same."[9]

It is unimportant whether Vico himself saw the importance of acknowledging his particularity, for he did write into the "Method" that the reader must remake the Science for himself. Any reading of the *New Science* must shift back and forth between remaking the Science oneself and speculating about how Vico would have made the speech of the *New Science* for himself. As a philosopher who emphasizes self-knowledge and *paideia*, Vico would prefer that we know ourselves and in that way know what he knew, rather than attempt to know him as he knew himself, forgetting to ask who we ourselves are.

Vico does not overestimate the importance of philosophy compared to religion even in the philosopher's life. But how limited is the role for philosophy in the human world? Recall Varro and Scaevola said natural theology was for the lecture hall, and was of little consequence in the marketplace (*CG* 6.5, 235; 4.27, 168). Augustine quotes Cicero who says that philosophy is for the few. *La Beata Vita* might be a case where the few achieve wisdom through philosophy, but the mature thought of Augustine is that these few still fall short from pride.[10] For Augustine, philosophy is not a way for the few to be wise, but a way of folly unique to a few. The distinction between the few and the many is also important in Vico, though it is not made a central theme (*NS* 129; *NS* 131; *IO* 6.14; *IO* 4. 8).

Vico says in axiom 6, that "philosophy considers man as he should be and so can be of service to but very few, those who wish to live in the Republic of Plato and not to fall back into the dregs of Romulus" (*NS* 131). I have already introduced the special role for which providence allows philosophy to arise in the third age, the age of humans, when religion is weakening, to cultivate virtue. Providence gives a real and significant role to philosophy. Nevertheless, a philosopher would completely misunderstand the gravity of the age in which he lives if he puffed himself up by thinking himself among a gifted few who can reach God through the intellect and disdained the remaining pious "many," because they lacked such sophistication of intellect. In fact, philosophy is far from the easiest way to become pious and humble. When one lives in the third age, the old age of humanity, then one must use one's intellect to recover the lost childhood through memory. To pretend one can completely return is also a denial of self-knowledge, since are we are not in heroic or divine times anymore. Nostalgia is another obstacle to self-knowledge.

The limits Vico places on philosophy and its importance in the human world should not be overstated. Vico does assert that reason is man in properly being man, and the age of humans is the properly human age (*NS* 918, 927). For Vico, being a pious non-philosopher is better than being an atheist philosopher. This judgment of relative worth stems from measuring by the goal of living well, wisdom and virtue. The goal of the lover of wisdom is to educate as many human beings as possible. Providence has provided many paths to arrive at this goal.

If philosophy only helps the very few, what about the many? What does piety dictate that the philosopher ought to say to a larger audience? Although the *New Science* does not engage in revealed theology, in the sixth inaugural oration Vico recommends revealed theology as the capstone of education understood as curing corruption (*IO* 6. 13). In the summary of this oration in the *Autobiography* Vico strongly states "pagan morality is insufficient to tame and subdue philauty or self-love," and that once students recognize this fact, "with humbled intellect let them make ready to receive revealed theology, from which let them descend to Christian ethics, and thus purged let them finally pass to Christian jurisprudence"(*A* 144–45). This statement is Vico's strongest for a Christian cure.

Vico may here be speaking from his identity as Christian citizen rather than philosopher. Otherwise the denial of a natural path to virtue seems inconsistent with the *New Science* and with the rest of the orations. This interpretation is supported by the fact the title for the sixth oration is "let us cleanse corrupt human nature and, as much as possible, thus help human society," and this oration is listed as the "Christian goal," which follows the two orations headed "Political Goals" (*IO*, Appendix, 142). If philosophy is only helpful for the few, it stands to reason that, to help the many, the study of Christian jurisprudence and theology would be essential *in a Christian commonwealth*. Vico knows that religion is the way most people are made virtuous, as he articulated in "Poetic Morals," so he is fully consistent in advocating fostering religion. Also in the sixth oration Vico says that jurisprudence involves moral theology "because we are interpreting the right within a Christian commonwealth" (*IO* 6.9). Vico continues to draw a distinction between the few and the many: "hence about the things divine and human, we either debate among the learned or converse among the common man, and with the former it is necessary that we discourse in truth, and with the latter it is necessary that we use a speech that is appealing" (ibid.). In a way, Vico might agree that "Christianity is Platonism for 'the people,'" though he would not mean this in a derogatory way.[11] Vico concludes that "you have been instructed in these studies of wisdom so that each of you may earn merit far and wide from human society and be of help, not only to yourselves or to a few, but to as many as possible, and to this end you should join with these studies those of elo-quence" (*IO* 6. 14; cf. *IO* 4. 8).

There is more than one way to govern oneself, to cure the corruption of the Fall, and the philosopher, if he is to help more than the very few, must understand and foster the religious as well as the philosophical way to virtue. Given the correlative roles of philosophy and religion, it is not surprising that Vico resolves the relationship between Platonism and Chris-tianity differently from Pico or Augustine. There are many levels to Vico's thoughts, many ways to see God, but not in the sense of a disingenuous double truth. For Vico unity is emphasized, which reflects his place in ideal eternal history, since the age of humans is characterized by equality. For Augustine, operating as he does from the divine age of the *ricorso*, there can be no such equality of multiple paths. For Augustine there is one true religion, and conversion is the only way to cure corruption. The abso-lute division of the two cities, city of God and earthly city, can be under-stood as the Christian equivalent of the first cities of the pagans, in which either you were a noble and had the sacred nuptials and auspices or you were a pleb and did not (*NS* 610). Augustine resolves the quarrel by siding with religion against philosophy. Vico does not choose sides in this way.

That Vico does not privilege faith, that he does not choose to make that authority absolute, is the real difference between Augustine and Vico. The way Vico preserves a place for religion would for Augustine undercut its absolute claims to authority on matters of salvation. Augustine would view Vico as still guilty of Platonic pride, namely, philosophy's pride that there are the few who do not need divine grace. The division itself, of human beings into the few and the many, the learned and the common man, would for Augustine be a manifestation of pride, which is the folly of the human beings who think they are wise. Augustine would not approve of Vico's universalization of religion and with it piety, wisdom, virtue, and eloquence. Vico still maintains the confidence that metaphysics is something human beings can do, that we can contemplate God, and make our passions into virtues. Vico preserves the dignity of Pico even as he embraces the piety of Augustine. The fact that Vico thinks there is more than one way to be pious, wise, and virtuous, is the most significant disanalogy with August-ine. The conditions of their births in the heroic and human ages of the *ricorso* illuminate how each answers the question of how to educate human beings as the fallen image of God, and how corruption is cured.

The most persuasive evidence of how Vico understood the complex relationship between Christianity and philosophy is in the way he lived his life. The same could be said of Augustine. Both leave philosophical autobiographies as proofs of their most fundamental ideas and as a way to instruct others as to how to live wisely. The question that the comparison of Vico and Augustine has led to is to what extent self-governing is really possible for fallen man, and to what extent it depends on divine grace.

The story of Vico's invitation to join an order by a priest is revealing (*A* 135). Vico identifies himself as a man of letters, and hence he does not make the transition that Augustine did from his liberal arts career to being a Servant of God which ultimately led to his ordination as priest and bishop. Vico nonetheless continued to bow humbly to the inscrutable plans of providence and grace. Vico's Lady Metaphysic must have a pure heart, one not sullied from pride. Vico does not abandon Platonism and philosophy, liberal arts, and eloquence. Vico agrees that man is fallen, and he incorporates some aspects of Augustine's critique of Platonism. Vico does not advocate conversion instead of humanistic education, or choose that life for himself. This choice is the greatest proof of what he really thinks.

After his conversion Augustine stopped working on liberal education, became a priest and then bishop, and turned his intellect to the interpretation of Scripture and church polemics against heresy, and other dogmatic writings. Vico made the other choice, and remained more like Augustine's earlier self. But Vico does not remain like the Neoplatonist Augustine was, because he is humbled by a broader perspective on philosophy as one part of the human world and history. This perspective was gained in large part by reading Augustine's providential understanding of history.

Vico's response to the *Acta* review of the *New Science* also illuminates in what sense Vico's humanism is a pious one. Of the Leipzig review which Vico calls "a gross misrepresentation of Vico and his *New Science*," Vico lists among the errors that the reviewer misunderstood the scope of the claims about religion. Vico says of the review that "it observes that the work is suited to the taste of the Roman Catholic Church, as if the conception of a Divine Providence were not basic to the Christian religion in all its forms, or indeed to all religions" (*A* 187). Vico objected to this reduction of his *New Science*'s universal claims about religion and providence to one denomination of Christianity and of himself to a Catholic apologist. Yet Vico is not objecting to being characterized as pious. Vico says that the Epicurean or Spinozist reviewer, "instead of the reproach he intended, pays the author the highest compliment, that of being pious" (*A* 188). Vico's *New Science* operates on multiple levels, and the reviewer misses the subtlety of Vico's reconciliation of religion and philosophy.

Judging from a claim he makes about his tendency to anger, Vico considers both the Christian religion and philosophy as providing standards for virtue. Vico writes of himself that "Vico was choleric to a fault. Though he guarded himself from it as best he could in his writing, he publicly confessed this failing. He would inveigh too violently against the errors of thought or scholarship or against the misconduct of those men of letters who were his rivals, which as a charitable Christian or a true philosopher he should rather have overlooked or pitied" (*A* 199). The "or" is very interesting, since it indicates that both would lead Vico to more virtuous action. Vico is certainly heretical in not accepting Paul's teaching that the only way to wisdom is through mediation of Jesus, and that human wisdom is folly. From Paul's point of view and Augustine's, Vico's straddling the ways of religion and philosophy is a contradiction, and one born of the vice of pride. About the charge of pride, Vico's confession of his fault in his *Autobiography* makes his pride less blameworthy, because confession, Augustine holds, is the opposite of presumption. The contradiction disappears when the question is seen from the point of view of the *New Science*. Vico honors religion as a child does his parents, but this respect does not mean that Vico is limited to its claims or must accept them completely on their own terms. When speaking to the common man, whom one is obligated to help as well as the few (*IO* 6. 14; *NS* 129), Vico will not jeopardize the authority of religion, but he will not ignore that providence allowed philosophy to arise in the human age once religion was weakening as another way to make human beings virtuous.

Vico reconciles the quarrel between religion and philosophy *in his life*. He is baptized, married, and buried in the Christian religion, and teaches as a professor of eloquence the knowledge possible for human beings through their own efforts. Vico is not syncretic, for the syncretist would blur and collapse the boundaries between religion and philosophy instead of seeing that they are different institutions ordained by providence to achieve the same goal. Augustine's stark either-or, either the earthly city or the City of God, is what one would expect from an heroic age; and just as one would expect from an age of equals, Vico allows many equally right ways to educate human beings into virtue and wisdom. Unlike the Renaissance Platonists who created hybrid forms of Christian Neoplatonism, Vico has a much more complex account of the respective roles of religion and philosophy in the human world.

Perhaps Vico would have viewed with humor, not anger, the incident that provides an image for the confusion surrounding his commitment to liberal arts and to the Christian religion. We are told in the continuation of Vico's *Autobiography*, that the Royal University professors and the confraternity of Santa Sophia fought over who had the right to bear Vico's body (*A* 207). Vico could not be carried by just the professors. He had to be carried by both, but no one could see that. After much confusion and delay, which Villarosa attributed to "human weakness and pride," both the professors and a cathedral group join to bear Vico's coffin (ibid.). How striking and emblematic this event is of the struggle between the the liberal arts and Christian religion in the *ricorso*. This event teaches us not to explain away either the philosophical or the religious dimension of the wisdom of the *New Science*. Wisdom is not a question to be answered by an either-or, but is a matter of discovering how we can have both-and. Even in death Vico generated fables.

PART THREE

THE PHILOSOPHICAL
HEROISM OF PLATO

Homer is the Plato of the poets;
Plato is the Homer of the philosophers.

Plutarch

Introduction

Vico's Ideal Philosopher and the Search for the True Plato

After descending through the layers of Vico's debts to the Renaissance Platonism of Pico and the "Christian Platonism" of Augustine, the reader of Vico can see the connections between Plato and Vico emerge in their own right. Plato does not have the additional complication of a starting-point in the *ricorso*, as did Pico and Augustine. Philosophy is close to its origin with Plato. In the terms of Vico's ideal eternal history, Plato lives in the human age of the *corso* and looks back to Homer as the teacher of the divine and heroic ages and to Socrates as a guide for his own human age.

Vico assigns to Plato a pivotal role in the development of his own thought. Having explored the mediation of some of the themes of Platonism found in Vico through Pico and Augustine, I can now turn to the question: what is the commonality between Plato and Vico which is not mediated through the later Platonists? In other words, when is Vico thinking about the Plato of the dialogues? What is Vico learning from Plato directly? There are many references to Plato in Vico's *Autobiography* which offer clues. With a sense of what role Plato played for Vico as he developed his thought it will be easier to understand the interpretations and misinterpretations of Vico's first author (*A* 139) which appear in the *New Science*.

In Vico's *Autobiography* Plato is the type for the philosopher who contemplates the ideal as opposed to the philologian who considers the historical (*A* 138; cf. *NS* 131). The interpretation of Plato as only concerned with intellectual not practical wisdom, however, is as much a distortion as the idea that Plato thought Homer was a philosopher. Plato is a poetic philosopher who contemplates the ideal, but he is poignantly acquainted with the actual world of generation and corruption. Plato not only acknowledges the gap between what human beings and cities ought to be and what they are, he continually draws attention to it.[1] There is a kernel of truth in both idealizations, but Plato's relationship to politics and to poetry is complex. Yet, as it was not Vico's purpose to give a comprehensive interpretation of Plato, the claims he makes are legitimate in context.

Vico explains in some detail his growing affinity for Platonic metaphysics as opposed to Aristotelian and more materialistic metaphysics (*A* 121; cf. 122, 131). Initially, Vico says that "he proceeded to study that of Plato, guided only by his fame as the prince of divine philosophers" (*A* 121). What Vico learns from Plato is that even the study of law, the most particular of human things, depends upon the ideal of justice. Seeing how Plato "founds a moral philosophy on an ideal or architectonic virtue or justice" leads Vico to contemplate a universal law and ultimately to discover ideal eternal history (ibid.). Vico writes that "consequently he devoted himself to meditating an ideal commonwealth, to which he gave, in his laws, an equally ideal justice. So that from the time that Vico felt himself dissatisfied with the metaphysic of Aristotle as an aid to the understanding of moral philosophy, and found himself instructed by that of Plato, there began to dawn on him, without his being aware of it, the thought of meditating an ideal eternal law that should be observed in a universal city after the idea or design of providence, upon which idea have since been founded all the commonwealths of all times and all nations" (*A* 121–22). Vico then distances himself from Plato by adding that "this was the ideal republic that Plato should have contemplated as a consequence of his metaphysic, but he was shut off from it by ignorance of the fall of the first man" (*A* 122).

What Vico accepts from Plato is more important than what he corrects. He embraces the Platonic insight that there are eternal truths which we did not make, and that these have more reality than physical substances (*A* 128). Vico continues that "by this principle of philosophy Plato establishes, in metaphysics, abstract substances as having more reality than corporeal ones. From it he derives a morality well adapted throughout for civil life, so that the school of Socrates, both in itself and through its successors, furnished the greatest lights of Greece in the arts both of peace and of war" (ibid.). Metaphysics and moral philosophy will remain linked for Vico as they are for Plato.

Vico is among the few interpreters of Plato who make the idea that "physics is a likely story" central to their own thought (*Ti.* 29d). In addition to this restriction of human knowledge of nature, there is a parallel emphasis on knowledge of history. One of the most intriguing references for Vico's own cyclic idea of history is that he associates Plato with the idea of "the Great Year." Vico mentions that he wrote a canzone "on Plato's idea of the 'Great Year,' on which Virgil had constructed his learned eclogue *Sicelides musae*" (*A* 131). In the cosmological myth of the *Timaeus* the return of the planets to their original positions is called "the perfect or complete year" (*ton teleon eniauton*) (39d). So there is a cyclic historical dimension to the metaphysics of the *Timaeus* which Vico admires.

Vico's poem "*Al medesimo*" on the subject of the "*massimo anno*," modeled on Virgil's fourth eclogue with roots in Plato, is among the strongest evidence that there is a link between Vico's ideal eternal history and Plato's metaphysics of cyclic history. [2] In this part of the *Timaeus* the cycles of the universe itself are the subject, but there are consequences for human life from these changes. The *Statesman* (*Politicus*) myth is clearer about the implications of the cycles of the universe for historical cycles closer to human life. In addition to Hesiod and the *Timaeus*, commentators on Virgil note the *Statesman* as source as well as the *Republic*, though in neither of these dialogues is there the formulation "great year." The proposal in the *Laws* for a liturgical year in which each god is given a month (*Leg.* 828c) is another acknowledgment of the cycles that also may be a source for Virgil, and therefore Vico. As a way of perceiving time in relationship to eternity, history is properly a subject of metaphysics. Perhaps this metaphysical understanding of history is why despite the acknowledgment of Plato's cyclic history of "the great year" Vico primarily associates Plato with the ideal. Plato writes a metaphysics of history rather than historical anecdotes, ethnologies, or reports of constitutions.

What the *Autobiography* depicts is the Plato who is a philosopher of the ideal; and, of course, his metaphysics does make the ideal more real than the corporeal. In another way, Plato is an "ideal" philosopher because he balances the eternal and the temporal, the philosophical and the poetic, the ideal and the actual. Vico dramatizes his own synthesis of ideal and historical, philosophical and philological, by trading on idealizations of Plato and Tacitus; the one as an ideal philosopher who ignores history, and the other as an historian without a sense of the ideal.[3] Vico says that "up until this time Vico had admired two only above all other learned men, Plato and Tacitus; for with an incomparable metaphysical mind Tacitus contemplates man as he is, Plato as he should be" (*A* 138). Vico elaborates this point by attributing intellectual wisdom to Plato and practical wisdom to Tacitus (ibid.). Then Vico applies this double movement of wisdom to his own discovery of the *New Science*. Vico links his own work to his first two authors when he states that "now Vico's admiration of these two great authors from this point of view was a foreshadowing of that plan on which he later worked out an ideal eternal history to be traversed by the

universal history of all times carrying out on it, but certain eternal properties of civil affairs, the development, acme and decay of all nations. From
this it follows that the wise man should be formed both of esoteric wisdom
such as Plato's and of common wisdom such as that of Tacitus" (*A* 138–
39).

Neither Plato nor Tacitus are said to combine the theoretical and the
practical, the ideal and the historical. This lack of a synthesis sets the stage
for the next author who can combine the two kinds of wisdom. Vico introduces his third author, saying "and now at length Vico's attention was
drawn to Francis Bacon, Lord Verulam, a man of incomparable wisdom
both common and esoteric, at one and the same time a universal man in
theory and in practice, a rare philosopher and a great English minister of
state . . . Vico concluded that, as Plato is the prince of Greek wisdom, and
the Greeks have no Tacitus, so Romans and Greeks alike have no Bacon.
. . . Vico now proposed to have these three unique authors ever before him
in meditation and writing, and so he went on elaborating his works of
discovery, which culminated in The One Principle of Universal Law" (ibid.).
Bacon is applauded for combining these two tendencies of human thought
and wisdom, and Vico seeks to imitate him.

Vico cannot stop with the third author, because Bacon does not have a
system of universal law. Vico acknowledges the limits of Bacon and introduces Grotius as his fourth author. About the transition from his third to
fourth author, Vico writes that "Bacon sees that the sum of human and
divine knowledge of his time needs supplementing and emending, but as
far as laws are concerned he does not succeed with his canons in compass-
ing the universe of cities and the course of all times, or the extent of all
nations. Grotius, however, embraces in a system of universal law the whole
of philosophy and philology, including both parts of the latter, the history
on the one hand of facts and events, both fabulous and real, and on the
other of the three languages, Hebrew, Greek and Latin" (*A* 154–55). That
Bacon's failure arises from not sufficiently embracing the ideal and eternal,
which are objects of intellectual contemplation, is revealing. Bacon did
not learn this lesson in metaphysics from Plato as Vico and Grotius did.

The development is less dramatic if one views both elements of philosophy and philology in differing emphases in Vico's authors, in particular the initial pair of Plato and Tacitus. Of course, it is true that Plato
emphasizes the ideal as the standard of the historical, and Tacitus focuses
on the historical. Vico's reasons for portraying his authors as he does are
understandable. Remarkably, Vico does acknowledge the connection between Plato's *Cratylus* and Bacon's *Ancient Wisdom*, even preferring the way

Plato handles the question of philology. Vico says that "by the reading of Bacon of Verulam's treatise *On the Wisdom of the Ancients*, more ingenious and learned than true, [he] was incited to look for its principles farther back than in the fables of the poets. He was moved to do this by the example of Plato who in the *Cratylus* had sought to track them down within the origins of the Greek language" (*A* 148). Here Vico acknowledges that Plato's influence on his thought is not only in terms of the ideal, but also in terms of the origins of language. Plato is a better guide to philology than Bacon, even though the latter is cast as the combination of philology and philosophy. Further evidence that Vico read Plato as more inclusive is clearly expressed by Vico's summary: "that a Plato (to take a conspicuous example) among the ancients was the equivalent of an entire university of studies of our day, all harmonized in one system" (*A* 199).

Even though rhetorically it is understandable why Vico described his authors as types, given the actual complexity of his authors, readers of Vico should not follow uncritically the portraits of the authors Vico provides in presenting his own thought. To do so would prevent the fruitful inquiries into these authors which Vico makes possible, and the further light they in turn shed on Vico himself. Although it is important to see how Vico himself envisioned the connection between his thought and Plato's, I will not limit myself to the parallels drawn by Vico. I will also investigate the thematic parallels Vico might have seen, if he had looked at individual dialogues of Plato from the point of view of his *New Science*. On this point of interpretation, I disagree in part with Alexander Pope's precept, "in every work regard the author's end, since none can compass more than they intend."[4] Readers ought to pay attention to the author's end, in this case how Vico himself is consciously appropriating Plato, but great authors often do compass more than they intend. In fact, Vico's injunction to the reader to fashion the Science for oneself can be understood as an endorsement of reaching beyond Vico's own way of making the Science true, which he shows in his *Autobiography* (*NS* 349).

In a sense, discovering the true Plato amid all the reinterpretations and distortions of his thought is as challenging as Vico's search for the true Homer. In another way, it is incomparably easier. Even if Plato's poetic philosophy is representative of the intellectual achievement of the Greeks, and he deserves to be called "the prince" of the political philosophers (*NS* 1109), Plato is one human being, not the Greeks themselves as Homer is. Plato is not a poetic character exactly, but in a sense Plutarch is correct that Plato is "the Homer of the philosophers." When Vico explains that the poets are the sense and the philosophers are the intellect of the human race, his primary instances, like Plutarch's, would be Homer and Plato. The difference is that Plato thinks in intelligible universals as we do, so the descent is not as arduous as the one Vico forged to discover the imaginative universals of the first humans (*NS* 34).

Vico undertook this project initially as a descent from Plato to the origins of human wisdom, but he realized the reverse to be necessary; one must begin from the origins of poetic wisdom and ascend to esoteric wisdom. In this way, the *New Science* fundamentally differs from the *Universal Law*, as Vico says, he "is dissatisfied further with the Universal Law because he tried therein to descend from the mind of Plato and other enlightened philosophers into the dull and simple minds of the founders of the gentile peoples, whereas he should have taken the opposite course; whence he fell into errors in certain matters"(*A* 194). In a sense to return to the origin requires that one descend first, before one can then ascend. Vico is emphasizing that the descent must overcome the conceits that would make what is found into something familiar. The descent into the mind before intelligible universals cannot hold on to its starting-point in "the mind of Plato" but must descend into the dark and find there a new light to find one's way back up.

The search for the true Plato is a Vichian project, though admittedly not one Vico himself undertook. The investigation of the family of Plato as opposed to an abstract thematic study of Platonism and the *New Science* or *Ancient Wisdom* is based on the Vichian principle that to understand something requires knowledge of the guise of its birth or origin. Plato agreed that the best method to understand something is to seek its origin (*Cra.* 426b). The origin of Platonism is not only Plato's dialogues, but also the hero of those dialogues, Socrates. Vico names Socrates the "father of the philosophers"(*HM* 240), and therefore Socrates is the origin of the family of Plato. Socrates is the philosophical falconer of this widening gyre of the history of philosophy. The heroism of Socrates inspired the philosophical poetry of Plato as the heroes inspired the Greek people to form poetic characters. It is enough for Plato to illuminate Vico, but it is breathtaking to watch Vico illuminate Plato. Vico enables us to see Plato with new eyes.

Chapter 7

Ideal Eternal History

Recall that Vico enumerates seven principal aspects of the *New Science* (*NS* 385–99). The fifth is "an ideal eternal history (*la storia ideale eterna*) traversed in time by the histories of all the nations. Wherever, emerging from savage, fierce, and bestial times, men begin to domesticate themselves by religion, they begin, proceed, and end by those stages which are investigated here" (*NS* 393). The questions multiply quickly. How could history be ideal much less eternal? What light could Plato shed on such a paradox? Further, what is the relationship of providence to ideal eternal history?

"Ideal eternal history" is an oxymoron, as are many key ideas in the *New Science*, because the newness of Vico's Science forces him to stretch language and ideas. As "rational civil theology" is the result of a division and collection, so "ideal eternal history" is the culmination of an inquiry into the nature of history. "Ideal eternal history" sums up the fundamental discovery of the *New Science* that there are stages of development that all nations undergo which make this temporal progression a universal one. Plato might seem to be only concerned with the ideal and eternal, neglecting the more practical subject of history, but in fact there are places in the *Republic* and other dialogues which examine precisely the question of the pattern nations go through from pre-political origin to decline. As Vico notes in his *Autobiography*, he wrote a poem about "Plato's Great Year," but in the *New Science* he does not elaborate on the parallels between his notion of ideal eternal history and the cyclic view of history in Plato's dialogues (*A* 131). The nature of history is an instance where there is more commonality between Plato and Vico than Vico either realized or acknowledged.

Vico invokes Plato in axiom 6 of the *New Science* about how philosophy considers human beings as they should be, just as he made Plato synonymous with this tendency in his *Autobiography*: "Philosophy considers man as he should be, and so can be of service to but very few, those who wish to live in the Republic of Plato and not to fall back into the dregs of Romulus" (*NS* 131). The allusion is to one of Cicero's letters to Atticus. This reference reveals Vico's tendency to view Plato as overly idealistic about politics, as Cicero comments about Cato using the same comparison. Cicero writes to Atticus: "For our friend Cato is not more to you than to me: but still with the best of intentions and unimpeachable honesty at times he does harm to the country: for the opinions he delivers would be more in place in Plato's Republic than among the dregs of humanity collected by Romulus" (*Lett. Att.* II.1.1). Vico follows Cicero when he identifies the essence of Plato's political philosophy with ideal city of the *Republic*.

Since Vico also refers to Plato's *Laws* and the *Timaeus*, why did he not consider the *Republic* in the context of other dialogues about the ideal city and actual politics? Part of the answer may be that to characterize Plato as on the extreme of utopianism emphasizes Vico's own ideal which combines theory and practice. In this way, the distortions would be more willful than the praise of Plato elsewhere would seem to warrant. Yet I do not suspect Vico of "anxiety of influence"; he knew his work was original as well as that he was indebted to his authors.[1] Also, Vico may have been thinking of Plato as mediated through other sources, and as I have already explored, that is often the case. The fact that Vico recast the later editions of the *New Science* in positive form may also account for his broad brushstroke references to predecessors, with no extended or detailed criticism of their views.[2]

Regardless of Vico's reasons for the sketchy nature of his own interpretation of Plato, to uncover the parallels between Vico and Plato the reader must answer a fundamental question about Plato's treatment of the human condition and Vico's accuracy in referring to it. The textual question about Plato is what evidence exists that Plato does consider human beings as they are in addition to as they ought to be; the interpretive question about Vico's texts is to what extent Vico recognizes this dimension of Plato. Though the utopian reading has a basis in truth, it is not the best reading of Plato's *Republic*. In particular, such a reading does not shed any light on Plato's description of pre-political human beings and the first cities in the *Laws*, to which Vico refers more often than to the ideal city.[3] A study of the *Republic* with the *Timaeus* and the *Critias* provides a different perspective on Plato's own account of the meaning of the ideal city in relationship to actual politics and history. In the application of the philosophical insights into politics in Greece in the *Laws* and the *Seventh Letter*, the ideal does not cease to be relevant; instead it serves as an eternal standard for the changing polities. In the *Statesman* the distinction between the ideal and actual levels of Plato's political reflections are brought most clearly into focus. The perfect ruler is not a human being, but a god. By revealing the centrality of this division of governing into divine and human, Plato avoids the conceit of scholars. Only in divine times when the gods were rulers has the ideal city existed in the past. Through a discussion of each of these works, I will show how Vico has more common ground with Plato than he realized. Reading Plato and Vico together illuminates the fundamental political and historical insights of both.

Plato's Ideal City and History

From the point of view of the *New Science*, the main interpretive puzzle is how to reconcile what Vico praises Plato for seeing and what he criticizes him for missing about history and politics. On the one hand, in addition to the axiom cited above (*NS* 131), Vico criticizes a central element of the *Republic*'s proposal, that the ideal just city would have kings who were philosophers or philosophers who were kings: "it is yet another vulgar tradition that the first kings were sages, wherefore Plato expressed the vain wish for those ancient times in which philosophers reigned as kings or kings were philosophers" (*NS* 253). Plato is charged with the conceit of scholars for misunderstanding the vulgar nature of the wisdom of the first lawgivers. On the other hand, Vico repeatedly credits Plato with the identification of the cyclopean fathers as the first families and the origin of commonwealths, and the starting-point of the delineation of the types of constitutions. Both moments are pivotal for Vico's own account.

I will first consider the validity of Vico's critique of Plato's ideal city as politically naïve. To understand the proposal of the philosopher-king, which Vico singles out for criticism, one must appreciate the movement of the *Republic*'s argument as a whole. Such a reading of the *Republic* corrects for the caricature of Plato as naïve about politics. A reading of the *Laws* and *Statesman* will complete the argument that Plato does not commit the conceit of scholars in his proposal of philosopher-kings. So how does Socrates relate the ideal city to the actual political world within the *Republic*?

Consider how the project of building the city in speech arises. Socrates is challenged to show that the just life is happier than the unjust, first by Thrasymachus (*R.* Book 1) and then the task is reframed by Glaucon and Adeimantus (*R.* Book 2). Socrates suggests to Glaucon and Adeimantus that it will be easier to see the nature of justice and injustice in a city, and then perhaps that in turn will illuminate justice and injustice in the soul

(*R*. 368d). It turns out after the city is built that it can be read into the microcosm effectively (*R*. 444a–b). Stated plainly, the reason Socrates suggests building the city in speech is to aid in the search for the nature of justice in the soul, not to construct a blue-print for utopia. The analogy of the city and the soul with the education proposed for each is the thread that unifies the *Republic*. Compare Rousseau who writes: "Do you want to get an idea of public education? Read Plato's *Republic*. It is not at all a political work, as think those who judge books only by their titles. It is the most beautiful educational treatise ever written."[4] I would not say that "it is not at all a political work," but I appreciate the overstatement which corrects for the neglect of the centrality of education and the move from the city back to the soul.

The most anti-political formulation of the relationship between the ideal city and actual politics is at the end of Book 9. Here the analogy of city and soul is completed; and as a middle term drops out of a syllogism, the city drops out once it serves to connect justice and the soul. In the final exchange of Book 9, Socrates says that the philosopher would do nothing to upset the "internal government of his soul," and Glaucon too quickly concludes that "he will not want to enter politics" (*R*. 592a).[5] Socrates answers "Yes, he will, by the dog. Perhaps not in the city of his birth, unless some divine contingency should intervene. But he certainly will in his own city" (ibid.). Glaucon then understands what Socrates means: the philosopher will only take part in the politics of a city such as they have built with their words, adding that he does not think it can be found anywhere on earth. Socrates responds that it does not matter whether this city exists now or in the future. He agrees that the philosopher will be a citizen of that city and no other, and that "perhaps its prototype can be found somewhere in heaven for him who wants to see" (ibid.).

The conclusion from building the city in speech is not about the ideal city or any city at all other than the metaphorical city in one's own soul. Whether the ideal city exists or not does not matter for the proof that it is better to be a just than an unjust human being. Even if the ideal city does not exist, it can still serve as a model for governing the city in the soul. The ideal city is an image of a pattern laid up in heaven which helps order one's soul; it is an image of the idea or form of Justice.

Even though the analogy builds to an anti-political conclusion, there is a crucial moment in the digression about the philosopher which must be considered together with the conclusion of Book 9. Despite the rarity of a just city, Socrates firmly states that it would be better both to be able to rule oneself and impart or participate in just rule of a city. If the philosopher tried to act as "a champion of justice" in a corrupt city, he would "find no ally" and would perish before he could do any good (*R.* 496c–d). From this fact Socrates concludes that in such cities the philosopher must be content with keeping himself free of injustice, and as if behind a wall in a storm, mind his own business as the lawlessness around him rages (*R.* 496d). Adeimantus responds that it would be no small achievement to preserve one's own justice and depart in peace (*R.* 497a). Socrates answers that neither would it be the greatest achievement, "unless he had had the opportunity to live in a city congenial to the philosophic nature. Only there would he have been able to attain his full stature and save the city as well as himself" (ibid.). This characterization of the full stature of the philosopher refines the nature of the ideal for human beings, but the conclusion remains essentially the same (cf. *Leg.* 702a–b). As in the end of Book 9, the question of which of the current cities would be suitable is answered by "none at all" (*R.* 497b). Since the right conditions are rare, the philosopher will primarily be concerned with becoming a just human being, since this is under his control. This self-mastery would not be the greatest achievement, but it is not a small one either. So Socrates agrees that the ideal life for the philosopher is a political and not only a private one, a life of action as well as contemplation. But divine intervention is required to have the right circumstances for such a life.

With full knowledge of the injustice that characterizes actual cities, Socrates makes the proposal that the ideal will come into existence only when philosophers become kings or kings philosophers (*R.* 473d–e). The opinion that philosophers would know the least, not the most, about politics is a distortion based on observations of corrupt politics. A just city must be ruled by just rulers and have just laws. Socrates's point is that the only way for this ideal to come into being is for those who have power also to have wisdom. Socrates attributes divinity to such a city, saying "if ever a philosopher's own best self finds a counterpart in the best of cities, the resulting regime will reveal a true divinity while all the others are human in principle and practice" (*R.* 497a–d). The philosopher is fundamentally one who contemplates the divine realities, and this vision leads to imitation of what is seen. The philosopher learns to govern his soul by imitating the forms, and Socrates asks: "if he goes beyond merely polishing his own intellect and feels under obligation to transfer the patterns he has seen in the divine order to both the public and the private natures of men, do you think he will lack the skill to move society toward justice, moderation, and all the virtues of ordinary men in civic life?" (*R.* 500 d; cf. *NS* 5). Glaucon responds, that he will not lack the skill, and agrees that the city can be happy "only if it is built by architects using measurements from the divine pattern" (ibid.). If he can, the philosopher will imitate divine realities by moving society toward virtue. This is the point of the philosopher-king proposal; the philosopher, who looks at the eternal realities and not the petty politics of the current cities, alone will be able to judge truly and rule justly.

Far from naïve about the likelihood of a philosopher ruling a city, Plato acknowledges the rarity, if not the impossibility, of a city of human beings living as they should, and paints a pessimistic portrait of the way human beings and their cities are. The *Republic* underscores the need to pursue private justice when public institutions prevent the philosopher from holding a position of political power. This acknowledgment of the difficulty of embodying the ideal does not mean that the ideal is irrelevant.

Against those who would laugh at Socrates's proposals, he answers that the conditions necessary for the city to exist are not impossible. Socrates repeatedly emphasizes that though rare, the ideal is possible, "and there need be only one such, if his city will obey him, in order that all that now seems distant and unachievable will become real" (*R.* 502b). Socrates concludes that "ours is the best constitution if it can be realized, and its realization, while difficult, is not impossible" (*R.* 502d). Only if it were impossible for a philosopher to be a king or a king a philosopher, "only if the charge were true, could we be justly ridiculed as dispensers of daydreams and futilities. . . . If, then, at any time in ages past the best of philosophers have been obliged to govern the state, or are now governing some barbaric land far beyond the limits of our knowledge—or will govern at some future time—we shall regard our position as vindicated. That is, the constitution we described is put into practice whenever the muse of philosophy holds sway in the state. It is not impossible for such a thing to happen. That there are difficulties, we readily admit" (*R.* 499c–d). This quotation reveals that it does matter whether the ideal is truly the ideal for human beings at their best, at their most imitative of the divine. There is a connection to *what is*, since what human beings can be at their best is a possible actuality. So the *Republic* leaves open the possibility that by divine dispensation it could occur that a city have a ruler who is also a philosopher, in other words, that power and wisdom would coincide for the good of the whole city. This possibility is never ruled out, but the extraordinary conditions required are not considered likely.

In its overall movement the *Republic* focuses primarily on the ideal, but there are important references to actual politics. The conversation does not concentrate on what the second best type of city might be, not because the latter is not a worthy or important investigation to undertake, but because it is simply not the task of *Republic*'s conversation, which is to choose which life is better for a human being, the just or the unjust. The grim pessimism or realism about the rarity of a just city, and the lament that none of the current regimes are conducive to the philosophic nature, hardly accord with a naïve optimism as some think the *Republic* represents. Notably, there is no mere dismissal of the political as the "solitary" philosophers (as Vico calls them) might propose (*NS* 130). Plato struggles with the social nature of human beings and the difficulty of imitating divine justice in the human world. Socrates says it would be an achievement, but not the greatest one, if the philosopher only succeeds in keeping himself from injustice. The philosopher is essentially an educator or a politician in the sense of one whose business is "to care for souls" as the *Laws* defines politics (*Leg.* 650b).[6] This is not the teaching of someone who only thinks about how human beings ought to be and not how they are.[7]

Within the *Republic* the nature of history and actual cities are subordinate themes, but they are certainly important counter-points. In addition to the comments about the actual cities already cited, in Book 2 the initial founding of the city produces a healthy city which is abandoned in favor of a more complex society. In this way the inquiry into the city begins with a history of the development of cities. At first the city arises from needs, and the result is a peaceful, primitive society held together by religion (*R.* 369d–72d). When Glaucon protests that such a city is a city for pigs not for human beings, the more complex human city that accounts for luxuries as well is said to be feverish (*R.* 372e). Socrates concedes that perhaps the feverish city is the better choice for finding injustice as well as justice, even though it has to be purged later in the discussion to find justice this way (ibid.). This means that the initial city, the first stage in the historical development of cities, might have been a way to see the ideal. Socrates is fond of the first city, and says "I believe that the city I have just described is well founded and that it will prove to be robust. But if you also want to examine a city in a state of fever, we can do that, too. It is in any case evident that many will not be content with simple fare and simple ways" (*R.* 372e).

Socrates says that few would choose the first city despite its superiority in virtue. This claim makes the exactly the same point as Vico's axiom that only a few would want to live in Plato's Republic (*NS* 131). The role of luxury in the decline from the initial peaceful city is consonant with Vico's account of how nations become corrupt.[8] Since philosophers are not part of the first city, that Socrates considers it "well-founded" is significant.

Socrates makes no mention of philosopher-kings here, nor does he refer to this healthy city later to prove that the ideal is possible, which he takes some effort to do. Nothing in the *Republic* itself suggests how such a city could be considered "well-founded." As I will later demonstrate, in the *Statesman* there may be a hint as to how this may be possible. In such divine times the ideal can perhaps exist without a philosopher-king at the helm.[9]

In the preamble to the descriptions of the degenerate types of cities and souls in Book 8, Socrates offers a perceptive reason why the analogy of the soul and city works. His insight is about how human beings are, not how they ought to be, and the claim is strikingly similar to Vico's own ideas on the subject. Socrates says that the character of a city comes from the character of its citizens (*R.* 544d), so there are as many forms governments as personalities. "Do you realize that there must necessarily be as many types of human personality as there are forms of government? Or do you imagine that governments spring from the proverbial oak and rock instead of from the inclinations that predominant among their citizens, which then tip the scales, so to speak, so that the rest will follow along?" (*R.* 544d–e). Glaucon agrees there is no other source of government. In the *New Science* Vico devotes two axioms to this point that "governments must conform to the nature of the men governed" (*NS* 246) and "this axiom shows that by the nature of the human civil institutions the public school of princes is the morality of the peoples" (*NS* 247). The human beings make the cities. Cities are not natural occurrences, springing from an oak or rock. Cities are natural, however, in the sense that a bird making a nest is natural, since it is part of who a bird is to make a nest. Thus, to be social or political is part of the nature of human beings, a claim with which Vico opens the *New Science* (*NS* 2). For Plato as for Vico, we make ourselves and our cities. The social nature of human beings as well as the fact that we make the civil world and so can understand it are implied at least in Socrates's claim that cities derive their character from the human beings who dwell in them.

Vico does not elucidate the types of cities as precisely as the *Republic* 8 does, but it is worth considering the exposition because the decline from one form to the next resonates with Vico's own cyclic account of history. The first is aristocracy, which is the city Socrates has described as the just and good city, and the type of soul of the philosopher is correlative. But the Muses teach that even that best city would decline; as all things, nations are subject to generation and corruption (*R.* 546a–47a). Plato cites Hesiod as the source for the Greek idea of the cyclic ages of history, and though Vico maintains that his idea of the cycles in history stems from the

Egyptians, his cycle contains Greek elements as well. Hesiod is the source both for the Greek division of the ages of the world into the golden, silver, bronze, and iron ages, and for the idea that Zeus destroys the wicked human beings by flood, from which remnant of survivors human beings now derive. In the *Cratylus* Socrates interprets Hesiod's golden race as follows: "I think he means that the golden race was not made of gold, but was good and beautiful. And I regard it as a proof of this that he further says we are the iron race" (*Cra.* 398a). This division of history according to metals persists in the Western imagination even into Dante, with his striking image of the old man based on *Daniel* (2: 31–33) (*Inferno* xiv, 100–20). Whether the division utilizes the metaphor of the metals, or the ages of gods, heroes, and humans, the meaning remains the same. History is a cyclic movement from a divine origin, to an all too human decline and destruction, and then a new beginning from the remnant of survivors. In the *Statesman* myth there will be even more striking resemblances between Vico's and Plato's cyclic vision of history. Within the *Republic*, the speech by the Muses reveals the necessity of the movement from the healthy city to feverish city, but no connection is explicitly articulated (*R.* 546a–47a).

Socrates explains the decline in terms of the failure of a father or a city to educate its successor to preserve its aims (*Leg.* 695a–e). In this way, the aristocratic father has a timocratic son because the son's spiritedness is stirred by seeing his father ridiculed; the timocratic father has a oligarchic son, for the son rebels against the code of honor that interferes with the acquisition of wealth; the oligarchic father has a democratic son, because he is miserly and the son wishes to give his desires freer rein; and finally the democratic father has a tyrannical son because he fails to teach the difference between lawful and lawless pleasures. The failure of education is not inevitable, but since, as the Muses teach, all things in the world of generation and corruption decline, at some point there will be the failures described (*R.* 546d).

The five types of soul are permutations of the three parts of the soul. If the highest part of the soul, reason, governs spirit and desire, then the soul is aristocratic or philosophical; if the middle part, spirit, rules reason and desire, then the soul is timocratic; if the lowest part of the soul, desire, rules, then there are three options: the oligarchic, democratic, or tyrannical soul, depending on whether the desires are for the lawful and essential, lawful and non-essential, or lawless, respectively. Since cities derive their characters from their citizens, the types of cities are also five. The ideal city here is identified with aristocracy, the rule of the best.

These types of degenerate or unjust cities in Plato, and the progression from one to another, must not have entirely escaped Vico's notice. One can easily imagine that he would have found congenial the speech of the

Muses that all things including nations are subject to generation and corruption. I will return to the types of commonwealths in Vico in the interpretation of the difficult reference to Plato in the conclusion of the *New Science* (*NS* 1097).

In addition to evidence in the *Republic* itself, the thematic links of the *Republic* to other dialogues refine the place of the ideal and its relationship to the historical in Plato. In the *Timaeus* there could even be a dramatic link, for Socrates refers to a conversation that sounds just like the one in the Piraeus recounted in the *Republic*. Regardless, the opening of the *Timaeus* depicts Socrates eager to hear what his ideal city would look like in motion (*Ti.* 19b–c). The part of the *Timaeus* with which I am concerned is more an introduction for the *Critias*, which is left as a fragment. But before Critias explains how such a city might live in history, the origin of time itself as "the moving image of eternity" must be established (*Ti.* 37d). Truly Plato and Vico agree that "doctrines must take their beginning from that of the matters of which they treat" (*NS* 314; cf. *Cra.* 436e, 426a). Timaeus's task is to tell "a likely story" of the creation of the natural universe down to the creation of human beings, and then Critias will take over (*Ti.* 27b–c). In Vichian terms, Timaeus will give the *coscienza* of what God made, and Critias will give the *scienza* of what human beings made. The *Statesman* and the *Laws* make up for the unfinished task of the *Critias* with their accounts of human history.

The themes of eternity and history are always linked in Plato. The eternal standard of the *Timaeus* is not loosely serving to set up the *Critias*. In the *Laws* one sees also that human governing must be understood in the context of divine providence (*Leg.* 713d–e). Likewise, the *Statesman* myth is even more explicit that the cycle of history has a divine epoch before the human epoch. History begins with the Demiurge's creation, and the actions of human beings come much later. Ignoring this preparatory cosmology or theology would lead to errors about politics, as the characters of the *Statesman* reveal (*Plt.* 275a).

In the introduction to the *Timaeus*, which is set some time after the conversation of the *Republic*, Socrates is depicted as anxious to consider politics in the sublunar realm and engage in further investigation about how an actual city might embody the ideal. After he summarizes his main theme of the day before, "the state—how constituted and of what citizens composed it would seem likely to be most perfect" (*Ti.* 17c), he asks "then have I now given you all the heads of our yesterday's discussion? Or is there anything more, my dear Timaeus, which has been omitted?" (*Ti.* 19a) Timaeus answers, "nothing, Socrates. The discussion was just as you have said" (*Ti.* 19b). Readers of the *Republic* will note that either this summary leaves out some of what was recounted the day before or Socrates relates only a partial account from the *Republic,* even in outline. For the summary of the ideal city in the opening of the *Timaeus* leaves out the proposal that philosophers be kings. Why does Timaeus say nothing is left out or why does Socrates leave out the proposal of the philosopher-kings he said was essential for the ideal city in the *Republic?* If it is Socrates's omission, it may reflect a difference in his audience on this occasion, or when he summarized the ideal city the day before he left it out also. The omission is hard to understand since the Socrates of the *Republic* was quite clear that a philosopher becoming the ruler was the only way the ideal could actually exist.

This omission could be linked to the peculiar opening of the dialogue, where Socrates counts the three present and asks where the fourth is (*Ti.* 17a). The absent member could be Glaucon, who walked back with Socrates from the Piraeus and could have been part of the summary given the day before. This guess is appealing because, if Glaucon had been present, Socrates would had to have included the philosopher-king proposal in his summary, for Glaucon would not have let that pass as Timaeus did. Regardless of who the unnamed absent fourth is, the absence of an expected interlocutor indicates something is left out of the account. I am suggesting that the philosopher-king is left out, to whose absence Socrates draws attention rather than entirely concealing. This interpretation is pure conjecture, however, and as far as I know the absent fourth remains a mystery.

After the summary of his remarks of the day before, Socrates draws attention to the gap between his ideal city and the actual world of politics. Socrates says "my feelings are rather like those of a man who has seen some splendid animals, either in a picture or really alive but motionless, and wants to see them moving and engaging in some of the activities for which they appear to be formed. That's exactly what I feel about the society we have described. I would be glad to hear some account of it engaging in transactions with other states, waging war successfully and showing in the process all the qualities one would expect from its system of education and training, both in action and negotiation with its rivals" (*Ti.* 19b–c). Socrates wants to see his ideal city brought to life. Socrates is searching for a way to bridge the gap between what ought to be and what is in politics, between the city in speech and actual cities.

First, Socrates says "I know that I am myself incapable of giving any adequate account of this kind of our city and its citizens" (*Ti.* 19d). Then he adds that he is not surprised at his own incapacity, since in his opinion all the poets, past and present, as well as all the sophists have failed to provide such an account. The reason is that no one can imitate what one has not experienced (ibid.). Who could give such an account? Socrates concludes, "there remain people of your kind, who are by nature and education imbued with philosophy and statesmanship. For Timaeus here comes from the Italian Locris, a very well run city . . . Critias, of course, all of us here know to be no amateur in these matters . . ." and Hermocrates is said to have genius and education to recommend him (*Ti.* 19e–20b). Socrates replies that when he told his audience yesterday about his ideal, he anticipated how they could repay him. "I had this in mind yesterday when I agreed so readily to your request for an account of my ideal society: I knew that there was no one more fitted to provide the sequel to it than you—you are the only living people who could adequately describe my city fighting a war worthy of her" (*Ti.* 20a–c). He sees the three as well-qualified to speak about politics, and he says he was even then looking forward to how they would repay him, now that he is the guest, and they are the entertainers (*Ti.* 17a).

The ones qualified to speak on bringing the ideal to life are those who are "by nature and education imbued with philosophy and statesmanship" (*Ti.* 19e). The omission of the philosopher-kings in Socrates's summary must not be because he has changed his mind; it must not be because he now rejects philosophers as the proper authority for political questions. For here he appeals to those who are both philosophers and statesmen, on the grounds that they are both, to explain how they think the ideal could be brought into existence. Socrates does not insist that philosophers must be kings in the ideal city for it to be the ideal city. This may mark a change of Plato's thought in a direction less susceptible to the charge of the conceit of scholars. Further meditation on the nature of history and the first cities may have led to a stronger sense that the real rulers of such times are the gods and their laws, not philosophers who are human beings and can rule only in human times.

The task of showing the city in motion falls to Critias, Plato's famous uncle and politician, and the fragment of the dialogue which bears his name is quite interesting for the question of the embodiment of the ideal in history. Socrates said that no poet in the past told of such an ideal city (*Ti.* 19d). Critias says that he knows from his grandfather that Solon could have been such a poet. Socrates agrees to listen to this tale to see if it meets his requirements (*Ti.* 20d).

Critias's grandfather, also named Critias, (who heard the tale from his father who was a dear friend of Solon) told his grandson a story about a meeting between Solon and the Egyptians in which he learned about ancient Athens. The occasion for the recitation was a poetry competition in which a kinsman said to Critias that he thought Solon was not only the wisest of men, but also the noblest of poets (*Ti.* 21c). As the story relates Solon went to Egypt where he had a conversation about history with one of the Egyptian priests. The priest chastised the Greeks for their ignorance of history. The priest explains that the ignorance of the past results from many deluges and other destructions of mankind (*Ti.* 22c–d). The Greek myth of Phaethon is explained as a faint memory of one of the disasters, where fire destroyed the earth (ibid.). The Egyptians are protected by the Nile from such disasters, and that is why they have the most ancient traditions, and know even more about the ancient Greeks than do the Greeks themselves (*Ti.* 22e–23a). Such disasters destroy the education and letters achieved by vulnerable civilizations, "so you have to begin all over again like children, and know nothing of what happened in ancient times, either among us or among yourselves" (*Ti.* 23b).

As Solon reports, the Egyptians chided the Greeks for being like children, unaware of their past. Vico does not cite the dialogue, but this is most likely the source for his claim in the *Autobiography* that "the Egyptians . . . twitted the Greeks for being always children and knowing nothing of antiquity" (*A* 169). Recall that the Egyptians are credited by Vico with remembering the ages of gods, heroes, and humans, as well as the languages that correspond to each age (*NS*, Chronological Table). Vico draws on the memory of the Egyptians for his account of ideal eternal history just as Plato had Critias draw on them for his, though Vico is more critical of the extent of the Egyptian claims to antiquity in favor of the Hebrews.

The story which follows is about the ancient Athenians. The priest begins with the revelation that "formerly there dwelt in your land the fairest and noblest race of men which ever lived, and that you and your whole city are descended from a small seed or remnant of them which survived. . . . there was a time, Solon, before the great deluge of all, when the city which is now Athens was first in war and in every way the best governed of all cities" (*Ti.* 23c). This city was founded by Athena, goddess of war and wisdom, nine thousand years ago, one thousand before the same goddess in Egyptian guise as Neith founded the city Sais, the home of the priest relating the story. The story of the battle of ancient Athens with the powerful Atlantis is suggested as a way to see the ideal city in motion as Socrates requested. Critias says he accepted the challenge yesterday because Socrates's city reminded him of this tale, since there were astonishing points of agreement in the descriptions of the cities (*Ti.* 25e–26a). Critias adds that he was confident they could succeed in providing what Socrates requested, "considering that in all such cases the chief difficulty is to find a tale suitable to our purpose, and that with such a tale we should be fairly well provided" (*Ti.* 26a).

The proposal is made and accepted in the opening of the *Timaeus;* after Timaeus's speech, in the *Critias*, more of the details of the city are recounted before the dialogue breaks off. In addition to the gods Timaeus invoked, Critias invokes Memory in particular to aid in giving such a difficult speech: "she is the power on whom the whole fortune of my discourse most depends" (*Criti.* 108d). Critias claims it is even more difficult to describe human beings than gods, for his audience is in a better position to judge errors about themselves than the gods (*Criti.* 107b–08a). By invoking Memory, Critias suggests there is a way to imitate what is not in one's own personal experience, but what is in the memory of one's race. The memory of ancient Athens is part of who they are in such a way that they can know it. They can know it as an adult remembers his childhood. Solon might have been a poet alongside Homer and Hesiod as Critias's grandfather suggested, if only political matters had not kept him from devoting himself to his poetry (*Ti.* 21c–d). The story has been handed down through Critias's family, and he even offers to show them the written record which he has inherited (*Criti.* 113b). The story purports to be "not a mere legend but an actual fact" (*Ti.* 21a), on the authority of Solon himself. Critias says "the city and citizens, which you yesterday described to us as fiction, we will now transfer to the world of reality. It shall be the ancient city of Athens . . . and there will be no inconsistency in saying that the citizens of your republic are these ancient Athenians" (*Ti.* 26c–d). Socrates replies "what other, Critias, can we find that will be better than this which is natural and suitable to the festival of the goddess, and has the very great advantage of being a fact and not a fiction?" (*Ti* 26e).

The *Critias* expands upon the origins, nature, and destruction of both ancient Athens and its adversary Atlantis. After the creation described by Timaeus, the gods divided up the world among themselves by lots. Athena and Hephaestus shared one lot, which was Athens; Poseidon's lot was Atlantis. Athena and Hephaestus "produced from the soil a race of good men and taught the order of their polity; their names have been preserved, but their deeds forgotten by reason of the destructions of their successors and the lapse of time. For the remnant of survivors, as has, indeed, been already said, was ever left unlettered among its mountains" (*Criti.* 109d). The remaining of the earthborn had to focus their efforts on obtaining basic necessities, and history is said to be the product of leisure (*Criti.* 109e–10a). At this point Critias draws a parallel between the way their soldiers were set apart and had no private property and the guardians of Socrates's ideal city; "in short, they followed all the practices we spoke of yesterday when we talked of those feigned guardians" (*Criti.* 110c–d). The city which emerged in this way had a reputation for righteousness and was famous for all the virtues (*Criti.* 112e). In order to show it in action, engaged in war, Critias turns to the description of the adversary.

The account of the origin and height of the commonwealth of Atlantis has elements of the ideal also, though the war begins when it has declined and lost its divine roots. The genealogy of the founding of Atlantis begins with the offspring of the god Poseidon and Clito, the daughter of "one of the original earthborn men of that region, named Evenor, with his wife Leucippe" (*Criti.* 113d). She bore five sets of twins, and these ten were the first ten kings of the ten parts of the island of Atlantis. Athens will be the city to defeat this great power when it loses harmony in itself. "Now this mighty and wondrous power, which then was in that region, the god arrayed and brought against this our own region, the cause, as the tale goes, being this. For many generations, while the god's strain was still vigorous, they gave obedience to the laws and affection to the divine whereto they were akin. They were indeed truehearted and greathearted . . . they thought scorn of all things save virtue" (*Criti.* 120d–e). The vigor and honesty of these citizens is a striking parallel to Vico's description of the ages of gods and heroes in the *New Science*.

The reason the Athenians became adversaries of another great virtuous city is that the citizens of Atlantis fell away from their divine roots. "But when the god's part in them began to wax faint by constant crossing with much mortality, and the human temper to predominate, then they could no longer carry their fortunes, but began to behave themselves unseemly. To the seeing eye they now began to seem foul, for they were losing the fairest bloom from their most precious treasure, but to such as could not see the true happy life, to appear at last fair and blessed indeed, now that they were taking the infection of wicked coveting and pride of power" (*Criti.* 121b). "The seeing eye" of Zeus is the highest judge of the virtue of cities, and he saw the decline of Atlantis: "Zeus, the god of gods, who governs this kingdom by law, having the eye by which such things are seen, beheld their goodly house in its grievous plight and was minded to lay judgment on them, that the discipline might bring them back to tune" (*Criti.* 121b–c). Both the decline and the remedy are similarly described in Vico's *New Science*.

The dialogue ends right before the speech of Zeus to the other gods is related, but from the *Timaeus* the reader knows that Athens will rise up to defend itself and the other cities from the attack of Atlantis, and so will be the agent of Zeus's discipline. Athens defeats Atlantis in battle (*Ti.* 25b–c), but the idea of bringing it back into tune is not fulfilled because violent earthquakes destroyed both the Athenian soldiers and the entire island of Atlantis (*Ti.* 25d). Perhaps Poseidon, since he is the god of earthquakes and father of the race of Atlantis, in anger over the defeat rose up to defend Atlantis in a quarrel among the gods and ended up destroying both of the cities. These are after all not gods in the Platonic sense necessarily, so they could still have the petty rivalries depicted in Homer. It certainly complicates the parallel with Vichian providence if the god disciplining the cities does not have the power to accomplish his plans, as it seems Zeus did not.

The parallels to Vico's description of the decline into a second barbarism which is worse than the first are the most interesting ones. Human times replace the divine times, and the ideal justice of the first cities, which were founded by the gods themselves, is replaced with pride and covetousness. This shift parallels the same transition from the healthy to the feverish city in *Republic* Book 2, and it confirms my earlier suspicion that the ideal city might have been the healthy city Socrates called well-founded. The ideal city is one that obeys the divine laws and has affection for the divine because it is like the divine (*Criti.* 120e). Piety and wisdom are linked, but the wisdom is not said to come from philosophy in these first virtuous cities. Even as a fragment, the *Critias* sheds much light on the way the ideal city could have existed in the past. Socrates would have his proof that the ideal is not impossible, for as he said in the *Republic*, there would only have to be one such city to prove that it was possible, however rare. Critias's grandfather praised Solon for his wisdom as well as his poetry, and said he would have been as famous as Homer and Hesiod had he been able to devote himself to his poetry. For a *mythos* that combines wisdom and poetry, the Greeks would have to wait for Plato himself. Before turning to the myth of Plato's *Statesman*, which shares many elements with that of *Timaeus* and *Critias*, I will consider the relationship of the ideal and actual in the *Laws*. Like the *Timaeus* and *Critias*, the *Laws* has significant thematic links to the *Republic* especially on the relationship of the ideal city to history.

The *Laws* is in many ways the best commentary on the *Republic*, and it can be read as a substitute for the completion of the *Critias* whose explicit task was to show the ideal city in motion. The conversation about founding a colony in Crete is another attempt to see how the ideal city might actually exist, this time in the near future instead of the distant past. The project of giving a new colony a constitution is as urgent a situation as is presented in the dialogues on the subject of statesmanship, surpassed only among Plato's works by the *Seventh Letter* which tells of Plato's attempts to influence political events in Syracuse which actually occurred. The story in the *Timaeus* and *Critias* was said to be fact not fiction, but it was a story outside the accepted poetic history of Greece.

In the *Laws*, the reader of the dialogues sees very clearly that Plato knows how human beings are as well as how they should be. In particular, this dialogue can shed light on Vico's charge of Plato's political naïvete stemming from considering human beings as they should be instead of how they are (*A* 138). The Spartan character Megillus even exclaims: "Stranger, you are belittling our human race in every respect!" (*Leg.* 804b). He is responding to the Stranger saying that human beings are like puppets, "sharing in small portions of the truth" (*Leg.* 804b; cf. 906b). This exchange follows the central distinction that divine things are serious and should be considered seriously, whereas "of course, the affairs of human beings are not worthy of great seriousness; yet it is necessary to be serious about them" (*Leg.* 803b). The Stranger defends his harsh words against human nature by saying that he was looking toward the god and spoke under the influence of that experience (*Leg.* 804c). The scrutiny of human weakness is present in the *Republic* and other dialogues, but it is especially prominent in the *Laws*, where with the honesty, and even humility, born from piety, old men realistically assess the human condition. Far from being tangential to the conception of human nature in the dialogues, such a recognition of human weakness is in fact the heart of the Socratic claim to wisdom as knowing one's own ignorance. The *Republic* shows how difficult education is and strongly states the rarity of the ideal, and such realistic claims are made stronger and clearer in the conversation of the old men in the *Laws*.

Consider what the Stranger says about the possibility of finding a philosopher-king to make the colony into the ideal city. They all agree that it is true now and always has been that the most efficient way for a city to change its laws is to have an all-powerful ruler. Taking over a city in this way is said not to be impossible or even difficult, but the rarity of such an individual is stated very strongly. "What is difficult is the following, which seldom comes to pass even in a great span of time, but which, when it does happen in a city, brings to that city myriads of all that is good . . . The possibility that a divine erotic passion for moderate and just practices should arise in some of the great and all-powerful rulers" (*Leg.* 711d). The quickest way to establish the ideal city is to have such a ruler be perfectly wise and moderate himself. If that were the case, laws would not even be necessary.

The temperament required is embodied by Nestor, who was as moderate as he was eloquent. Nestor "lived in the time of Troy, as they claim, though never among us; but if such a man has ever existed, or will exist some day, or is now among us, then he himself lives a blessed life, and blessed are those who join in paying heed to the words that flow from his moderate mouth" (*Leg.* 711e). The conclusion drawn from the Nestor example is the same as the one in the *Republic*, that the best regime emerges when power and wisdom coincide in a ruler: "when the greatest power coincides in a human being with prudence and moderation, then occurs the natural genesis of the best regime, and laws to match: but otherwise it will never come to pass" (*Leg.* 712a). These remarks are a restatement of the proposal of the necessity for philosopher-kings, but here the Stranger acknowledges that they serve as a myth, or oracle. The Stranger concludes by saying, "let these remarks be like a myth pronounced in oracular fashion, revealing, on the one hand, that it would be difficult for a city with good laws to come into being, but, on the other hand, that if what we discussed did occur, such a city's origin would be the quickest and by far the easiest of all" (ibid.).

Why does the Stranger think it is so hard for a human being to be wise and moderate like Nestor? Consider the strongest statement against the likelihood of one individual having power and wisdom, and hence the need to pursue the second best, that of framing just laws: "it's necessary for human beings to have laws, so they differ in no way from the beasts that are the most savage in every way. The cause of these things is this, that there is no one among human beings whose nature grows so as to become adequate both to know what is in the interest of human beings as regards a political regime and, knowing this, to be able and willing always to do what is best" (*Leg.* 875a). "There is no one among human beings" is a strong statement; the reasons are twofold. First, "it is difficult to know that the true political art must care not for the private but the common—for the common binds cities together, while the private tears them apart—and that it is in the interest of both the common and the private that the common, rather than the private, be established nobly" (*Leg.* 875a–b). This reason is the chief obstacle that the education of the guardians in the *Republic* is intended to overcome; they are taught to value the common over the private.

The second reason given in the *Laws* is that "even if someone should advance sufficiently in the art to know that this is the way these things are by nature, and after this should rule the city, without being audited, and as an autocrat, he would never be able to adhere to this conviction and spend his life giving priority to nourishing what is common in the city, while nourishing the private as following after the common; mortal nature will always urge him toward getting more than his share and toward private business, irrationally fleeing pain and pursuing pleasure, and putting both of these before what is more just and better" (*Leg.* 875b–c). The ability to sustain one's knowledge is acknowledged elsewhere in Plato (*Smp.* 208a), and in the *Republic* the rarity of the temperament needed to be a philosopher-king includes the ability to moderate one's passions as well as to attain knowledge (*R.* 503d). Saying that a human being "would never be able to adhere" to the knowledge of the common good he attained underscores the opening pessimistic claim these reasons support, that "no one among human beings" could be as wise and moderate as the philosopher-king would need to be.

I would agree that this is a step beyond the realism of the *Republic* about the difficulty of the ideal if the *Laws* did not preserve the possibility that by divine dispensation a human being could overcome these two considerable obstacles. Such a human being could exist, and the Stranger gives the example of Nestor, though some doubt is cast on his reality ("so they claim"). Reserving the possibility that someone could have the right nature and follow through in every case doing the right thing is all the *Republic* claimed as well. In the *Laws* the focus is shifted, because this possibility is considered so rare that the conversation should turn to the second best option. For these reasons the Stranger concludes that "of course, if ever some human being who was born adequate in nature, with a divine dispensation, were able to attain these things, he wouldn't need these laws ruling him. . . But now, in fact, it is so nowhere, in any way, except to a small extent. That is why one must choose what comes second, order and law—which see and look to most things, but are incapable of seeing everything" (*Leg.* 875c–d; cf. 746a–b). This statement of the ideal of a philosopher-king is the same, but the likelihood is diminished to such an extent, that choosing the second best is advocated.

As lawgivers, they first have to state what the best regime is, which gives them a model to imitate in the less than ideal situations (*Leg.* 739b). The best city is one where the common good is honored before private advantage; "no one will ever set down a more correct or better definition than this of what constitutes the extreme of virtue. Such a city is inhabited, presumably, by gods or the children of the gods (more than one), and they dwell in gladness, leading such a life. Therefore one should not search elsewhere for the model, at any rate, of a political regime, but should hold on to this and seek with all one's might the regime that comes as close as possible to such a regime. If the regime we have been dealing with now came into being, it would be, in a way, the nearest to immortality and second in point of unity" (*Leg.* 739e). Admitting that in practice the second best is all human beings are usually able to achieve does not mean that there is no place for articulating the ideal. To imitate the model one has to know what it is. The Stranger acknowledges the importance of practical as well as theoretical wisdom for the actual lawgiver; he states plainly the double movement between how things are and should be that this requires: "he who presents the model for what should be attempted should depart in no way from what is most noble and most true; but, when some aspect of these things turns out to be impossible for a fellow, he should steer away and not do it. Instead, he should contrive to bring about whatever is the closest from the things that remain" (*Leg.* 746b–c). This is a Platonic defense of considering how human beings should be, given that one also knows how they are.

Unlike Plato's attempt to make Syracuse better through educating the tyrant in philosophy, the three old men in the *Laws* acknowledge that since a philosopher-king is so rare, they had better consider the next best, which is to establish good laws. Even if there is no opportunity to realize the ideal city in one's homeland, or even the second best using it as a model, one can learn from such an ideal city how to govern one's own life. The parallel with the conclusion of the analogy of the city and soul in the *Republic* could hardly be clearer: "All these things have been discussed for the sake of understanding how a city might best be established sometime, and how, in private someone might lead his own life" (*Leg.* 702b; cf. *R.* 591e–92b). I cannot emphasize enough that I see no contradiction between the teaching of the *Republic* (and the actions described in the *Seventh Letter*) and the *Laws;* rather, there is a difference of emphasis and context. There is no absolute reversal where Plato learns that the ideal city is not possible. Before Plato went to Syracuse he knew it was unlikely to succeed, depending as much on divine luck as human effort, and perhaps his faith in the slim possibility was shaken, but it is not as if he were optimistic in the *Republic*. He had already seen Socrates executed when he wrote the *Republic*, and that was more formative intellectually than the incident with Syracuse, though that experience is important.[10]

Vico never discusses the commentary on the ideal city or the import of the claims about human limitations in the *Laws*. Vico refers to the *Laws* primarily to praise Plato for realizing the cyclopes are the first fathers and origin of commonwealths (*NS* 338, 503, 522, 547, 547, 950, 962, 982, 1005). But the parallels between the description of the origins of cities in *Laws* 3 and 4 and Vico's own in the *New Science* go beyond the reference to Homer's discussion of the cyclopes. Just as in the *Timaeus* and *Critias*, and as will be evident in the *Statesman* as well, the idea that nations are born when a remnant of human beings survive a catastrophe like a flood and proceed through the stages of civilization and decline is prominent in the *Laws*. Vico's frequent recognition of Plato's reference to the cyclopes as the origin of commonwealths is the most explicit acknowledgment of the Greek roots of Vico's ideal eternal history. Wherever Plato discusses the first humans he also explains how human beings fall away from these divine times of their origins through luxury and are ultimately destroyed by Zeus and begin again from a remnant who lack memory and are again pious and honest. Vico's reference to Plato's correct identification of the first stage of ideal eternal history is the strongest evidence in the *New Science* that he knew of the significant parallels between his ideas of history and Plato's.[11]

Faced with a question about history, Plato in the *Laws* as in the *Republic* (*R.* 545d, ff.) turns to the poetic history of myth. Vico cites Strabo's reference to one such appeal to Homer's *Iliad* in the *Laws* (*Leg.* 680b–82e). "In Strabo there is a golden passage of Plato saying that, after the local Ogygian and Deucalionian floods, men dwelt in caves in the mountains; and he identifies these first men with the cyclopes [*Leg.* 680b, 682a], in whom elsewhere [*Leg.* 680e–81b] he recognizes the first family of fathers of the world. Later they dwelt on the mountainsides, and he sees them represented by Dardanus, the builder of Pergamum, which later became the citadel of Troy [*Leg.* 681e–82d]. Finally they came down to the plain; this he sees represented by Ilus, by whom Troy was moved onto the plain near the sea, and from whom it took the name Ilium [*Leg.* 682b]" (*NS* 296, references added). Vico considers this passage of Plato important enough to be an axiom.[12] It immediately follows the series of axioms (66–96) called "the principles of ideal eternal history" (*NS* 294). Axiom 97 states the same point without the reference to Plato: "let it be granted, as a postulate not repugnant to reason, that after the flood men lived first on mountains, somewhat later came down to the plains, and finally after long ages dared to approach the shores of the sea" (*NS* 295). "The golden passage of Plato" makes exactly this point about the development of cities. The interlocutors of the *Republic* accept this postulate on the authority of the muses (*R.* 545e; 547a), and the interlocutors of the *Timaeus* and the *Critias* on the authority of Solon. Since it is a matter of memory that exceeds any personal experience, one must rely on the authority of others for its truth.

In what context does Plato refer to the cyclopes? The question that opens *Laws* 3 is: how do cities become corrupt? This is another way of asking the question of *Republic* 8: how does faction emerge even in the best cities? Socrates suggests that Homer might contain the answer: "Shall we follow Homer and pray that the Muses will tell us 'how faction first befell them,' pretending that the mock-heroic tones they adopt to tease little children are to be taken seriously?" (*R.* 545d–e) Glaucon's response is not a yes or a no, but a question as to what they would say. Once the Muses have given their speech, which features the idea that "destruction is the portion of everything created" (*R.* 546a) including the nations, the teaching is accepted, at least as a fruitful avenue of discussion. The authority of the poets is not accepted uncritically, but the kernel of truth is not rejected because of its source. On the other side of the Platonic moral critique of poetry, however, is the idea of its occasional divine inspiration; "for the race of poets is divine, and becomes inspired when it sings: each time, singing in the company of certain Graces and Muses, they hit upon many things that truly happened" (*Leg.* 682a).

Homer is also the answer to the question posed in *Laws* 3. In order to answer the question of the origin of political regimes the Stranger suggests that the viewpoint needed is the same one needed to see "the progression of cities as they change toward virtue and at the same time towards vice" (*Leg.* 676a). The viewpoint is "one that embraces an infinite length of time and the changes during that time" (*Leg.* 676b). In terms of the *New Science*, the perspective required to understand the origins and the changes in virtue and vice of nations is ideal eternal history. Kleinias does not understand what the Stranger means, so the Stranger elaborates. The Stranger persuades him of the impossibility of conceiving how long there have been cities, how long human beings have been involved in politics (ibid.), how many cities have come into being and been destroyed in that immeasurable length of time, and how they must have gone from better to worse and worse to better (*Leg.* 676c). They agree that discerning the cause of this change "might perhaps show us the first origin and transformation of political regimes" (ibid.). At this point the Stranger asks: "do you both believe that there's some truth in the ancient sayings? . . . The ones that tell of many disasters —floods and plagues and many other things—which have destroyed human beings and left only a tiny remnant of the human race" (*Leg.* 677a). The reply is "this sort of thing seems entirely credible to everyone" (ibid.). Compare Vico's axiom which states that this commonplace is "not repugnant to reason" (*NS* 295); he asks his reader for a similar agreement as the Stranger does.

In addition to the steps of the generation of cities, their decline is also mapped by the *Laws*.[13] Is there a resemblance between the *Laws* and the *New Science* on the corruption as well as the generation of nations? Vico does not address the extent of the resemblance between *Laws* 3 and his own ideal eternal history. In fact he only notes the similar description of the generation of cities, not the corruption, although the latter is the guiding question of *Laws* 3. The explanation may be that Vico was thinking of the passage as mediated through Strabo (which is how he cites it)(*NS* 296), and for whatever reason did not pursue the connection. Nonetheless, the parallels are significant. This similarity alone strongly demonstrates that Plato, like Vico, knew how human beings *are* not only how they *should be*.

The corruption of the cities brings the reader of the dialogues or the *New Science* closer to the present, as neither audience lives in the golden age. The types of unjust cities in the *Republic* are presented as devolving from the ideal city. Unlike the *Republic* which begins with the peaceful, healthy city, in the *Laws* the starting-point is the savage cyclopes. This harsh rule of the father over the family is the origin of all commonwealths (*NS* 338). This prepolitical state of nature is not itself the first commonwealth. Out of this initial barbarism the first city emerges when the family monarchies join into a heroic aristocracy. These cave-dwelling cyclopes, exemplified by Polyphemus in Homer's *Odyssey*, are the first humans of Vico's cycle (*NS* 243). They are just beginning to practice the Vichian principles of humanity. Although the distinctions between the state of nature and the early phases of the process of civilization are not clearly demarcated in the *Laws*, in general the depiction of the giants or titans and the cyclopes corresponds to Vico's first barbarism of sense. There is a brutality as well as honesty to the first humans, which is often masked by stories of the golden age.

There follows also a second barbarism described as arising from luxury which undermines the balance between order and freedom (693e, ff). Vico describes that this second barbarism is "darker than the first" (*NS* 1046; cf. 331). In the *Laws* the second barbarism is characterized by fearlessness and shamelessness, just as in the *New Science*. Fear and awe or piety are essential for a good city (*Leg.* 699c), and when these are lost (*Leg.* 701a–b), human beings are again like the titans (701c; cf. *NS* 502, 1106). The final phase of the decline from excess of freedom stands in opposition to obeying laws and brazen impiety: "after this comes the ultimate freedom when they cease to give any more thought to oaths and pledges and everything pertaining to the gods, but instead display and imitate what is called the ancient Titanic nature—arriving back again at those same conditions, and introducing a harsh epoch in which there is never a cessation of evils" (*Leg.* 701c).

The progression described is the same, here as in the *Republic*, *Timaeus*, and *Critias*, as Vico's own: "Men first feel necessity, then look for utility, next attend to comfort, still later amuse themselves with pleasure, thence grow dissolute in luxury, and finally go mad and waste their substance. . . . The nature of peoples is first crude, then severe, then benign, then delicate, finally dissolute" (*NS* 241–42). Vico's most detailed description of the two barbarisms which mark the beginning and the end of the cycles of ideal eternal history is found in the conclusion of the *New Science*: "through long centuries of barbarism, rust will consume the misbegotten subtleties of malicious wits that have turned them into beasts made more inhuman by the barbarism of reflection than the first men had been made by the barbarism of sense. For the latter displayed a generous savagery, against which one could defend oneself or take flight or be on one's guard; but the former, with a base savagery, under soft words and embraces, plots against the life and fortunes of friends and intimates" (*NS* 1106). When a commonwealth reaches this extreme, Vichian providence destroys it just as Critias said Zeus intended to punish Atlantis in order to restore harmony (*Criti.* 121 b–c; *NS* 1106).

Humanity is something that must be generated and will be lost in the course of the history of all the nations which is the history of corruption. The initial commonwealths are not the most human; nevertheless, although lacking the perfection of human virtue, they also avoid the extreme vices that accompany the development of the intellect. The reason for this necessary progression is not explained in any of the accounts in the dialogues considered so far (*Republic*, *Timaeus*, *Critias*, and *Laws*), but the *Statesman* suggests how the cycles make sense metaphysically.

Before turning to the *Statesman*, another description of the origins of the human commonwealth should be examined, going back even further than the previous account which began with the cyclopes. The discussion of the golden age in Book 4 of the *Laws* provides an insight into the pessimism about human cities as well as indicating that divine rule is the ideal that lawgivers attempt to imitate.

In *Laws* 4 the conversation turns to founding a city in speech, now that the origins and fates of cities are evident. When the Stranger asks which type of regime they want for the colony, his interlocutors cannot even identify their own cities's types, so he asks: "Should a little more use be made of myth, if it will allow us somehow to clarify, in a harmonious way, the answer to the present question?" Kleinias is not enthusiastic, saying "is that then the way one has to proceed?" The Stranger replies, "by all means," and tells of the rule of Chronos without further explanation: "Now long before the cities whose formation we described earlier, there is said to have come into being a certain very happy rule and arrangement under Chronos. The best of arrangements at the present time is in fact an imitation of this" (*Leg.* 713b). The ideal city, which was said to be so rare in human times that they needed to turn to a second best, in fact existed in divine times and with divine rulers.

The *Laws* here resembles the search for the ideal in motion of *Timaeus* and *Critias* for, in both, the ideal city is said to have existed in a golden age in the distant past. So distant is the ideal city, that even with the immeasurable perspective of the opening of *Laws* 3, the search does not reach back far enough. The flood that left the cyclopes on the mountain tops was the remnant of an earlier civilization, and the Stranger now turns to describing those divine times. All the cities discussed in *Laws* 3 were cities of human times, as Vico would say, taking the heroic and human times together in distinction from the divine times (*NS* 1057). Nestor is of heroic times, living in the time of the Trojan war, but there existed before that a golden age which is a memory even for Nestor.

The Stranger explicitly states that the golden age did not rely on human rulers, for "Chronos understood that, as we have explained, human nature is not at all capable of regulating the human things, when it possesses autocratic authority over everything, without becoming swollen with insolence and injustice. So reflecting on these things, he set up at that time kings and rulers within our cities—not human beings, but daimons, members of a more divine and better species" (*Leg.* 713c–d). Just as in the *Republic* the ruler is compared to a shepherd of herd animals, the gods are said to be shepherds of human beings in the golden age just as human beings are to animals now. "He did just what we do now with cattle or sheep and the other tame herd animals. We don't make cattle themselves rulers of cattle, or goats rulers over goats; instead, we exercise despotic dominion over them, because our species is better than theirs. The same was done by the god, who was a friend of humanity: he set over us the better species of daimons, who supervised us in a way that provided much ease both for them and for us. They provided peace and awe and good laws and justice without stint. Thus they made it so that the races of men were without civil strife, and happy" (*Leg.* 713d–e).

This argument leads to an even deeper resignation about the prospects for a good city ruled by human beings: "What this present argument is saying, making use of the truth, is that there can be no rest from evils and toils of those cities in which some mortal rules rather than a god. The argument thinks that we should imitate by every device the way of life that is said to have existed under Chronos; in public life and in private life—in the arrangement of our households and our cities—we should obey whatever within us partakes of immortality, giving the name 'law' to the distribution ordained by intelligence" (*Leg.* 713e–14a). This additional observation that human beings ought to imitate the way of life under the reign of Chronos in private as well as public recalls the analogy of the city and the soul I traced above in the *Republic* and other passages of the *Laws*. In the same way, here the conclusion about the corruption of cities applies to souls as well: "But if there is one human being, or some oligarchy, or a democracy, whose soul is directed to pleasures and desires, and needs to be filled with these, and retains nothing, but is sick with endless and insatiable evil—if such a one rules a city or some private individual, trampling underfoot the laws, there is, as we just now said, no device of salvation" (*Leg.* 714a). There is a severity to the portrait of the destruction of civilizations in *Laws* 3 which seems to hold out no hope of rebirth.

Laws 3 does not address the possibility that there is a remedy for the corruption in the action of divine providence bringing humanity back to life as a phoenix. Despite the central discussions of divine providence in *Laws* 10, the role of providence at the end of the cycle is not considered in these earlier discussions. An obvious opportunity to do so is side-stepped, for in the quotation from the *Iliad* which is the authority for the origin of the cities, Aeneas says: "Zeus builds up and Zeus diminishes the strength in men, the way he pleases, since his power is beyond all others" (*Il.* 20, 242–43).[14] Later in the *Laws*, there is the strong claim that God governs (*Leg.* 709b, 716c). Not making this explicit earlier renders the account harsher, as if providence did not guide history.

Recall that Vico accuses Plato of having "a vain wish for those ancient times in which philosophers reigned or kings were philosophers" (*NS* 253). Nevertheless, in the descriptions of the most ancient times, Plato does not attribute wisdom to the human beings at all, for they are like sheep of a divine shepherd. The golden age of Plato so described is not the *Republic*'s city in speech transported back in time. The *Critias* comes closer to having wise and moderate human beings ruling in the distant past, but there the past unfolded in the iron age, not the golden age. As I understand Vico's claim about the conceit of scholars, the error lies in attributing the esoteric wisdom of the human times to the divine times. In the *Republic* itself, *Critias*, and here in the *Laws*, there is never an instance where Plato's characters fall into this error. In the *Statesman* one can see that Plato identifies a form of this error himself, and cautions about committing it.

The first sentence of the *Laws* is a question: "Is it a god or some human being, strangers, who is given credit for laying down your laws?" (*Leg.* 624a). This is the essential first question in a dialogue "on lawgiving," and is equally crucial with respect to "the statesman" or "the king" (*Plt.* 259d). The reader of Plato might not notice how important a correct answer to this question is in the *Laws*, but the *Statesman* makes this evident. Kleinias responds by answering, "A god, stranger, a god—to say what is at any rate the most just thing" (*Leg.* 624a). This answer lacks conviction, perhaps because Kleinias himself has been given the task of being a human lawgiver or because he dismisses the myths as not serious. The dramatic setting of the *Laws* is a journey along the road from Knossos to the Cave and temple of Zeus where the Spartans believe their laws were entrusted to Minos. The setting recedes into the background as the human lawgivers discuss their task. Again, the distinction between divine and human lawgivers arises. Regarding the task of legislating for a second best city, the Stranger replies that "it is indeed in a certain way shameful even to legislate all the things we are now about to lay down, in a city such as this, which we claim will be well administered and correctly equipped in every way for the practice of virtue . . . . But we aren't in the same position as were the ancient lawgivers who gave their laws to heroes, the children of gods . . . we're humans, and legislating now for the seed of humans" (*Leg.* 853c). The division is not fully explored in the *Laws*, but in the definition of the statesman it is essential.

As I said above, in the *Laws* there is no explanation for why these stories are to be believed other than the authority of the poets. Likewise the *Republic*, *Timaeus*, and *Critias* all left their accounts of history at the level of *mythos*. The *Statesman* takes one difficult step further toward explaining why the true *mythos* is true. The *Statesman* uniquely claims to give the reason why there are these stories. Instead of taking the *mythos* as the starting-point (as the *Critias* does explicitly, and the others do by appeal to Homer and Hesiod), the *Statesman* gives the origin of these stories (*Plt.* 269b). The myth in the *Statesman* is a philosophically appropriated myth; it is a cosmic history which explains the metaphysical reasons for the periodic disasters remembered through the poets. The *Statesman* can be regarded as the first philosophy of history because it makes this move from *mythos* to *logos*. The other dialogues I have examined for their accounts of history have considered the myths about history philosophically relevant, of course, but they do not take the next step to give a *logos* of why these myths must be right about history. The stories are true because the Muses say so, but they are also true because metaphysical insights about the divine and the mortal require the cyclic history to be true.

The myth enters the discussion when it seems as if the characters have quickly achieved the goal of defining the statesman through the method of division. The statesman is "a shepherd of a hornless herd" (*Plt.* 265d), and with some refinement, this definition becomes the conclusion, when all the threads are gathered (*Plt.* 267a). Immediately the Stranger asks whether there is not a grave error, and the definition is really not complete at all. The interlocutor is surprised by this, and requests an explanation. The first explanation of the problem is that unlike other herdsmen, the statesman is not the only one who claims to be the shepherd of the human herd (*Plt.* 268c). Now they agree to take a longer road to discover the real nature of the statesman. So they begin again, taking as their starting-point "a mass of ancient legend, a large part of which we must now use for our purposes; after that we must go on as before, dividing always and choosing one part only, until we arrive at the summit of our climb and the object of our journey" (*Plt.* 268d–e).

The first story focuses on a portent which resolved the quarrel between Atreus and Thyestes. Zeus reversed the rising and setting of the sun and all the other planets to attest to the justice of Atreus, and then returned them to their present courses (*Plt.* 269a). The second mythic *topos* for their philosophical speech is the golden age ruled by Chronos, which the stranger says they have heard from many story-tellers (ibid.). The myths teach that "men of that former age were earthborn and not born of human parents" (*Plt.* 269b). The Stranger links these stories, saying: "all these stories originate from the same event in cosmic history, and so do hosts of others yet more marvelous than these. However, as this great event took place so long ago, some of them have faded from man's memory; others survive but they have become scattered and have come to be told in a way which obscures their real connection with one another. No one has related the great event of history which gives the setting of all of them; it is this event which we must now recount" (*Plt.* 269b). He promises that "once it has been related, its relevance to our present demonstration of the nature of a king will become apparent" (*Plt.* 269c).

The Stranger turns the portent of Atreus to his purposes and posits that the universe's capacity to rotate in reverse is a necessity of its nature (*Plt.* 269d). The cycles of history remembered obscurely by the poets are explained by the metaphysical principle that perfect motion is the attribute of divinity alone, and all mortal, created things, including the universe itself, are subject to corruption: "Ever to be the same, steadfast and abiding, is the prerogative of the divinest of things only. The nature of the bodily does not entitle it to this rank" (ibid.). God gave the universe, and with it human institutions, the most perfection possible for that which is not divine (*Plt.* 269d–e). The motions are cyclic or circular because that is the most perfect kind of change in motion, since only the divine remains eternally the same.

What is the nature of the universe's forward and reverse motion? How does it affect human beings? The second and third points, that Chronos ruled the golden age and in this age human beings were earthborn, are in this way incorporated into the account. God governs the initial era instead of a human lawgiver, with a divine constitution, not human, or rather no constitution. "There is an era in which God himself assists the universe on its way and guides it by imparting its rotation to it. There is also an era in which he releases his control. He does this when its circuits under his guidance have completed the due limit of the time thereto appointed. Thereafter it begins to revolve in the contrary sense under its own impulse—for it is a living creature and has been endowed with reason by him who framed it in the beginning. Now this capacity for rotation in reverse is of necessity native to it" (*Plt.* 269c–d). This must be the way the universe rotates because the other possibilities are said to contradict the first principle about divine sameness and mortal change (*Plt.* 269e–70a). If these other options are so ruled out, then the only possibility which remains is that "in one era it is assisted on its way by the transcendent divine cause, receiving a renewal of life from its creator, an immortality of his contriving. In the other era, when it has been released, it moves by its innate force and it has stored up so much momentum at the time of its release that it can revolve in the reverse sense for thousands of revolutions, because its size is so great, its balance is so perfect, and the pivot on which it turns is so very small" (*Plt.* 270b).

The interlocutor agrees that this is a probable and consistent account (ibid.), so they turn to the implications for human beings of "this great cosmic fact underlying all these miraculous stories . . . the fact that the revolution of the heaven is sometimes in its present sense, and sometimes in the reverse sense" (ibid.). The question of the relevance of these cosmic changes for human beings is raised explicitly: "we must believe, then, that at the time such changes take place in the universe we human beings have to undergo the most drastic changes also" (*Plt.* 270c). What is the nature of these drastic changes? I have already pointed out the destruction of the human race except for a remnant in some detail from the *Republic*, *Timaeus*, *Critias*, and *Laws*, and now the *Statesman* enables the reader of Plato to place this fact in metaphysical context. "So it must needs be that in the cosmic crisis there is widespread destruction of living creatures other than man and that only a remnant of the human race survives. Many strange new experiences befall this remnant, but there is one of deeper import than all. It follows on God's first taking over the rewinding of the universe, at the moment when the revolution counter to the one now prevalent begins to operate" (*Plt.* 270c–d).

The account continues that human beings at this juncture stop growing old but reverse also, and become younger and younger until they fade into nonexistence (*Plt.* 270d–e). The same happens to the bodies of those killed in the cataclysmic events. Although the explanation may be as unlikely as the event it is meant to explain, the Stranger says this is why the children of this era were not born to human parents, but were earthborn. From a Vichian perspective, this can be taken as a metaphorical transformation of developed societies back to the more animalistic pre-civil state in which there was no longer the human institution of marriage (as *Plt.* 272a attests) so children were born like other animals, and so from the earth, not in terms of a human culture.

All the needs of the human beings of this age of Chronos are provided without labor, so that it is made clear that this era is not the present one (*Plt.* 271c–d). These earthborn human beings are the subjects of Chronos, not any human lawgiver or statesman. "In that era God was supreme governor in charge of the actual rotation of the universe as a whole, but divine also, and in like manner was the government of its several regions, for these were all portioned out to be provinces under the surveillance of tutelary deities. Over every herd of living creatures throughout all their tribes was set a heavenly daimon to be its shepherd. Each of them was all in all to his flock—providing the needs of all his charges" (*Plt.* 271d–e). Just as described in the *Critias,* the universe is divided up among the gods who found and rule the various regions directly as shepherds take care of their flocks (*Criti.* 109b–c). The assumption that rulers are like shepherds is crucial to *Republic* 1 (*R.* 343b–d; 345c). This image of god as shepherd is also found in the *Laws* account, where the error initially made and then discovered in the *Statesman* is not made (as it was in the *Republic* perhaps), for they agree that just as human beings do not make cattle rulers over other cattle, so the gods did not let human beings rule over other human beings (*Leg.* 713d).

The Stranger relates that there were many consequences of the divine rule of the golden age, so he limits the scope to human beings. "So it befell that savagery was nowhere to be found nor preying of creature on creature, or did war rage or any strife whatsoever. There were numberless consequences of this divine ordering of the world, but we must leave them all aside save those concerning man's life in that paradise. A god was their shepherd and had charge of them even as men now have charge of the other creatures inferior to them—for men are closer to the divine than they are. When God was shepherd there were no political constitutions and no taking of wives and begetting of children. For all men rose up anew into life out of the earth, having no memory of the former things" (*Plt.* 271e–72b). Recall that in the *Laws*, human beings are described in their pre-political state as peaceful, when after the flood the remnant of human beings live peacefully under divine governance (*Leg.* 713c–14a). The initial healthy city in the *Republic* is likewise described as free of war and in harmony with the gods, though the rulers are not said to be the gods themselves (*R.* 372b).

In the context of the *Statesman*, however, the fact of divine rule takes on a particular importance so it is emphasized, for it reveals the error in their definition of the statesman. Now the reason for the digression is becoming apparent. "We were asked to define the king and statesman of this present era, and of humanity as we know it, but in fact we took from the contrary cosmic era the shepherd of the human flock as it then was, and described him as the statesman. He is a god, not a mortal. We went as far astray as that" (*Plt.* 275a). The grave mistake was to think that human beings could be shepherds over other human beings, when in fact only gods could fulfill the analogy of herdsman over human beings. "The divine shepherd is so exalted a figure that no king can be said to attain to his eminence. Those who rule these states of ours in this present era are like their subjects, are closer to them in training and in nurture than ever shepherd could be to flock" (*Plt.* 275e). Human beings can only properly be said to rule as shepherds over other animals, but not each other (cf. *Leg.* 713c–d). The rule of human beings over human beings is judged to be a grave fault or error (*Plt.* 267d, 274e), most likely because it is impious to attribute to human beings what properly belongs to the gods. For completeness, the proper division should have included the shepherd king of the age of Chronos as well as the mortal ruler of the age of Zeus (*Plt.* 276a; 276d). Governing and lawgiving is not something purely human, as the first sentence of the *Laws* indicated. Any definition of the statesman or a king must be broad enough to cover both divine and human governing.

In the *Statesman* the story of cosmic origins corrects a mistake based on reasoning about kingship without regard to the era of the universe which one is considering. At first the characters compare the king to the shepherd, but then the philosophical appropriation of the myths of the golden age demonstrates that this properly describes only the divine shepherd king of the reign of Chronos. In the reign of Zeus, which is the present era, the ruler is a human being governing human subjects more like himself than not (*Plt.* 275c). This similarity breaks down the analogy of shepherd to flock. In the golden age, the gods were to us as shepherds to sheep (*Leg.* 713d).

Recall that in the *Laws* the Stranger said in conjunction with the description of the rule of Chronos, that "there can be no rest from evils and toils for those cities in which some mortal rules rather than a god" (*Leg.* 713d). On this account, and the one in the *Statesman* and *Critias*, the ideal human city is not one with a human philosopher-king, but one ruled by a being as superior to human beings as they are to the animals they care for as shepherds. This insight is the key to understanding that Plato is not committing the conceit. It requires some speculation to answer Vico's charge on these grounds, but is clear that Plato thinks one could make an error about statesmanship based on misunderstanding what epoch one is governing. The claim in the *Statesman* about that error is closer to overcoming the conceit about the wisdom of the lawgivers than anything else before Vico.

As long as Plato is not attributing philosophical wisdom to human kings in the golden age, he has not committed the conceit, however important he thinks philosopher-kings are for the later human times. The ideal ruler of human times would have a rare knowledge, but it is a human knowledge nonetheless. In a way this line of argument suggests a recognition of the conceit of scholars who think the past rulers were the same as the present ones. It reveals that the knowledge of what statecraft is must differ in the age of gods from the age of humans. Plato is not thinking that the philosopher-king would govern in divine times, but in human times such a ruler would be required for human cities to be made divine or to approximate the peace and harmony of the divine rule of the golden age.

Another new element in the *Statesman* is the explicit question of whether it is better for a human being to live at times under rule of Chronos or under Zeus. This question also underlies Vico's meditations on history. In the *Statesman* we discover a discussion of the era of Zeus, elaborated to contrast with the golden age already described. I have postponed this part of the account in order to make clear how the error about the definition of the statesman was revealed by the account of the golden age. The role of luxury is not stated as a cause or contributing factor of corruption as it was in the *Republic*, *Laws*, and *Critias*, but impiety and forgetfulness are clearly evident. In contrast to the golden age when the universe was "guided by the divine pilot," and good prevailed over evil, "when it must travel on without God, things go well enough in the years immediately after he abandons control, but as time goes on and forgetfulness of God arises in it, the ancient condition of chaos also begins to assert its sway. At last, as this cosmic era draws to its close, this disorder comes to a head. The few good things it produces it corrupts with so gross a taint of evil that it hovers over the very brink of destruction, both of itself and of the creatures in it" (*Plt.* 273c–d). Once the universe has in this way wound down, God will behold its troubles and sickness and once again take "control of the helm once more. Its former sickness he heals; what was disrupted in its former revolution under its own impulse he brings back into the way of regularity" (*Plt.* 273d–e).

The *Statesman* provides a cosmic explanation for the description in the *Critias* of the degeneration from peaceful honesty to luxury which occurs when the connection between human beings and the race of gods weakened. During the first era when God rules, the connection is strong and life is peaceful; the later corrupt era is when the universe is released from divine governance and unwinds following its own inertia. God governs the first era, the first rotation, but as the reversal occurs, the universe unwinds on its own inertia, following destiny, back into chaos, from which it is rescued by God reestablishing the order. As in the *Timaeus* and the *Critias* human beings are said to forget the previous ages and calamities, and memory is therefore required. From all these moments in the dialogues concerning the political dimension of human existence, one can glimpse what can be called the Platonic philosophy of history.

The answer to which cosmic era is preferable is not an easy one. In the *Statesman* the answer turns upon whether the human beings under Chronos engage in philosophical inquiry. If they do so, then the answer is clearly that human beings then were a thousand times happier than human beings now. But if not, then the answer is less clear. As in the *Republic*, the most human city is not the healthy city or golden age, but the feverish city, which through philosophy can achieve wisdom. Vico agrees that reason is necessary for the proper expression of human nature (*NS* 919; 927), and his ideal would be wisdom and piety together. Vico considers human nature proper as intelligent nature (*NS* 927). Following Socrates, Vico would pause before rejecting such a pious city, though philosophy were not yet possible in such a city. Vico would caution against a judgment that privileges philosophy's goods, which are admittedly only for the few. Do human beings who have not developed the intellect truly have human happiness? Granted that piety and wisdom together would be the perfection of human nature, what if there must be a choice? If piety and wisdom are separated in the human times, then is it preferable to live in the pious divine times, where wisdom is not fully human? These questions can only be raised here, not answered, as they lead from the philosophy of history to the very heart of human nature and happiness.

Vico's Form of History

Now that I have demonstrated how Plato does consider both how human beings and cities "are" as well as how they "ought to be," the parallels between Plato and Vico are more visible. Vico's criticism of Plato for committing the conceit of scholars is resolved by a study of the dialogues themselves. But even with this detailed account of parallels between Vico and Plato's dialogues on the nature of history, which arose from exploring this criticism, questions regarding the differences between them still remain. Vico's remarks in the *Autobiography* and the conclusion of the *New Science* help refine the differences. What emerges in the conclusion of the *New Science* is that Vico looks at distinctive elements from Plato and recombines them in his account of history as ideal and eternal in a way that moves beyond Plato. Vico's innovation is to see history itself as an object of intellectual contemplation, which as such is universal, ideal, and eternal. In other words, Vico makes "history" one of the Platonic forms, or in Neoplatonic language, one of the ideas in the mind of God (*NS* 2).[15]

There are two prominent moments where Vico acknowledges Plato in the "Conclusion of the Work" (*NS* 1097–1112) of the *New Science*, first in the opening sentence (*NS* 1097), and then at the conclusion of the summary of ideal eternal history (*NS* 1109). The subtitle of the conclusion— "On an Eternal Commonwealth, in Each Kind Best, Ordained by Divine Providence"—serves as a guide to understanding how Vico adapts Plato's ideal city in summarizing his ideal eternal history.[16] It is significant that Vico's conclusion begins with Plato: "Let us now conclude this work with Plato, who conceived a fourth kind of commonwealth, in which good honest men would be supreme lords. This would be the true natural aristocracy. This commonwealth conceived by Plato was brought into being by providence from the first beginnings of the nations" (*NS* 1097). The most obvious of the many questions embedded in this statement is what does Vico mean by the kind of commonwealth he cryptically identifies as the fourth? I will treat this question first, and then I will return to the more difficult questions.

Vico could be employing any one of many lists of types of commonwealths in political philosophy from Plato and Aristotle, to Tacitus and

Machiavelli. Vico may be attributing another author's division to Plato and not have a specific text of Plato in mind. Nevertheless, several possibilities in Plato's dialogues exist from which Vico could draw this division. Both the fact that Vico further identifies the fourth type as "a true natural aristocracy," and the clue from the subtitle that it is "an eternal commonwealth" rule out several possibilities.

For instance, although he knows the passage, Vico probably is not referring to "the fourth city" in the *Laws*, where four types of cities are extrapolated from Homer's *Iliad* (*Leg.* 683; cf. *NS* 296, and note by Nicolini on that passage). In *Laws* 3, the progression of the generation of cities builds to four cities: "now we've gained this much by the meanderings of the argument, by going through certain regimes and settlements: we have seen the first, the second, and the third city, settled one after the other, as we believe, over immense stretches of time. And here this fourth city—or nation, if you wish—comes before us, having been settled in an earlier time and now being settled once again" (*Leg.* 683a–b). This second monarchy does resemble the mixed monarchy Vico describes (*NS* 1004), but this genuine parallel between Vico and Plato is not the same as that meant in the conclusion. To call this fourth mixed monarchy of the *Laws* and Vico's discussion of the returned monarchy of the human times either "an eternal commonwealth" or "true natural aristocracy" simply does not follow. So although only the "fourth city" from Plato's texts has any plausible parallel to a fourth city in Vico (*NS* 1026), it cannot be the one meant in the conclusion.

The description that "good and honest men" rule the fourth kind, as well as its eternal character, seems to mirror the ideal city of the *Republic,* or the city laid up in heaven (*R.* 592b). If the allusion is to the *Republic,* then Vico is projecting another division onto Plato because the *Republic* clearly states there are five constitutions, just as there are five kinds of souls (*R.* 445d). In the *Republic*, the ideal is counted as the first and is identified as the "true aristocracy" (*R.* 545a). The other four are the degenerate or unjust forms: timocracy, oligarchy, democracy, and tyranny. Vico's calling the city the fourth could be a mistaken memory of the *Republic's* types. Regardless, the *Republic's* account of the true aristocracy or the ideal city suggests that this is what Vico means by his "fourth" type.

Let us examine textual support in Plato for adding the ideal as an additional type to the number of human governments, however one divides the human governments. In the *Statesman*, Plato subdivides the three types to result in six, then adding the ideal city as the seventh (*Plt.* 302c). Vico's likely source is the *Statesman*, where the principle of the division is the number of rulers, which is exactly how Vico himself divides the common-wealths (*NS* 1026). In adding the ideal as fourth, Vico may be thinking that Plato also had three types of human cities.

There is also another fourth (or fifth if one counts the recurrence of monarchy as a fourth human type), which is the golden age under divine administrations. If one reads three and only three types of human com-monwealths (*NS* 29, 1004), then the fourth is divine. Vico does not count the divine rule when he enumerates his otherwise exhaustive division of three types of commonwealths, so this could explain why he identifies the fourth with Plato's ideal aristocracy. Such is the divine origin of all the human types of governments. The rule of the best, eternal rule, would be divine rule (*NS* 1098). Both the *Statesman* and *Laws* support a strong sepa-ration of divine commonwealths from human ones. Whether the golden age when gods ruled, as described in the *Critias*, *Laws*, and *Statesman*, is the same as the ideal, that is, the true natural aristocracy, is more difficult to ascertain. In the *Laws*, the golden age is located even further back in time than the cyclopean starting-point of the earlier discussion. In the triads of Book 4, Vico counts the divine as first, and the heroic and human monarchy as second and third. Why he does not consider the eternal com-monwealth (the subject of the conclusion) the first kind, based on his own earlier distinction (*NS* 925), must be explained by the fact that Vico at-tributes a list of four kinds of commonwealths, different from his own and including the divine, to Plato.

Regardless of how Vico arrived at the number four, the idea behind dividing according to the number of human rulers into three and the addi-tion of a fourth for the divine rule is the best explanation of why Vico calls Plato's ideal the fourth type. The subtitle supports strongly that the fourth is an eternal city ruled by a divine ruler, and that the other three are the only human types. Tactius, not Plato, is the most likely source for Vico's exhaustive division in terms of the number of rulers (*NS* 29, 1004). Tacitus is drawing on Plato, and Vico must have known that Plato is the origin of the division of commonwealths present in most political philosophies. Vico could be aware of the same division in Plato, or attribute Tacitus's account to Plato as he does with the later Neoplatonic mistakes about poetry. Plato is identified with political philosophy (*NS* 1109), so this truth about the types of commonwealths is perhaps attributed to him in principle, rather than based on a reading of a particular dialogue. It would be odd for Vico to collapse Plato and Tacitus on this point given that he usually keeps them distinct, but there does seem to be real continuity between Plato and Tacitus on the types of cities.

In addition to reinforcing the reading that the fourth commonwealth is the ideal city of Plato, the subtitle of the conclusion—"On an Eternal Commonwealth, in Each Kind Best, Ordained by Divine Providence"— indicates that the eternal commonwealth is governed by providence. The first sentence elaborates on this point, saying that the fourth kind "conceived by Plato was brought into being by providence from the first beginnings of the nations" (*NS* 1097). This point is connected to the second reference to Plato in the conclusion where Vico praises Plato as the prince of political philosophers who shows that providence governs human institutions (*NS* 1109). As noted earlier, Vico credits Plato with deserving to be called "divine" for his doctrine of providence, in opposition to Stoic fate or Epicurean chance (*NS* 365). Although Vico praises Plato for acknowledging some form of divine providence, he does not mention that Plato conceived of this temporal unfolding of the ideal city ruled by a "Greatest and Best" God (*NS* 1098). Plato is credited with knowing that providence governs the universe, but not with tracing how that governing manifests itself in history. Vico moves beyond Plato regarding the relationship of providence and history.

Consider how in the conclusion Vico describes the way providence acts in history: "Here was formed a state so to speak of monastic commonwealths or of solitary sovereigns under the government of a Greatest and Best whom they themselves created for their faith out of the flash of the thunderbolts, in which this true light of God shone forth for them: that he governs mankind" (*NS* 1098). Vico describes the first cyclopean monarchy rising indirectly from the power of individual fathers through their fear of Jove, the thundering sky (ibid.). To whom else would the fierce, proud giants bow but to God? In this way Vico begins with the giants who invent the idea of Jove, and are guided to do so by God's plan for human beings. Human beings act freely, neither by fate, nor by chance, since the results are always the same (*NS* 1108). Plato does not explain how the transition from giants to first citizens and rulers occurred in this way, guided by providence. Vico establishes that the first idea of providence, the truth that "he governs mankind" (*NS* 1098), is itself the result of divine guidance.

Providence governs the first rulers and enables them to govern others with this divine source of authority. In this way, God is the first instance of "the two great lights of natural order," that "he who cannot govern himself must let himself be governed by another who can. Second, that the world is always governed by those who are naturally fittest" (*NS* 1105). Plato agrees with these political principles, which are true for God ruling humankind, heroic human beings ruling others, and human reason ruling individual passions.

Vico presents another way to see the relationship of Plato's ideal city and history. Vico does not locate the ideal city in the past, as Critias did for the ancient Athens of the age of Zeus, nor in the more distant past as the *Laws* and *Statesman* did for the golden age ruled by Chronos, nor in the future as projected as possible in the *Republic* and, to a lesser extent but on similar grounds, in the *Laws*. All of Plato's dialogues agree that the ideal city does not exist in the present. Recall that for the *Republic* and the *Laws* the conditions for the ideal city are that power and wisdom coincide. In human terms, the ideal city exists when philosophers are kings or kings are philosophers. In divine terms, God governs under these conditions, as both Greatest and Best, as the most powerful and most wise ruler of "the great city of the human race" (*NS* 342). So what Vico is suggesting is the real existence of the ideal city, but not as a human city existing in the past, present, or future. The ideal commonwealth does not exist in any one of these dimensions of time, but in them all eternally. The history itself, past, present, and future, is ideal. For Vico, God governs "the great city of the human race" eternally, and ideal eternal history is the pattern of that eternal governance, in past, present, and future. History is the face of time which reveals its divine guidance. Plato sees that "time is the moving image of eternity" (*Ti.* 37d), but he does not glimpse the face of God in that movement in the same way Vico does.

From Vico's perspective, when Plato sought the intersection of the ideal city and history, he missed how his idea of providence could contain the answer. Vico praises Plato for his idea of providence, but Plato does not envision the whole history of the human race as the ideal city with God as its governor even in corrupt human times. Thinking of the human race as itself one city ruled by God is not present in Plato, though in the *Statesman* the cycles of history apply to humankind universally. The mediation of Augustine between Plato and Vico becomes clear in this move by Vico concerning providence in the "Conclusion." Whereas in the *Statesman* myth, there is an epoch of unwinding when God is absent, and God only returns to rescue the remnants of humanity, for Vico God works throughout history turning the evil human beings do to good. Vico's providence is distinctively Augustinian in this respect, as I have shown above.

Vico also echoes Augustine when he criticizes Plato for his ignorance of the Fall of man in the *Autobiography*. Recall that Vico reports that he was led to "the thought of meditating an ideal eternal law that should be observed in a universal city after the idea or design of providence, upon which idea have since been founded all the commonwealths of all times and all nations" by his study of Platonic metaphysics (*A* 122). Immediately following this acknowledgment of his intellectual starting-point in Plato's metaphysics, Vico distinguishes himself from Plato by adding that "this was the ideal republic that Plato should have contemplated as a consequence of his metaphysic; but he was shut off from it by ignorance of the fall of the first man" (ibid.). Vico sees himself as appropriating Plato's ideal for his own purposes in the *Autobiography*, just as he will do in the conclusion of the *New Science*.

What is the reader to make of Vico's linking the acknowledgment of "the fall of the first man" and his ideal eternal history? Vico's ideal eternal history is not the linear sacred history of Fall, Redemption, and Judgment. The criticism cannot be understood in the same light as Augustine's charge against Porphyry's denial of the incarnation, or Dante's relegation of the virtuous pagans, including Plato, to a shadowy circle of the inferno. In both cases, Augustine and Dante are opposing the Christian linear history to the false pagan cyclic history. There is no such simple interpretation of Vico's charge against Plato, because Vico's own use of the Fall of man, as well as the linear history it implies, is far from central.[17] Unlike Augustine or Dante, Vico singles out the first stage of sacred history, the Fall, and then grafts that element onto the cyclic history of the pagans. The result is that Vico's ideal eternal history resembles Plato's views of history more than it does Augustine's or Dante's. Vico considers the Fall as part of a philosophical, not theological, description of the human condition. If this is a truth accessible without faith, then Plato is not kept from this insight because he did not have access to revelation.

Even more perplexing is that Plato does have a sense of the falleness of human beings, though not the incarnation and redemption through a divine mediator. Plato describes how far the human soul has been distorted from its immortal beauty in the image of the statue of the sea god Glaucus who, once beautiful, is so covered in barnacles and worn down that it looks like a monster not a god (*R.* 611d). The image of the souls being dragged down from their essential nature and losing their wings in the *Phaedrus* myth is another way in which the idea of the Fall is a central part of the Platonic account of human nature (*Phdr.* 248a–c). Education becomes necessary to remedy this fallen state of being.

If Plato's ignorance of the Fall is not a clear explanation of how he differs from Vico on providence, then what is a better explanation? What is it that kept Plato from contemplation of the eternal commonwealth which exists in history, and discovery of the ideal eternal history in Vico's sense?

One plausible reading would view Plato as lacking the biblical idea of a personal God who "counts the number of the stars, to all of them He assigns names" (*Ps.* 147: 4), and knows the plight of each sparrow and the number of hairs on an individual's head (*Matt.* 10: 29–30). Plato incorporates the image of fallen souls himself, and his entire work is animated by the need for education to make us human. Plato also knows that God governs the universe. It is concerning the nature of the governing that Vico sides with Augustine, not Plato. Plato does not inherit as Vico does the fundamental myth of the *ricorso* that God enters history. Since God is omniscient for Christian theology, historical details are objects of divine knowledge. In this way, history itself can become an object of divine knowledge and governing in all its details, including what Plato excluded as purely human, when God is not guiding the unwinding of the universe. Vico adds to the pagan historical cycles a Christian dimension, when he asserts that God governs all the phases, good and bad, turning the evil into good. The Augustinian development of providence beyond Plato's idea of God as the measure and governor of all things places Vico closer to Augustine than to Plato on the nature of God, though all three agree on the existence of a divine governor.

The conclusion amplifies the *Autobiography*'s recognition that Plato deserves praise for making philosophy of history and divine providence central to his thought, though differently from Vico. As closely as the *Statesman* approximates ideal eternal history with its cosmic perspective, it does not claim that God governs the history of the human race as a universal city. Even so, Plato's influential definition of time as "the moving image of eternity" (*Ti.* 37d) is essential for understanding what Vico means by ideal eternal history. Vico preserves this debt to Plato in the *Autobiography* and the conclusion of the *New Science*.

The uniqueness of Vico's discovery is that in his metaphysics, history is the primary object of contemplation. Lady Metaphysic "contemplates in God the world of human minds, which is the metaphysical world, in order to show His providence in the world of human spirits, which is the civil world or world of nations" (*NS* 2). Plato approximates this level of metaphysical contemplation of history in the *Laws* and *Statesman*, but he did not list "history" as among the highest objects of knowledge (e.g., goodness, justice, beauty, etc.) in his description of the Divided Line (*R.* 509d–11e). The fundamental division of the Line is into being and becoming, and insofar as history is identified with becoming, it is not the object of knowledge, but only of opinion. Vico, on the hand, places history among the *archai*, as objects of *nous* or contemplative knowledge. Saying that history is something Lady Metaphysic can contemplate "in God" is the most striking evidence that history for Vico is an idea in God's mind. In effect, Vico discovers a new Platonic form (*idea*).

Platonic descriptions of eternity and time initially make an idea of history seem impossible, for that would be equivalent to having an idea of becoming itself, when becoming is "what is not," while ideas are "what is." Nothing in the realm of coming to be and passing away perfectly embodies any of the forms, and the nature of the participation between individuals and ideas is a vexed problem in the interpretation of the Platonic dialogues. But the *Timaeus* insight that "time is the moving image of eternity" reinforces the kinship, not just the difference, that exists between the realms of being and becoming (*Ti.* 37d). The appearances in the realm of becoming are the appearances of the realities.

Vico begins to unravel the paradox of ideal eternal history when he explicitly states that "though this world has been created in time and particular, the institutions established therein by providence are universal and eternal" (*NS* 342). History can be an object of human knowledge and a subject of philosophy's concern, because history contains this universal dimension. As mentioned earlier, the idea of history as philosophical is a new one. Aristotle ranked poetry as more philosophical because he considered history as wholly particular. Vico agrees that knowledge must be of what is universal, but he thinks history is universal. The matters of history are particular, and philology must study these particulars. Philosophy sees the "forms" providence creates in the "matters" of history (*NS* 629). The *New Science*, through the combination of the two, reveals an ideal eternal history which is the pattern that underlies and is embodied imperfectly in the courses that all the nations run in time.

The idea of history is discovered by studying historical particulars, so Vico is not guilty of making history into a theoretical construct imposed upon historical particulars. Vico's idea of history emerges when philosophy discovers a pattern from the details of history itself. If there is a form or pattern that can be discerned, then the paradox is made intelligible. There can be a way that time is eternal if it unfolds itself in universal, unchanging patterns. The *New Science* as a combination of philosophy and philology was required to discover such an idea of history.

Reading Plato with Vico generates an understanding of Platonic form as dynamic not static. In defense of this approach, consider the desideratum of the *Sophist* that life and being coincide as what is most real. "But tell me in heaven's name, are we really to be so easily convinced that change, life, soul, understanding have no place in that which is perfectly real—that it has neither life nor thought, but stands immutable in solemn aloofness, devoid of intelligence?—That, sir, would be a strange doctrine to accept"

(*Sph.* 249a). This strange doctrine is precisely what gets misattributed to Plato under the epistemological category "the Platonic theory of the forms" which are devoid of all life and change because they are considered apart from their participation in life. The conclusion of the *Sophist* on this question is that both change and the unchangeable are real: "it seems that only one course is open to the philosopher who values knowledge and the rest above all else. He must refuse to accept from the champions either of the one or of the many forms the doctrine that all reality is changeless, and he must turn a deaf ear to the other party who present reality as everywhere changing. Like a child begging for both, he must declare that reality or the sum of things is both at once—all that is unchangeable and all that is in change" (*Sph.* 249c–d).

Plato is suggesting a middle way between Parmenides and Heraclitus. In contemplating ideal eternal history, Vico brings Platonism closer to achieving this desire to understand the participation between the eternal and the temporal, the most real and that which comes to be and passes away. The immanence of the transcendent God in the human world through the aspect of divine providence brings divinity and the realm of becoming closer than any other Platonic metaphysics.

Chapter 8

The Serious Poet: Divine and Human

I have explored how Vico's central theme "ideal eternal history" resonates more with Plato than is usually recognized. This connection about the nature of the human world brings their thought much closer together. Now I will return to the question of the quarrel between philosophy and poetry, where first impressions place Vico and Plato on opposite sides of the quarrel. I argued in chapter 1, that Vico's criticism of Plato for leading all other philosophers in his train in the belief that Homer was a philosopher is more an indictment of the Neoplatonic allegorization than anything in Plato himself (*NS* 780). In chapter 4, I picked up this thread again with Augustine who explored the other side of Plato's engagement with the poets, in considering his moral critique of Homer in the *Republic*. As I said, though Vico does not acknowledge it, his own search for the true Homer is motivated by a moral critique of Homer similar to Plato's in the *Republic*.

Plato's Poetic Metaphysics

Vico does not raise the most paradoxical question about his first author; namely, how is it that the same Plato, who is so harsh in judging the poets, is also himself a great poet?[1] Understanding how Plato leaves a place for a truthful use of images, such as his own, requires insights from the *Laws*, *Timaeus*, *Sophist*, *Republic*, and the *Symposium*. The crucial point for seeing that Vico and Plato do not stand far apart even on poetry, where they seem furthest apart, is that Plato does not reject all uses of the imagination and all poetry in principle, but makes a division between true and false images, and true and false poetry. What poetry imitates determines its worth, just as the object of *eros* determines its worth. Just as Diotima teaches about *eros* in the *Symposium*, the use of language in poetry as well as in rhetoric is itself neither good nor bad.

In the *Laws* serious and playful activity is contrasted. What is serious is the divine not the human. But serious poetry (*poiesis*) can be either divine or human, since some human beings imitate the divine in their poetry. In the *Republic* only serious poetry is admitted into the just city, and one who composes it is called "an austere and less pleasing poet" (*R.* 398a). Divine poetry has already been alluded to, with the definition "time is the moving image (*eikon*) of eternity" from the *Timaeus* in the discussion of history. The Demiurge's making of the cosmos is the model for true human image-making. Vico draws upon the analogy of divine and human making in the inaugural orations, as I pointed out in chapter 2. In one of the most Platonic of the inaugural orations, Vico overlooks the objections of the theologians about comparing God to an artist or craftsman, and states plainly that "God is the master artist of nature; the mind, we may say, the god of the arts" (*IO*, 1.5).[2] Notably, Vico does acknowledge that the way God creates is very different from human making, so the point the theologians seek to preserve is maintained in Vico.

Vico explicitly acknowledges the Platonic dimension of the *Ancient Wisdom*. As I mentioned in the introduction to this third part on Plato, the debt of the *Ancient Wisdom* to the *Cratylus* is among the direct references to Plato's dialogues in Vico (*A* 148; *NS* 401, 431, 444). Vico explains that just as Plato sought wisdom in Greek etymology, so he would do so in the Latin language. The strongest statement is in the *Second Response*, where Vico says, "I was stimulated to this enterprise by the example of Plato's *Cratylus*, where he sought to investigate the ancient wisdom of the Greeks by the same method; and also by the authority of Varro . . . " (*AW* 155). Plato, and Iamblichus following his example, was right to resist the rival view that names were arbitrary. Confronted with ignorance about the origins of words, such theorists wrongly declare their meanings arbitrary and as a result "have given peace to their ignorance" (*NS* 444). But the speculation of these Platonists on what the words meant was "mere conjecture" and "vain" (*NS* 401).

Vico thinks Plato as well as Iamblichus looked for the natural meanings of words (rightly rejecting the idea that they were arbitrary) in vain because they lacked the insights of his "Poetic Logic." There Vico explains that in order to find the true origins of words, one must realize that the first humans thought radically differently from humans now. Plato, along with everyone else, is guilty of thinking that his kind of language is as old as the world. "For that first language, spoken by the theological poets, was not a language in accord with the nature of things it dealt with (as must have been the sacred language invented by Adam, to whom God granted divine onomathesia, the giving of names to things according to the nature of each), but was fantastic speech making use of physical substances endowed with life and most of them imagined to be divine" (*NS* 401). The etymologies of Plato's *Cratylus* suggest or assume much more extensive powers of abstraction than were present during the divine and heroic time of the origins of articulate speech. Plato's *Cratylus* is central to Vico as a springboard for the investigation of poetic logic. No one before Vico understood the origin of the meaning of names, but at least Plato had the intuition that the meanings of names were significant, and for this Vico acknowledges him.

I will not explore further here the parallels stemming from Vico's reading of Plato's *Cratylus*, since it does not directly shed light on the question of their respective solutions to the quarrel of philosophy and poetry.[3] Indeed there are frequent references to Plato's dialogues in the *Ancient Wisdom*, each of which could take the reader into another set of questions. For example, in addition to the *Cratylus*, the reader of the *Ancient Wisdom* can see Vico incorporating the metaphysics of the *Timaeus*, which he mentions in his *Autobiography* (*A* 122) that he admired and followed, as I noted in chapter 7. I will focus specifically on how Vico illuminates divine and human making in the *Ancient Wisdom*, since the model of divine making is essential for understanding how Plato and also Vico understand the truth of images. Images are evaluated for both Plato and Vico in terms of a metaphysics in which one of the central ideas (and perhaps even the middle term) is *poiesis*.

The analogy of divine and human making is clearly stated in the opening section of the *Ancient Wisdom* which introduces the *verum esse ipsum factum* principle. Historicistic interpretations of Vico cite the very paragraphs where the proof of their error is made clear. Vico does not separate ideas of human making and truth from divine making and truth. Immediately after stating his discovery of the convertibility of *verum* and *factum* in Latin, Vico writes: "and therefore the first truth is in God, because God is the first Maker; this first truth is infinite, because He is the Maker of all things; it is completed truth, because it represents to Him all the elements of things, both external and internal, since He contains them" (*AW* 46). Vico continues in this Platonic vein, when he delineates the reason for divine knowledge being complete and human incomplete in terms of the distinction between discursive (*dianoia* or *ratio*) and non-discursive thought (*nous* or *intellectus*) (ibid.). Vico explains that "to know (*scire*) is to put together the elements of things. Hence discursive thought (*cogitatio*) is what is proper to the human mind, whereas intelligence (*intelligentia*) is proper to God's mind" (ibid.).

Vico illustrates these ideas with an analogy which resembles Nicholas of Cusa's mathematical images. In fact, the entire discussion resembles Cusa's, since the pairs of opposites, infinite and finite, complete and incomplete, *ratio* and *intellectus*, are fundamental in Cusa.[4] Vico compares divine truth to "a solid image like a statue," and contrasts human truth as "a monogram or a surface image like a painting" (ibid.). God's truth is knowledge of the inner and the outer, not seeing just surfaces, but analogous to seeing all three dimensions of a figure as opposed to only two. The explanation of this analogy is that "just as divine truth is what God sets in order and creates in the act of knowing it, so human truth is what man puts together and makes in the act of knowing it. Thus, science is knowledge of the genus or mode by which a thing is made" (ibid.). Then Vico returns to the image for further clarification: "As we said, God makes a solid thing because He comprehends all the elements, man a plane image because he comprehends the outside elements only" (*AW* 46–47).

Vico repeats the model of divine making when he refers to the *verum-factum* principle in the *New Science* as well, so this cannot be dismissed as a part of Vico's earlier thought which was later abandoned. In the "Principles" of the *New Science* Vico concisely restates the analogy of knower and objects of knowledge at the divine and human levels: "Whoever reflects on this cannot but marvel that the philosophers should have bent all their energies to the study of the world of nature, which, since God made it, He alone knows; and that they should have neglected the study of the world of nations, of the civil world, which, since men had made it, men could come to know" (*NS* 331). Vico's *Scienza nuova* in its very title shows that Vico maintains his earlier distinction between what human beings can know (*scienza*) because they have made it, and what they cannot know, but can only witness (*coscienza*) because God made it. Vico draws this same distinction in his *Autobiography* (*A* 127).

What God makes is serious, for it is more real than what human beings make, as a statue has more reality than a painting of a statue. But human beings are capable of making serious things as well. Human activities can be divided into those which imitate the truth and those which represent falsehood. Insofar as the human imitates the divine, the creation should be taken seriously (cf. *NS* 1410). The Vichian scientist meets the requirements of serious human making by taking God's making as the model. Both Vico and Plato embody in their own writing the ideal for human making, namely that it be "*vero e severo*" and "austere" (*NS* 814; *R.* 398a). Given Plato's famous critique of poets, first it is important to show how Plato leaves room for such serious human poetry. The *Sophist* and *Symposium* will clarify the role of images in the philosophical life for Plato.

The *Republic* dwells almost exclusively on the misuse of images. There are two important exceptions; first, there is the allowance for a human "austere and less pleasing poet" (*R.* 398a), and second, the description of God's making of real objects as a model for all other making in the Divided Line and in the critique of imitation (*mimesis*) as three removes from reality in *Republic* 10.[5] The culmination of the *Sophist* is the definition of the sophist as a maker of false images, which is appropriate to the subject of the dialogue. Yet in the division which leads to this definition, the possibility of a human truthful maker of images appears, though it remains tangential to this conversation. This thread might have been picked up in the projected dialogue *The Philosopher*, but it was never written.[6] Even so, the division of images in the *Sophist* suggests the role images could play for philosophers as opposed to sophists.

Just as in Vico, *poiesis* for Plato must first be divided into divine or human (*Sph.* 265b). This division of making into divine and human is as essential to avoid errors as the division of governing into divine and human was in the *Statesman*. If one thinks that all governing is merely human, or all creation or image-making is merely human, then there is no standard for justice or truth of regimes or images. If there is providence and not merely fate or chance ruling the cosmos, then one must begin with divine making, knowing, and governing, to understand their human counterparts. One must look to the originals before one can judge the images.

The sophist thinks there are no originals so that knowledge is not defined by imitation (*mimesis*) of originals.[7] This denial is also fundamental to the *Republic*'s famous images of education as well as the *Sophist*. For the sophists who live by the light of the fire in the Cave rather than the Sun outside it, images are not copies of any greater reality. If all is appearance, the distinction between appearance and reality disappears. If one takes the sophist's point of view, the division between knowledge and opinion collapses, and Plato's images of the Cave as well as the Line depend on this distinction. All knowledge is relative to what human beings make, and there is no further standard to judge its truth.[8] Hearing this description of the sophist, a reader of Vico might place Vico in this category based upon his *verum-factum* principle, that we can only know what we make. As I have already pointed out, for Vico this principle is true for God as well as human beings, and the truth we make is only two dimensional compared to the divine which is three dimensional. Just as Plato's *Laws* (*Leg.* 884a–907d) opens with an eloquent prelude to a law defending providence against atheism, so Vico's *New Science* seeks to persuade the reader that wisdom is inseparable from piety (*NS* 1112). The apprehension of Jove is the beginning of humanity as well as wisdom, for then there is a judge and model outside the human. The philosopher must remember that there is something which transcends what human beings make. For Vico as for Plato, Protagoras's formula that "man is the measure of all things" must become "God is the measure of all things" (*Leg.* 716c).

After the initial division of productive art into divine and human, and the subdivision of each into production of originals or of images, there is a further division of human images. The *Sophist* leaves room for truthful human making by dividing images (*eidolon*) into likenesses (*eikones*) as well as phantasms (*phantasma*). The former are truthful and the latter deceptive. This division is first made early in the dialogue (*Sph.* 235a–36c), and after a long digression it is completed at the end to refine the definition of the sophist (*Sph.* 264b–68d). In both of these parts of the conversation, the crucial division is between making likenesses and making phantasms. The making of likenesses (*eikastike*) "consists in creating a copy that conforms to the proportions of the original in all three dimensions and giving moreover proper colour to every part" (*Sph.* 235d). Not all image-makers seek to imitate the truth in this way, but instead "leaving the truth to take care of itself, do in fact put into the images they make, not the real proportions, but those that will appear beautiful" (*Sph.* 236a). In such semblance-making (*phantastike*) the image only appears to be a likeness (*eikon*).

At this point in the conversation the characters are unsure under which of these arts the sophist belongs (*Sph.* 236d). Near the end of the dialogue this division and the question of where to put the sophist is recalled (*Sph.* 264b). The sophist will be caught finally in the net of their division, cornered in the category of maker of phantasms.[9] Since the goal is to define the sophist, the other side of the division is not pursued. As Francis Cornford comments "the sophist creates 'images (*eidola*) in discourse' (*Sph.* 234c); but if there is such a thing in discourse as the production of exact replicas, we are not concerned with it. All the 'images' we are going to consider fall under the inferior branch, the production of semblances, that are not complete reproductions of the original, but involve an element of deceit and illusion."[10] For understanding the sophist, one does not need to pursue the nature of the *eikon*, but to understand the philosopher, and specifically Plato, this is exactly what must be considered.

What is so intriguing about the notion of *eikon* in the *Sophist* is that what remains true to the original is the proportion. Recall Vico's analogy of divine and human truth. What would be the same in a statue and a monogram would not be the depth and inner dimension, but the proportion. A sketch of a statue, which is essentially how Vico describes human truth, is a truthful representation of the relationship of the parts to the whole in the statue itself. Human beings can imitate the proportions of divine truth.

So Plato does not reject all images or all poetry, only those which do not imitate what is real and true. On the other hand, the *Sophist* does not pursue this left side of the division, for it does not lead to the definition of the sophist. Unlike what the reader of the *Republic*'s Divided Line might expect, in the *Sophist* all images and image-making are not restricted to the lowest level of *phantasma*. The Divided Line itself does not depict true human making, though it does show divine making of the physical objects of the cosmos. When one maps the *Symposium*'s Ladder onto the Divided Line, then one discovers that part of being a philosopher is to create both *logoi* and true virtue in himself. The *Symposium* is about the philosopher, not the sophist, so the place given to images here sheds light on truthful *eikones*. The philosopher loves what is real, not what merely appears to as does the sophist. If the philosopher incorporates images, they would have to be products of *eikastike* (the art of making *eikones*) not *phantastike* (the art of making *phantasma*). Of all the dialogues, the *Symposium* reveals the most about the relationship between philosophy and *eikastike*.

The Ladder image in the *Symposium* depicts the ascent which distinguishes the philosopher from those who love not wisdom but lower things. The *Symposium* is explicit that the lover of beauty will bear fruits of his love at each stage of the ascent, some being pregnant in body, others in soul (*Smp.* 206b; 208e–09a). Thus, the ascent involves creation as well as passionate knowing. There are two moments of each rung; first one loves what one sees or knows, and then one responds by creation. In the lower mysteries which precede the ascent of the philosopher, Diotima tells Socrates that all creatures express the desire for immortality in procreation (*Smp.* 206e–07a; 208b). How does the philosopher express this desire to be immortal?

The answer is discovered in the second to the last rung of the ladder of *eros* where there is a crucial acknowledgment that the philosopher uses language to create in response to what he sees. "After customs he must move on to various kinds of knowledge. The result is that he will see the beauty of knowledge and be looking mainly not at beauty in a single example . . . but the lover is turned to the great sea of beauty, and, gazing upon this, he gives birth to many gloriously beautiful ideas and theories, in unstinting love of wisdom (*philosophia*), until, having grown and been strengthened there, he catches sight of such knowledge, and it is the knowledge of such beauty. . . " (*Smp.* 210c–e). Instead of children, philosophers beget discourses. Plato employs this same analogy in his critique of written speeches as analogous to orphans in the *Phaedrus* (*Phdr.* 275e). Also in the *Phaedrus* one finds the idea that a speech "ought to be constructed like a living creature, with its own body, as it were" (*Phdr.* 264c).

What sort of *logoi* would the philosopher beget at this point in the ascent? The best answer is that the lover of wisdom would create works like Plato's own. If one maps the Line onto the Ladder, the creation of hypotheses and theories from the third level seems to match. Rising above opinion to knowledge is first achieved through *dianoia*. This stage is not the end, not the highest moment of vision or creation in the ascent of the *Symposium*. The sudden sight of Beauty itself must be by *nous*, which is how the philosopher knows forms. The philosopher who has seen the forms could still produce discourses, informed by this direct apprehension of Beauty, but the proper creation after *nous*'s vision of the forms is to become like that oneself.

Consider the transition from the penultimate to the last rung: "'from these lessons he arrives in the end at this lesson, which is learning of this very Beauty, so that in the end he comes to know just what it is to be beautiful. And there in life, Socrates, my friend,' said the woman from Mantinea', there if anywhere should a person live his life, beholding that Beauty" (*Smp.* 211c–d). The creation which manifests at this level is nothing external to oneself; rather it is a virtuous life. Diotima concludes that "in that life alone, when he looks at Beauty in the only way that Beauty can be seen—only then will it become possible for him to give birth not to images of virtue (because he's in touch with no images), but to true virtue (because he is in touch with the true Beauty). The love of the gods belongs to anyone who has given birth to true virtue and nourished it, and if any human being could become immortal, it would be he'" (*Smp.* 212a–b).

This conclusion was anticipated when Diotima explained how souls could be pregnant as well as bodies. Before the ascent passage, she said "they are pregnant with what is fitting for a soul to bear and bring to birth. And what is fitting? Wisdom and the rest of virtue, which all poets beget, as well as all the craftsmen who are said to be creative" (*Smp.* 209a). The true philosopher, who is said to be dear to the gods if anyone is, has as his greatest creation his own virtuous life. The only adequate response to seeing Beauty itself is to try to become beautiful oneself. In this sense, Plato would embrace Pico's idea that one is as a human being "maker and molder of thyself" (*O*, 225). This viewpoint is not Protagorean relativism, since it is in imitation of divine reality that we make ourselves.

This last step is the begetting of true virtue, writing not in a treatise, but on one's own soul. Recall that discourses were compared to children in the *Symposium* and to orphans in the *Phaedrus*. The *Phaedrus* also explains that "there is another sort of discourse, that is brother to the written speech but of unquestioned legitimacy . . . The sort that goes together with knowledge, and is written in the soul of the learner: that can defend itself, and know to whom it should speak and to whom it should say nothing. —You mean no dead discourses, but the living speech, the original of which the written discourse may fairly be called a kind of image" (*Phdr.* 276a). Socrates's claim that he is the "midwife" is significant in this context (*Tht.* 148e–51d). He certainly was the midwife for Plato's *logoi*. Yet Socrates did create, in his own soul and in his life, true virtue. Plato and others were mesmerized by him, and as the fruit of this love of beauty in Socrates, Plato depicted his life as the image of virtue. Socrates did not write anything down, but created his own life which Plato used as an *eikon* of spiritual beauty, goodness, justice, and truth. This act of self-creation gave Socrates the fame, a sort of immortality, for which Vico invokes Socrates at the end of his *Autobiography* (*A* 200). Philosophical writing at its best would imitate this true virtue, and that is what Plato does by making the heroic life of Socrates the central image in the dialogues. Such images born of *eros* for the good, true, and beautiful, will be not the empty *phantasma* on the wall of the Cave manipulated by sophists, but *eikones* created by philosophers for the sake of the conversion of others to see beyond that *eikon* to what it imitated.

The paradox from which I began was that Plato banishes the majority of the artists from his ideal city, but he himself is a great artist. This paradox disappears once one understands how Plato distinguished between images which were likenesses and those which were merely phantasms. The *Sophist* leaves open the possibility of a human maker of images who makes likenesses not phantasms, truthful not false images. Seeing how Plato can consistently incorporate images in his own writing reveals that he is not like some philosophers who criticize rhetoric and the imagination and at the same time masterfully employ them in spite of themselves.[11] It is true that the Divided Line in the *Republic* does not explore the positive place of images, but the Line itself, along with the Ship, the Sun, and the Cave, are essential to the *Republic*, and they are *eikones*, not *phantasma*. Plato not only leaves open the possibility of true images, but the dialogues themselves illustrate the existence of such images without fully accounting for them discursively.

The philosopher is not reducible to the poet, so the quarrel remains. Unlike the sophist, the philosopher is not defined by image-making. For the philosopher, unlike the poet, the image is not judged in itself, but for its ability to make human beings better morally. The philosopher who creates *logoi* which use *eikones*, as Plato himself does, is not primarily encompassed by the divisions which begin from art and divide into acquisitive and productive (*Sph.* 219d). There are also practical and theoretical divisions of knowledge to consider in defining the philosopher. Unfortunately, Plato does not write a dialogue in which he defines the philosopher using this method of division and collection. As I will explore in the final chapter, instead of a definition of the philosopher, Plato presents us with a portrait of Socrates.

Vico's Frontispiece as Platonic *Eikon*

Since Plato wrote dialogues which develop characters, plots, and settings, classifying Plato as a serious poet possesses an inherent plausibility. But how can Vico be read as a serious poet? The key to grasping Vico as a serious poet is understanding the frontispiece of the *New Science* as an *eikon* in Plato's sense.

Vico does not speak of serious philosophical poems as explicitly as Plato does, when he invents the "austere and less pleasing poet" with his philosophical hero (*R.* 398a). When Vico uses the phrases "serious poetry" or "serious poem," he means that of the vulgar poets whose poetry is history (*NS* 1037). For instance, Roman law is an example of a "severe poem" (ibid.). Vulgar wisdom is "*vero e severo*" (*NS* 905), which means true and severe. In the ages of gods and heroes, it is not an aesthetic flourish to say that the sea smiles, but a way to convey information about the world to others. There is no indication that Vico noticed the similarity to Plato's "austere and less pleasing poet." Although Vico's original discovery is this "*vero e severo*" poetry of the theological poets (ibid.), Vico himself is a serious and truthful maker of images as a philosopher in a human age, just as Plato is.

In the *New Science*, Vico explains the use of images to describe abstract ideas in the human age in contrast to the nature of images in the serious poems of the vulgar, theological poets. As Vico had already written when he commissioned the frontispiece of the *New Science*, "when we wish to give utterance to our understanding of spiritual things, we must seek aid from our imagination to explain them and, like painters, form human images of them" (*NS* 402). Unlike the first poets, who described spiritual ideas in physical terms without an intervening metaphorical distance (for instance saying "the sea smiles," "fields were thirsty," and many others (*NS* 405)), "we nowadays reverse this practice in respect of spiritual things, such as the faculties of the human mind, the passions, virtues, vices, sciences, and arts; for the most part the ideas we form of them are so many feminine personifications, to which we refer all the causes, properties, and effects that severally appertain to them" (*NS* 402). The vulgar poets lacked intelligible universals, so their language at the divine and heroic times had to be stretched to accommodate intangible objects. In vulgar poetry, what looks to us like metaphors are in fact true and severe poetic descriptions. On the contrary, in human times the philosophical poets contend with an excess of abstraction and a deficiency of imagination. In the former case, the images have univocal meanings, in the latter, metaphorical or allegorical (*NS* 210).

Vico writes, "it is noteworthy that in all languages the greater part of the expressions related to inanimate things are formed by metaphor from the human body and its parts and from the human senses and passions" (*NS* 405). Vico gives many illustrations of this aspect of language, as mentioned above, to help us understand what cannot be imagined (*NS* 34), and then adds an intriguing explanation. Vico maintains that these facts about language are all "a consequence of our axiom that man in his ignorance makes himself the rule of the universe, for in the examples cited he has made of himself an entire world. So that, as rational metaphysics teaches that man becomes all things by understanding them (*homo intelligendo fit omnia*), this imaginative metaphysics shows that man becomes all things by *not* understanding them (*homo non intelligendo fit omnia*); and perhaps the latter proposition is truer than the former, for when man understands he extends his mind and takes in the things, but when he does not understand he makes the things out of himself and becomes them by transforming himself into them" (*NS* 405). The way human beings know by making is the most famous idea in Vico; but how they make because of ignorance is often overlooked, even though it is this ignorance that sows the field of poetic wisdom out of which philosophical wisdom can grow.

How do human beings move from making images to compensate for their ignorance to knowing through their making? Providence is the answer to the question of how this transition happens, for in this aspect God brings knowledge out of ignorance just as He brings good out of evil. Vico does hold that human beings understand things because they make them (*verum esse ipsum factum*), but he maintains that this quintessential human knowledge is based on the initial making because of ignorance. The initial ignorance of human beings leads to the original fantastic making of the world in the image of human beings, and then out of that ignorance providence ordains the development of human knowledge in which human beings make what they know. If it were not for divine providence, human beings would never move beyond the initial ignorance by which they made themselves the measure of all things. Without the action of providence itself, human beings would never discover the limits of their knowledge of the divine and natural worlds and never turn inward to seek self-knowledge. Socrates's quest for self-knowledge began in wonder and with an acknowledgment of ignorance. Without the initial ignorance that led to primitive language and out of which articulate speech evolved, Socrates could not have asked the questions that founded Western philosophy.

What is heroic for the earliest humans is to find a way through the dominant sense to express spiritual or intellectual meanings; what is heroic for the later intellectuals is to reinvest the abstractions with the robust passion and wonder of the first humans. This insight is consistent with Vico's moral philosophy which holds that the passions should be moderated, not mortified or indulged (cf. Plato, *R.* 571e). The most human speech is not wholly intellectual or wholly sensual or fantastical. Vico shifts the balance of his own language back to a moderate position by adding the mute language of, or the metaphors of, the frontispiece to stir the imagination of the reader as well as to challenge the intellect.

Vico is a serious poet, a serious maker of images, which are meant to instruct and move, in the terms of Horace's ideal (*Ars. Po.* 1. 333).[12] At the same time, there is a sense in which the images also delight. The reader who understands the *New Science* will delight in it, and Vico explicitly tells the reader he will experience a "divine pleasure" when he narrates or makes the Science for himself (*NS* 349). What does Vico's *eikon* teach us? In what way does it summarize how Vico's *New Science* is "a metaphysics compatible with human frailty"?

The answers are found in "The Idea of the Work" which is a remarkable document. Most emblems placed before similar Renaissance books did not have any explanation much less a lengthy explanation like Vico's; and only through an accident of publishing do we have this one. Vico's anger at the printers, coupled with his subsequent decision not to print the correspondence as he had intended, is turned by providence to good by leaving blank a significant number of pages. The pages had to be filled to avoid an embarrassing gap in numbering. Vico explicitly states the purpose of the engraving in these new pages: "we hope it may serve to give the reader some conception of this work before he reads it, and, with such aid as imagination may afford, to call it back to mind after he has read it" (*NS* 1).

The panoramic intent and moral dimension of the frontispiece are underscored by Vico's comparison with the Tablet of Cebes, saying that as it was a table of moral things (*cose*), so was Vico's of civil things (*cose*) (ibid.).[13] Vico calls his commentary on the engraving, "The Idea of the Work." In Greek "*idea*" is from "*orao*," "I see," whose perfect tense is "*oida*," "I know," and so the title is an illustration of the use of the physical to express the spiritual. Just as Vico said, there are insights to be discovered through the study of the etymology of other languages, such as Greek and German, as he did for Latin, "far beyond their expectations and ours" (*NS* 33). With the Greek roots uncovered, the reader can see that the frontispiece is what Vico saw with his mind's eye. To know is to have seen as well as to have made.

I cannot explain all of the symbolism here; that task is accomplished by Vico himself in "The Idea of the Work: Explanation of the Picture Placed as Frontispiece To Serve as Introduction to the Work" (*NS* 1–41). Instead I will highlight the aspects which illustrate the Platonic themes, and especially how philosophy relates to the human world. Since understanding what Vico means by "a metaphysics compatible with human frailty" is the underlying question of this study, the most important image is that of Lady Metaphysic.

Of Lady Metaphysic, Vico first simply says she stands above the natural realm as "the name means as much" (*NS* 2). Recall that in "On Wisdom in General" Vico defines metaphysics as wisdom: "'wisdom' came to mean knowledge of natural divine things; that is, metaphysics, called for that reason divine science, which seeking knowledge of man's mind in God, and recognizing God as the source of all truth, must recognize him as the regulator of all good. So that metaphysics must essentially work for the good of the human race. . . " (*NS* 365). Following Cicero (*De Off.* I. 153), who was in turn appropriating Plato (*R.* 598d), Vico holds that "true wisdom, then, should teach the knowledge of divine institutions (*cose*) in order to conduct human institutions (*cose*) to the highest good" (*NS* 364). (*De Off.* I. 153). In the introduction to the *Ancient Wisdom*, Vico praised his friend Doria for applying metaphysics to human matters, so metaphysics was already seen in light of the human realm, and therefore had to be "compatible with human frailty." Lady Metaphysic is the embodiment of this sort of wisdom, which is the knowledge of divine things and at the same time sheds light on the human things. This makes sense of the difficult claim that Lady Metaphysic "contemplates in God the world of human minds, which is the metaphysical world, in order to show His providence in the world of human spirits, which is the civil world or world of nations" (*NS* 2).

Frontispiece to Vico's *New Science*, 1730/1744

Vico imagines metaphysics as a lady with winged temples, whose hands tremble in ecstasy, while she balances precariously on the globe and reflects what she sees in God into the human world. For the ray of providence to be reflected, the heart of metaphysic, represented as a jewel, must be "pure and clean" (*NS* 5). Vico explicitly contrasts this metaphysics with that of the Stoics and the Epicureans. The heart of the Stoic metaphysicians is not "pure and clean" but "dirty or befouled with pride of spirit" and the heart of the Epicurean metaphysicians is likewise unclean because of "vileness of bodily pleasures" (ibid.). This division is the same one which Vico makes an axiom, when he admits the political philosophers, chiefly the Platonists, and excludes the Stoics and Epicureans (*NS* 130). Lady Metaphysic is among the political philosophers, and resembles the Platonists more than any other sect.

The "pure and clean heart," as I mentioned in part 2, chapter 6, shows the Augustinian dimension of Vico's thought. Augustine conjures a similar image, when he describes the act of offering "on the altar of the heart, the sacrifice of humility and praise, and the flame on the altar is the burning fire of charity" (*CG* 10.3, 375). The Christian scriptures's beatitude that the pure of heart see God informs both images (*Matt.* 5: 1–12). Lady Metaphysic is neither guilty of excessive self-love nor inordinate love of physical pleasures.

The jewel is also the clearest expression that Lady Metaphysic represents the ideal philosopher, who not only contemplates but also educates the human race. Such a metaphysics acknowledges the social nature of human beings (*NS* 2). Vico explains that the jewel also "indicates that the knowledge of God does not have its end in metaphysic taking private illumination from intellectual institutions (*cose*) and thence regulating merely her own moral institutions (*cose*), as hitherto the philosophers have done. For this would have been signified by a flat jewel, whereas the jewel is convex, thus reflecting and scattering the ray abroad, to show that metaphysics should know God's providence in the public moral institutions or civil customs, by which the nations have come into being and maintain themselves in the world" (*NS* 5). Again Lady Metaphysic is the image for the axiom about philosophy's relationship to the human world. She does not withdraw as a solitary philosopher would (*NS* 130); rather she understands that "to be useful to the human race, philosophy must raise and direct weak and fallen man" (*NS* 129).

What enables Metaphysic "to raise up" the human race are the wings at her temples. Vico introduces Lady Metaphysics as "the lady with the winged temples" (*NS* 2), but he does not elaborate on the philosophical history of wings as the image for *eros* from Plato's *Phaedrus* to the Renaissance commonplaces, nor does he mention his own discovery of the identification of wings and heroes in poetic wisdom. Both of these poetic and philosophical resonances amplify the nature of Vico's metaphysics.

In the *Phaedrus*, when *eros* for the beautiful is stirred, the wings which were lost by the fallen soul begin to grow back (*Phdr.* 248e–52c). In the famous image of the soul as charioteer of white and black horses, each part of the soul is winged. The charioteer has winged temples, just as Vico's Lady Metaphysic does. Recall that in Pico's *Oration*, he said "we shall fly up with winged feet, like earthly Mercuries" (*O*, 231). In Ficino's commentary on the *Phaedrus*, he distinguishes two erotic impulses of the higher soul, that of the will for the good and the intellect for the truth. Ficino says that "there are twin wings, a double impulse innate to the intelligence and lifting the soul to supernals: one is the impulse in the intellect which turns back with all its strength towards the divine truth, the other, the impulse in the will which turns back with all its strength towards the divine good."[14] The second idea of love directed to the good as a characteristic of the will reveals the Augustinian influence on Renaissance Platonic views of love, and this idea of the will is evident in Vico as well (*NS* 399; cf. *AW*, 105–06, *IO*, 1.14).

For a more complete amplification of the idea of *Eros* behind Lady Metaphysic's winged temples, one must turn to Plato's dialogue devoted primarily to *eros*, the *Symposium*. This dialogue was greatly emphasized in the Renaissance. Both Lady Metaphysic and the figure of *Eros* in the *Symposium* are images for the nature of the philosopher and philosophical *eros*, but in Plato's image the balance of opposites is emphasized, while it remains only implicit in Vico's figure. Like many fables about the gods and heroes, Diotima's story begins with the birth of *Eros* (*Smp.* 203b). *Penia* or Poverty is his mother, and she contrived to conceive with *Porus* or Resource at the birthday party for Aphrodite. *Eros* is characterized by lack or poverty as well as by a resourceful mind. *Eros* loves the beautiful and the good which he himself lacks, for love is for that which one lacks and wishes to possess or become. This lack means that *Eros* is not himself a god, but "in between god and mortal" (*Smp.* 202e). This is also how Lady Metaphysic is depicted by Vico.

Another important image of mediation between the divine and human is also echoed in Dante's image of Beatrice. For instance, Lady Metaphysic standing on the Zodiac is reminiscent of the ascent in the *Paradiso* (*Canto* 1), when Dante looks back on the planets below with Beatrice. The Platonic account of *eros*, especially as mediated through Augustine, contributes to Dante's portrait of his guide to the divine mysteries after he leaves Virgil behind. Beatrice is Diotima as well as Heavenly *Eros* for Dante. But Dante's portrait of Beatrice is more like Agathon's of the beautiful *Eros* than Diotima's needy and yet resourceful *Eros*.

Unlike Dante's Beatrice, Vico's Lady Metaphysic is more like Virgil, for her knowledge is a rational civil theology of divine providence, instead of a revealed faith in divine grace. So Vico transforms the imagery of the Tuscan Homer just as Plato does Homer himself. In Vico, Beatrice becomes a human woman with frailty as well as strength. She is not an unreal idealization of a woman, and she is not even especially feminine. She is struggling to maintain balance, with her hands trembling in ecstasy, and the face seeing beauty is not itself especially beautiful. For Vico as for Dante, "to know . . . is to love, to love is to see, to see is to know," but Vico emphasizes the love which is the love of what one lacks, and of which as a human being one can only get a glimpse.[15] As Aristotle says, a glimpse of what one loves is better than seeing up close something else (*Par. An.* 644b–45a). Vico does not make the mistake Agathon does of making *Eros* itself beautiful (*Smp.* 201e). Vico does not divinize Lady Metaphysic, but she is more than human.

As I suggested above, in addition to the wings signifying the *eros* of philosophical wisdom, in the *New Science* the wings are primarily associated with their meaning in poetic wisdom. When one explores Vico's explanations of the wings as a hieroglyph in the *New Science*, one uncovers a connection between metaphysics and heroism. Consistently Vico describes the wings as symbolizing something belonging to the heroes (*NS* 508; cf. 604, 713). The heroes gave *Eros* a name similar to their own to signify that they alone had solemn nuptials (*NS* 508; cf. *Cra.* 398c–e). Metaphysic's wings mark her as heroic, and her placement relative to the human and divine realms accords with the claim that "the heroic nature is midway between the human and the divine" (*NS* 508, 515). If one looks at the picture closely one can see a counterpoint between the philosophical heroism of Lady Metaphysic and the poetic heroism of the heroic age. The winged helmet of Mercury lies on the ground motionless, and the moving force of the picture is the winged temples of the heroic mind of Metaphysic cooperating with divine providence to educate the human race. Now she is the messenger between the divine and the human.

Most interpretations of the *New Science* ignore the upper half of the frontispiece, with Lady Metaphysic and the Eye of God with its Rays of Divine Providence, as well as Vico's explanation of these in the "Idea of the Work."[16] Even from a narrowly aesthetic point of view, it is impossible to

understand the image unless Lady Metaphysic is the pivot. The best interpreters of Vico fasten on to his insights about *fantasia*, memory, the axioms, or the cyclic pattern of history, which are all important, but none of
these parts in themselves can provide a vision of the whole the way the
frontispiece does by featuring Vichian metaphysics. None of these selec-
tive studies can answer the question of how Vico's work might meet Horace's
standards: to instruct, delight, and move (*Ars. Po.* l. 333). None can answer how Vico's frontispiece can be considered an *eikon* in Plato's sense.
For recall that Plato defined an *eikon* as an image that is true to the proportion of the original (*Sph.* 235d), and to see proportion one must consider
not only the parts separately but how they fit into the whole. Vico's aesthetic as well as philosophical achievement in the frontispiece is represent-
ing the proper proportion of human wisdom in relationship to the divine.
The part which is the key to the whole is the one whose function is the
contemplation of the whole, and whose ideal is eloquence as wisdom
speaking.

To see how Vico intends the image as a whole, it is best to begin at the
end: "last of all, to state the idea of the work in the briefest summary, the
entire engraving represents the three worlds in the order in which human
minds of the gentiles have been raised from earth to heaven. All the
hieroglyphs visible on the ground denote the world of nations to which
men applied themselves before anything else. The globe in the middle represents the world of nature which the physicists later observed. The
hieroglyphs above signify the world of minds and of God which the metaphysicians finally contemplated" (*NS* 42). This paragraph delineating the
world of nations, the world of nature, and the world of minds and God, or
the metaphysical world, organizes the profusion of detail in the picture to
reveal an upward movement. The passive construction that the human
minds of the gentiles "have been raised" conveys that providence governs
the development of human wisdom.

Providence is the object of Metaphysic's contemplation, and through it
she understands the civil world. The world of nations occupies a crucial
place as the subject matter of human Science, but without providence there
would be no ideal eternal pattern to discover. The world of nature, represented by the globe, is not the subject matter for Vichian metaphysics.[17]
Vico plays on the Greek etymology that metaphysic's name means it is
above nature (*NS* 2). Vico follows Plato's *Timaeus* more closely than did
Dante and others, when he takes up the position that physics is "a likely
story " (*Ti.* 29d). Vico's adoption of the Socratic teaching that human
beings should first know themselves is one of his most fundamental debts

to Plato's dialogues. The idea that providence governs the universe and that what human beings can know is the human world are deep parallels between the thought of Plato and Vico. These two points alone make the metaphysics of the *New Science* more closely akin to Plato's metaphysics than to any other.

The image of Lady Metaphysic shows that metaphysics is at the heart of how the *New Science* seeks to instruct, delight, and move. The reader who experiences "divine pleasure" will achieve this through contemplation of providence's governing of history. But the contemplation of Vichian metaphysics is not introspective; instead, metaphysics knows itself in relationship to what it is not: namely, the Divine Eye and the vulgar poetic wisdom of Homer. There are the two distinct but interrelated moments of wisdom: vulgar, poetic wisdom and esoteric, philosophical wisdom, with the philosophical growing out of poetic which is its matrix. Metaphysics is a latecomer in the human world, and as such does not provide its own, certain starting-points. Unlike poetic wisdom, philosophical wisdom imitates God and knows the true as well as grasps the certain.

The statue of blind Homer with a cracked base represents the true Homer behind the corrupted versions of the poems we inherited, which is all that remains of poetic wisdom, along with etymological traces in ancient languages (*NS* 6). Homer lacks the intellectual light of philosophy, but philosophy lacks the firm foundation in the world of nations. The relationship between Lady Metaphysic and the statue of Homer becomes even more significant when one recognizes that Vico's metaphysics is Platonic. Nothing less than "the ancient quarrel of philosophy and poetry" is being depicted silently through that diagonal ray. Vico solves the ancient quarrel by giving the dominance in the heroic age to the vulgar poets and dominance in the age of humans to the philosophers. This solution preserves both as the teachers of humanity, but their wisdom is of a different nature.

As much as Vico was fascinated by his discovery of the poetic wisdom of the first humans, he lived in the human age of the *ricorso*, and therefore his heroism had to be philosophical. No amount of persuasion could make a human being in our age into an Achilles or an Odysseus; but philosophical heroism is possible. Vico seeks to instruct human beings about the entire spectrum of wisdom, and how the poetic is the ground and provides the certainty for later philosophical versions of the principles of humanity. What Vico wants is to encourage human beings to be as heroic as possible in an age when intellect is ascendant and religion has lost its ability to protect the principles of humanity (religion, marriage, and burial) as the foundation of civilization.

Philosophy later proves these certain principles to be true. Vico explains that "D. M." on the urn "represents the common consent of all mankind in the opinion later proved true by Plato, that human souls do not die with their bodies but are immortal" (*NS* 12). Vichian metaphysics can locate all three principles of humanity in the world of nations: religion by the altar and the fire and water on it which were used in taking auspices, marriage symbolized by the torch lit from the fire on the altar, and burial by the urn. Lady Metaphysic sees these certain principles of humanity, and links them to their philosophical correlatives. As I have noted before, the philosophical level of the principles of humanity are strikingly Platonic: divine providence, moderation of the passions, and immortality of human souls.

The duality of the principles of humanity, expressing themselves as certain and poetic, and true and philosophic, demonstrates the beautiful symmetry of Vico's insight into the human world. Just as humanity has two levels, so does the education of human beings. Initially providence is the educator of the human race, establishing the first institutions. As a result of this governing of the world of nations, philosophy can emerge. Philosophers can imitate God because their minds are made in the image of God, and they can claim like the poetic heroes to be sons of Jove (*HM* 244). Just as the Demiurge in the *Timaeus* is described as "free from envy" (*aphthonos*) (*Ti.* 29e), so the philosophical hero wants to share the knowledge of the true for the good of the human race. Vico's God is not self-absorbed like Aristotle's, but a craftsman whose Reason must persuade Necessity (*Ti.* 48a). Likewise Vico's philosopher is not a solitary specialist absorbed in the workings of his own mind, but a hero who seeks to persuade others of the truth of what providence wrought.

The philosopher must be eloquent in order to stir the passions of the audience to endure the difficult path of making oneself human through self-governing and self-knowledge. There is nothing more difficult for a human being than to imitate God in this way, and nothing more satisfying than to stir this *eros* in others as God has in oneself. In the *Symposium*, *Eros* is called "the greatest workmate of *paideia*" (*Smp.* 212b). The work of raising human beings up from their weak and fallen state to wisdom requires a powerful motivating force like *eros*. Through *eros* the human is raised to a state in between the merely human and the divine, for as God rules the universe, the philosophical hero rules his passions. It is the love of the beautiful, the good, and the true that draws human beings to imitate God in their own souls and lives. If the poetic hero had ever denied his divine lineage, he would have no longer been a hero. If a philosopher renounces the true Jove, he cuts himself off from the source of his wisdom; this is why "he who is not pious cannot be truly wise" (*NS* 1112). Vico stirs in the readers of the *New Science* "a productive desire for wisdom," which is a feeling not corrupted by any of the conceits, to "admire, venerate, and desire to unite themselves to the infinite wisdom of God" (*HM* 233; *NS* 1111).

Vico argues that philosophy itself plays a role in what God ordained for the course of nations. Lady Metaphysic as philosophical hero recognizes the role providence has given her in this human age: to replace the poetic hero with a new philosophical heroism, with its new kind of self-mastery and new kind of courage. Philosophical courage is required to moderate or master *eros* from pain and pleasure. She must embody both "know thyself" and "nothing in excess." The knowledge of the dignity of human beings when they imitate God will spur her to heroic acts on behalf of the rest of humanity. At the same time, the awareness of the limits and humble origin of her knowledge will give her a heart that is not befouled by pride, but burns instead with a pious love of God. This stance is rightly called "a metaphysics compatible with human frailty" for it both acknowledges the limits of human knowledge and at the same time demands the maximum of human ability. Vico calls this balance "heroic mind." As the embodiment of Vico's own heroic achievement, the *New Science* is balanced, a metaphysics that neither claims to know all truths nor lacks the courage to find what truths human beings can know.

The frontispiece is essential to a study of Vico's philosophy because Vico intended it to help the reader remember the wisdom of the *New Science* (*NS* 1). Vico's perspective of ideal eternal history adds another dimension to the discussion of the nature of serious philosophical poetry. In particular, Vico's wider context of the changing relationship of sense and intellect aids the reader in understanding the complex nature of Vico's serious philosophical poetry. The frontispiece is a true and serious image of what Vico saw with his mind's eye. Just as the frontispiece is invaluable for grasping Vico's vision of the things divine and human which constitute wisdom, so Plato's portrait of Socrates is a summary image for the philosophical teaching which inspired the entire family of Plato.

Chapter 9

Conclusion: Socrates as Philosophical Hero

I have established the place that Plato leaves for philosophical *eikones,* which the serious poet makes instead of *phantasma,* and the relevance of this division of images for understanding Vico's frontispiece of the *New Science.* Now I can turn to the question: how does Plato himself meet the standards he set for a serious poet? Vico does not ask this question, just as he does not thematize how his *New Science* is itself serious poetry, how the frontispiece is an *eikon,* and how he is a serious philosophical poet. Vico does not credit his first author with inventing this unique philosophical poetry. Instead, Vico criticizes Plato in his *Autobiography,* saying that "Plato adorns rather than confirms his esoteric wisdom with the common wisdom of Homer" (*A* 154). Vico does not see how important Plato's critique of Homer is and how his response is more complex than that of later Platonists; for Plato primarily views Homer as a rival moral teacher of the Greeks, not the source of imagery for allegorical interpretation.

What Vico does point out is that Plato invents "philosophical heroism" (*NS* 1041). Socrates is the hero of Plato's philosophical poetry. Having reached the end of this study's descent through the family of Plato, I will explain what the portrait of Socrates as philosophical hero means for interpreting Vico and his kinship to Plato. The ideas of Plato and Vico on philosophical heroism, which Vico also calls "heroic mind," reveal their kinship more than any other aspect of their thought, for it is the shared educational goal of their philosophy. Further, this aspect of Platonism in Vico comes not from any later Platonist, but from Plato himself.

In what sense is Vico correct in his interpretation that Plato adorns rather than confirms his wisdom with Homer? It is true that Plato does not discover the true Homer as Vico does, and as a result he does not see that poetic wisdom is the foundation of all the arts and sciences, including philosophy. Plato does not speculate as Varro did about the ancient Romans. Recall that Varro held that the stories were once true and, only in their corrupted state as handed down to his own time, committed the serious errors about the nature of gods, heroes, and humans. Vico makes the argument for the Greeks which Varro made for the ancient Romans. Viewed in this light, Vico agrees with Plato that as the poetry of Homer reads now, it is false and does not contain the original poetic wisdom Vico champions. Since Vico posits the corruption of the tales of Homer, he too criticizes the morality of the Homer that Plato knew. If persuaded that there were an earlier poetry of Homer which were true to the nature of the gods, heroes, and humans, Plato could have no disagreement about admitting it.

The reader of Plato can only speculate, based on the reasons behind Plato's judgments and the nature of his own philosophical poetry, whether he would have been persuaded by Vico's argument for the dependence of all arts and sciences on vulgar, poetic wisdom. Plato is understandably not as self-conscious about his relationship to Homer as Vico is. For Vico, Homer represents the summary of the divine and heroic ages, and Plato the high point of the age of humans of the *corso*. It is not surprising that Plato himself, without the benefit Vico had of observing the *ricorso*, does not see their roles in ideal eternal history. So Vico is right that Plato does not discover the poetic grounds of philosophy in the vulgar wisdom of the true Homer. What Vico does not point out is that Plato would have no objection to myths which were "true and severe" (*vero e severo*), since the *Republic*'s critique addresses the poems which do not tell the truth. I do not claim that Plato had a doctrine of poetic wisdom; rather that nothing in Plato's critique of poetry is incompatible with Vico's search for the true Homer. On the other hand, Vico did not recognize the similarity between his search for the true Homer and Plato's moral critique of Homer. These are the fruits of the search for the true Plato which Vico did not undertake.

Although Plato does not give Homer the same role Vico does, Plato does take Homer very seriously. Recall that the *Statesman* comes close to acknowledging a philosophical dependence on myth, since the grounds for believing in periodic cataclysmic events in history are that all the poets sing of it (*Plt.* 269b). Moreover, Plato knows that the poets like Homer have been the educators of the Greeks. The centrality Plato gives Homer as a rival educator distinguishes him from Aristotle, for example, for whom the quarrel between philosophy and poetry is not definitive of his own conception of philosophy. Aristotle takes as his starting-point not Homer but other philosophers. Vico is one of the first major philosophers (if not the only one) since Plato to consider poetic wisdom as a serious rival to philosophical wisdom.

Even though it is true that Plato does not use Homer, or rather the true Homer which is what Vico means, to confirm his philosophy, Vico could not use the Homer Plato knew to confirm the wisdom of his philosophy either. The fact that Plato did not discover the true Homer makes "confirming with Homer" two different things for Plato and Vico. Vico's criticism is correct as far as it goes, but he is not saying more than that Plato did not discover the true Homer, so he did not solve the quarrel between philosophy and poetry as Vico himself could. Vico does not consider how Plato himself reappropriates Homer in his philosophy in casting serious poetry as its rival. Vico does not give Plato credit for trying to invent a truer Homer in his own work. Plato does not look for the true Homer, but seeks *himself* to be a truer poet than Homer. Homeric references do sometimes adorn rather than confirm Plato's thought, but he also recognizes the role of Homer as moral teacher of the Greeks. Vico is not quite fair to say that Plato merely adorns his wisdom with Homer, because Plato takes Homer as the starting-point for his revised ideal of heroism.

Let us now conclude this work with Socrates, whose heroic life Plato makes the central *eikon* of his philosophical writing. Plato transforms Homer, and presents himself as a rival poet and educator.[1] Just as Homer had Achilles and Odysseus as heroes, so Plato has Socrates. Vico approaches this parallel when he says Plato invents "philosophical heroism," for one could extrapolate from this connection that Plato sets his account of heroism against the heroic poets. Vico does not draw this conclusion. Vico views Socrates as the key to both philosophical heroism and to how Plato rivals Homer. Now I will turn to the details of Plato's portrait of Socrates as the *eikon* of philosophical heroism in the *Republic* and the *Symposium*.

In *Republic* 2–3, the argument of the critique of poetry unfolds, stating that Homer, as well as Hesiod, did not tell the truth about gods, heroes, or human beings. Plato does not advocate abolishing all poetry. Plato is ready to embrace "an austere and less pleasing poet" (*R.* 398a), so it is not the craft of poetry itself that is false. The poetry of Homer and Hesiod taught falsehoods not only about the gods and heroes, but also about the good life for human beings. It was not serious about serious things (*Leg.* 803c) and took petty matters, such as Achilles's anger, as serious. The poets failed as moral teachers, and Plato's dialogues offer a revision and substitute for their role in Greek society. Plato is an "austere and less pleasing poet;" as a serious poet, Plato is a human poet who imitates the divine.

The *Republic* hints at the fact that Plato is making himself a truer Homer by its use of images which in a subtle manner identify Socrates and Odysseus. Consider for example the opening line where Socrates says "I went down" (*kateben*)(*R.* 327a), which identifies him with Odysseus's descent (*katabasis*) to the underworld (*Ody.* 11). There is also the echo of Odysseus's difficult homecoming, when Socrates is repeatedly interrupted by "waves" of objections (*R.* 453d; 457c; 472a; 473c). In the opening scene Socrates is headed homeward, but he is detained, and not by his own consent (*R.* 327b; 327b–328b). Plato is not allegorizing Odysseus as the soul seeking home with God, as the Neoplatonists such as Plotinus would do. Instead, Plato substitutes Socrates's journey for Odysseus's, and by implication makes Socrates a hero. Plato is a better teacher about heroes than Homer, for he judges what is good and evil according to the true models agreed upon in the conversation of the *Republic* itself.

The *Republic* is a masterpiece on many levels, yet I would add as further evidence of his genius the way that Plato's self-implicating models account for the status of his own philosophical poetry as a new moral teacher of the Greeks in place of Homer. Adeimantus says there has never been anyone who has spoken the truth, in verse or prose, about the gods, heroes, and humans, specifically defending justice for its own sake (*R.* 366e–67a). No one, that is, until Plato. The interlocutors even agree that the final model for how human beings ought to be depicted depends on the outcome of the defense of justice over injustice as what makes human beings happy, which is the subject of the *Republic* itself (*R.* 392a–b). The models for austere poetry cannot be completed until *Republic* 9, when the proof is finally given that the just life is better than the unjust for a human being (*R.* 392a–b; 580b–c). When Glaucon proclaims this truth, he does so as "son of Ariston": "Shall we fetch a herald, or shall I sound the word myself? By proclamation of Ariston's son the best and most righteous man is also the happiest" (*R.* 580b–c). This may be one of the thinnest veils between Plato and a character in a dialogue, as he is, like his brother Glaucon, the son of Ariston. So Plato's patronymic declares the truth of the final model for austere poetry, and the conclusion of the central argument of the *Republic* (*R.* 392a–b).

The culmination of the call for an austere poet is the myth of Er, which meets the models established, and in this myth especially Plato reveals his unique gifts. The *Republic* itself takes seriously the divine things, calls heroic that which approaches the divine, and teaches that human beings are ridiculous unless they express the most divine part of their nature. The *Republic* does not give a detailed portrait of the philosophical version of the hero, because the hero is telling the story. It is as if Homer's *Odyssey* were told exclusively from Odysseus's point of view, as if the entire work were told in the way that the Phaiakians's books (*Ody.* 8–12) are, as the memory of the hero himself. It is necessary to turn to another dialogue to get an external view of the philosophical hero. In the *Symposium*, after an evening of speeches praising *Eros*, Alcibiades praises Socrates. In this speech of Alcibiades, the figure of Socrates as hero is most manifest.

First, an interesting identification of Socrates and *Eros* develops, since all the other encomiasts praised *Eros*, and Alcibiades insists he can praise no one but Socrates in his presence (*Smp.* 214d). The images Alcibiades uses to describe Socrates echo precisely the description of *Eros* in Diotima's speech as child of *Porus* (Resource) and *Penia* (Poverty) (*Smp.* 203b–d), a speech given before Alcibiades's arrival. Like *Eros*, Socrates is bare-foot and needy as well as resourceful. Socrates is always looking for the knowledge he says he lacks, just as *Eros* loves what it lacks. Just as *Eros* is in between the divine and human, as a kind of intermediary, so Socrates is compared to statues of Silenus, which are ugly on the outside, but when opened reveal gods inside (*Smp.* 215a–b; 216e). Socrates as philosophical hero expresses the divinity of the human mind when it burns with *eros* for the truth. Alcibiades recognizes the beauty of Socrates's soul, and his description of his experience is the one a mere mortal feels when confronted with a hero or god. Alcibiades is ashamed of his own life by comparison (*Smp.* 216b).

Alcibiades spends a great deal of his speech of praise on Socrates's extraordinary powers (*Smp.* 216c). He relates how Socrates withstands the cold (*Smp.* 220b), how he can stand in contemplation oblivious for hours (*Smp.* 220c), how courageous he is in the face of danger in battle (*Smp.* 220d), and, in the most personal anecdote, Alcibiades tells how Socrates slept under his cloak with perfect self-control despite the great beauty of Alcibiades as a temptation (*Smp.* 219c–d). It is not only the speech of Alcibiades that highlights Socrates's uniqueness. The beginning of the dialogue illustrates how Socrates is inhuman in his ability to contemplate (*Smp.* 174d–75b), and at the end of the dialogue after staying up all night talking, Socrates spends his day as usual while the others must sleep (*Smp.* 223d). Like a hero, Socrates is set apart from human weaknesses, especially those regarding the body.

That no one has seen Socrates drunk, no matter how much wine he drinks, links the *Symposium* itself to the discussion of symposia in *Laws* 1. In the *Laws*, the Stranger argues that there ought to be a way to test lack of moderation in regard to pleasure just as there are tests of courage in facing pain (*Leg.* 633d). Courage does not only consist in proper boldness in the face of pain, but also a proper fear of giving in to immoderate pleasures (*Leg.* 634b, 647c–d). Symposia can be used to test for excessive boldness, and so complete education into virtue. In such philosophical symposia, one person remains sober (*Leg.* 640d), and Socrates's always being sober reveals his self-mastery and ability to instruct others. *Eros* must be stirred to boldness to overcome pain, but it also must be held back in order to have the proper shame. Shame is what Socrates triggers in Alcibiades, who is infamous for immoderate boldness to the point of impiety.

Socrates's knowledge of *ta erotica*, the only knowledge he claims (*Smp.* 177e), is the source of his heroism, for he knows how to moderate *eros*. Since the *Cratylus* is playful in its etymologies, perhaps a syllogism based on its identification of "*eros*" and "hero" would not be inappropriate here (*Cra.* 398c–e; cf. *NS* 508). The *Symposium* suggests the identity of Socrates and *Eros*, as I have pointed out, and the *Cratylus* adds the other premise, that "*eros*" and "hero" are linked, sharing the same spelling with a different breathing mark. Thought of in this way, *eros* is the middle term connecting Socrates and hero, with the conclusion that Socrates is a hero.

As I said above, Vico credits Plato with inventing the idea of "philosophical heroism" (*NS* 1041). Vico may imply, as I am suggesting, that Plato is transforming Homeric poetry in his own philosophy. Regardless, Plato's description of Socrates as a hero exemplifies precisely the qualities Vico attributes to the philosophical hero in the *New Science*. With a sense of how Socrates was Plato's philosophical hero, I can turn to what Vico says about Plato's invention of philosophical heroism. This similarity between Vico and Plato is especially significant because it represents agreement on the goal of the philosopher. For both, the idea of heroism is taken over from the epic poetry of Homer as an image for the goal of philosophical *paideia*.

In the *New Science*, Vico traces how he thinks that Plato arrived at the idea of philosophical heroism. First Plato observed how most human beings act in their own private interest, then he contemplated the idea of the common good or justice, and from there "he raised himself to the meditation of the highest intelligible ideas of created minds, ideas which are distinct from these created minds and can reside only in God, and thus he reached the height of conceiving the philosophical hero who commands his passions at will" (*NS* 1041). If the "philosophical hero" is one "who commands his passions at will," the *Symposium* (as well as other dialogues) supports the idea that Socrates is an exemplar of such a hero. Commanding one's passions at will does not mean eliminating all passions for Vico or for Plato. Recall that Vico opposes "Stoics, who seek to mortify the senses" as well as "Epicureans, who make them the criterion" (*NS* 130). These are the psychological errors about the nature of the passions which correspond to the metaphysical errors of fate and chance. The principle of humanity involved here is "the moderation of the passions" in its philosophical form, which is grounded in the certain institution of marriage (*NS* 360). Compare Vico's claim that control of concupiscence makes us human, so here too Vico advocates control of passion not its elimination (*NS* 1098). *Republic* 9 makes the similar call for moderation, holding that that the healthy man "neither sates nor starves his appetites" (571e).

Socrates knows the truth about *eros*, and that is all he claims to know (*Smp.* 177e); but it is exactly what a human being must know to be wise. Socrates knows how to moderate his *eros*, and raise his humanity to its heroic limit, approaching as nearly as a human being can the image of divinity. The knowledge of the limit of humanity is the fruit of a proper love for the divine, and this is the virtue of piety. The proper love for oneself and other human beings is justice. Justice is being "a friend to oneself" as well as others (*R.* 443d). Plato's invention of the philosophical hero, Vico says, prepared the way for "the divine definition which Aristotle later gave us of a good law as a will free of passion, which is to say the will of a hero" (*NS* 1042). Vico adds that Aristotle "understood justice as the queen of the virtues, seated in the spirit of the hero and commanding all the others" (ibid.). Aristotle follows Plato's *Republic* closely on this point.

In both the cases of piety and justice what is necessary is moderation. This proper proportion of the parts of one's soul is born from moderation not complete humiliation. To be human one has to moderate one's passions, or one is no better than a beast, but to be a hero one must master one's passions. By the philosophical hero's example of mastery, he inspires in others at least the desire to be moderate.

Vico declares firmly that philosophy is only useful to the human race if it advocates *moderation* of the passions. This axiom bears repeating in this context; "to be useful to the human race, philosophy must raise and direct weak and fallen man, not rend his nature or abandon him in his corruption" (*NS* 129). In the age of humans, religion loses its capacity to make human beings virtuous, and philosophy must warn those who scoff at religion, marriage, and burial, that they are transgressing the bounds of humanity itself (*NS* 360). Philosophy was brought into existence by providence in order to make those who stray feel shame at their vice. Although it is easy to criticize philosophers for merely talking about virtues, Vico makes clear that in an age when virtue needs champions, this is a noble enterprise. Likewise Plato delivers his prelude against atheism, and by doing so he does not betray his own piety by allowing argument about the subject, since it is in defense of providence that he argues with those who deny it (*Leg.* 884a–907d).

Vico links philosophy and the idea of the hero again, when he explains how providence ordained philosophy's role in the moral education of human beings. The popular commonwealths give rise to an interest both in the idea of the hero and truth and hence to philosophy itself: "these commonwealths gave birth to philosophy. By their very form they inspired it to form the hero, and for that purpose to interest itself in truth. All this was ordained by providence to the end that, since virtuous actions were no longer prompted by religious sentiments as formerly, philosophy should make virtues understood in their idea, and by dint of reflection thereon, if men were without virtue they should at least be ashamed of their vices. Only so can peoples prone to ill-doing be held to their duty" (*NS* 1102). Recall that Alcibiades admits that Socrates makes him ashamed, and that no one else does (*Smp.* 216b). Socrates most exemplifies the philosophical hero in Vico's sense when he stirs Alcibiades to want to be good like Socrates himself is. The goal of the philosopher is not only to be a friend to himself, but also to befriend others; and if he is lucky, to serve the common good of his city.

The gift, which the philosophical hero brings to the human race, is the teaching of moderation. The fruit of the highest mastery of *eros* is not withdrawal from human life, but "a productive desire for wisdom" (*HM* 233). The philosophical hero embodies both imperatives inscribed on the Temple of Delphi, "know thyself" (*gnothi seauton*) and "nothing in excess" (*meden agan*). This same temple was the birthplace of Socrates's philosophical heroism. When Socrates heard that the oracle had said that there was no one wiser than Socrates (*Ap.* 21a), he embarked upon his quest to find someone wiser than himself (*Ap.* 21b–c). Socrates asked questions of those who believed that they were wise, and found that they were not (*Ap.* 21c–22d). Socrates finally understood that the truth of the oracle lay in the acknowledgment of his ignorance (*Ap.* 22e–23b). Socrates was wise because he did not pretend to know that which he did not know. Recognition of the limits of one's wisdom is human wisdom (*Ap.* 20d–e; 23a–b).

Vico does not dwell elsewhere in the *New Science* on the philosophical hero or his task in relationship to the rest of the human race; so making the philosophical heroism reference central to a reading of the *New Science*'s fundamental philosophical significance might appear to be an exaggeration. I raise this possible criticism since my project is the study of Vico's kinship to Plato, and Vico credits Plato with inventing philosophical heroism. The theme does occur elsewhere in Vico in such a way that supports my attention to the passage in the *New Science*. Vico makes philosophical heroism the primary theme of his oration to the Academy of Oziosi, "On

Heroic Mind." In this eloquent oration, Vico instructs prospective philosophical heroes about the serious responsibility they bear for raising up
and directing weak and fallen human beings (*NS* 129). "On Heroic Mind"
supports the reading that the educational ideal of philosophical heroism
was central to his thought as a whole. In this "solemn oration" Vico says he
will address his audience "with the weight and gravity inherent to its own
subject matter" (*HM* 229; cf. 235). From this oration and others, it is clear
that Vico does not take the custom of giving an inaugural oration lightly
(cf. *A* 146).

What Vico says about the original meaning of "hero" sheds further light
on the idea of philosophical heroism, by clarifying that philosophical heroism transforms or replaces poetic heroism: "when I speak of your mani-
festing the heroic mind through studies, I am not choosing those words
lightly. If heroes are those who, as poets say or as they invent, were wont to
boast of their divine lineage from 'all-judging Jove,' this much is certain:
the human mind, independent of any fiction and fables, does have a divine
origin which needs only choosing and breadth of knowledge to unfurl
itself. So you see, I do ask of you things greatly surpassing the human: the
near-divine nature of your minds—that is what I am challenging you to
reveal" (*HM* 230).

In addition to this articulation of the analogy between the poetic hero
who boasts of divine lineage and the philosophical hero who possesses the
divinity of the mind, Vico gives another example of this kind of transference. Vico speaks of a gymnasium as "a term consciously transposed from
bodies to minds" (*HM* 234).[2] Just as a gymnasium as a place to train the
body is transferred to the development of the mind in the university, so
does the physical ideal of the heroic warrior or king become the intangible
ideal of the philosophical hero. Whereas a gymnasium cured ailments of
the body and led to physical health, so the university provides opportuni-
ties for students, suffering from false opinions, corrupt desires, and imprecise tongue, "to be healed, restored, made perfect by wisdom" (*HM* 234–
35). The *Republic*'s ideal education is based on the analogy of the health of
the body and the justice of the soul. In both cases proportion is the ideal
(cf. *HM* 239). As Benedetto Croce said, "the only philosophy which carries with it a true ethic seems to Vico to be the Platonic," and this Platonic
ethic adopted by Vico is based on proportion (ibid.).[3]

Vico also incorporates the image of "the mind's eye" (ibid.), which is
even more recognizably Platonic than the health analogy. It is not clear
whether Plato is self-conscious about the necessity of beginning abstract
thought with such physical universals. In the *Sophist*, the image of the

mind's eye occurs in the description of the quarrel always going on in metaphysics between the giants and the gods; for those on the side of the giants measure what is real by touch, and those on the side of the gods consider as more real what is seen by the mind's eye (*Sph.* 246a–c). Plato does not suggest that humanity itself first measures by touch before it learns to see with the mind's eye. Vico may credit Aristotle with approaching this insight, however, when he agrees with him that there is nothing in the mind that was not already present in the senses (*NS* 263).

Vico's "master key" to the *New Science* is discovering the imaginative universal and its relationship to the intelligible universal (*NS* 34). As the disciple of Socrates, who first asked the difficult questions of essence (*NS* 1040), such as what is piety, Plato describes the struggle to see with the mind's eye intelligible universals or immaterial forms. Most interlocutors, failing to understand what Socrates is asking, give examples of piety, or maxims about justice from the poets. Plato freely extends the familiar qualities of physical bodies to the soul's operations, but he does not explore as Vico does the necessity of this dependence on myth as the origin of philosophy. The poets make philosophy possible, and not some individual poet, but the vulgar poets of each of the nations. Neither Plato nor Aristotle discovered the imaginative universal, despite the central roles they assign to myth and imagination in their work.

Vico knows exactly what he is saying (he even tells the students he is not choosing his words lightly), when he articulates the ideal of "heroic mind." This heroism is not of the heroic age. Just as Achilles is a hero of the heroic age, so Socrates is a hero of the human age. The analogy points out differences as well as similarities. Health resembles justice in significant respects so as to be a useful analogy, and so the epic hero sheds light on the philosophical hero. Vico recollects the heroic ideal in such a way that it can exist in the human age. There are no more literal heroes once the third age begins. As Achilles once mastered his body and pre-reflective life, now there can be philosophical heroes, who master the mind and spiritual life.

In the *Republic*, Plato sketches the ideal life of the lover of wisdom (philosopher-aristocrat) and the four deficient forms (timocrat, oligarch, democrat, and tyrant). These five ideal types are the intellectual versions of the characters of the stories of epic history. What justice means for Plato is the configuration of the soul where reason rules spirit and desire, and injustice where it does not. Socrates serves as the primary example of the just human being, for he comes the closest to being an *eikon* of the type itself. In the myth of Er, Odysseus becomes Socrates when the heroic adventurer chooses the private life of someone who minds his own business (*R.* 620c), which is the definition of justice.

With this dimension of Plato in mind, consider what Vico writes about students reading the poets to discover the nature of virtues and vice: "Compared with these ideal types, men in everyday life will seem rather to be the unreal characters, for where men are not consistent their lives do not cohere. So consider, with a certain godlike mind, human nature as portrayed in the fables of great poets: even in its wickedness it is most beautiful, because always self-consistent, always true to itself, harmonious in all its parts . . . " (*HM* 236–37). Vico then informs the students that once they have read the poets and "thrilled with delight" that there are even greater pleasures in "the sublime orators" (*HM* 237; cf. *NS* 349, *SM* 12–14). Vico has already mentioned that "hero" is defined by philosophers as "one who ever seeks the sublime" (*HM* 230), so the adjective sublime can also mean heroic. Vico predicts that the students will be caught up in as great an admiration for these whose "art is marvelous in its adaptation to our flawed human nature: appealing to the passions originating in the body, they twist men's minds around, no matter how settled, into wishing the direct opposite" (*HM* 237). This comment sounds as if rhetoric is reduced to sophistry, but the next claim makes clear that there is a proper use of such persuasion: "In this, moreover, Almighty God excels and He alone, but by His own vastly different ways of triumphant grace. Who draws the minds of men to Himself by heavenly delight, no matter how pinned down they are by earthly passions" (ibid.). The eloquence Vico says that the philosopher must have in the *New Science* to educate human beings into virtue (*NS* 1101) is perfectly possessed only by God, who is the true knower, maker, and governor. To be a sublime or heroic orator, one also must be a philosopher who imitates God in educating human beings. For eloquence is never separated from wisdom for Vico, even though some orators fall short of eloquence in their practice of rhetoric.

In a final reference to how he is adapting the poetic hero, he instructs the students as follows: "Undergo herculean trials, which, once passed, vindicate with perfect justice your divine descent from true Jove, Him the greatest and best. Prove yourselves to be heroes by enriching the human race with further giant benefits" (*HM* 244; cf. *NS* 1098). Vico ends with this series of imperatives calling the students to action. Philosophical heroes go through a contemplative stage, but without the culminating active dimension of giving gifts to humanity, one is not a hero.

Not only does Plato invent philosophical heroism, as Vico says, he also embodies it, as a true disciple of Socrates. In the story of Plato's life we are told that first he wrote plays, and given his gift for language there is every reason to believe he would have taken his place among the great Greek tragedians.[4] What happened? Plato met Socrates who questioned him about the truth of what he wrote in his plays, and as a result Plato burned his plays and began his philosophical life as a follower of Socrates.[5] Plato turned his gifted literary imagination to the expression of the truth as he discovered it through the midwifery of Socrates. This is why Plato made Socrates the hero of his philosophical poetry. Plato's philosophical poetry is the fruit of a moderated *eros* that knows its poverty and resource (*Smp.* 203b), and as a result has proper fear and boldness (*Leg.* 649b–c). This moral courage and balance is lived by Plato as well as imitated in his dialogues for the benefit of future generations who would not be as fortunate as he was to know Socrates, the greatest midwife of philosophical heroes.

Vico also represents in his own life the heroism he advocates in speech. The best explanation for why Vico wrote the *Practica* is that he wished to avert the charge that his own wisdom was restricted to contemplation, and that he fails to be a political philosopher but is himself among the inactive solitaries he criticizes (*NS* 130). Perhaps Vico realized such a defense was redundant, and that is why he omitted it. Whatever the reading of the *Practica*, the discovering, writing, and publishing of the *New Science* itself is a heroic act. This accomplishment was heroic even though Vico had no one who really understood him to memorialize his achievement. While embodying heroic mind, Vico exhorts his audience to manifest it in themselves in "On Heroic Mind." He is an eloquent "sublime orator," and, as such, he attempts to imitate the Divine Orator.

Like Aeneas, Vico undertakes an heroic journey. Vico descends to the origin of humanity and brings back the wisdom he finds to our present age of barbarism. When he introduces "the golden bough" of the *New Science*, the imaginative universal, he relates the labors he endured for its sake (*NS* 34).[6] This act of recollection transforms Vico himself into a philosophical hero, just as he exhorts the students to become. Vico discovers something "new," as he tells them they can (*HM* 235). The *New Science* and "On Heroic Mind," an oration on a theme "wholly new" (*HM* 229; cf. *NS* 1096), are the gifts Vico gives. Plato casts Socrates as his Odysseus; Vico casts himself as Aeneas. Vico ends his *Autobiography* with a reference to the original philosophical hero of Plato, Socrates. Vico's work culminated in the discovery of the *New Science*, and despite his detractors, the promise of future audiences made him consider himself "more fortunate than Socrates, on whom Phaedrus has these fine lines: 'I would not shun his death to win his fame; I'd yield to odium, if absolved when dust'" (*A* 200). Vico's heroism may finally be appreciated now that the signs of barbarism of reflection are clearer than they were in 1744. He was writing for his times to avert something like the imbalance of our own. The confidence that he had in the divinity of the mind, and the human capacity to rise to heroic heights, excludes any wholly pessimistic reading of Vico.

A serious admission of the fallen condition of human beings is an essential moment in Vico's philosophical anthropology, but so too is an exuberant proclamation of the dignity of the human mind and its heroic potential for good. The metaphor of hero as the highest achievement of humanity is a perfect one when one recalls that pagan heroes had one parent who was mortal, and the other immortal. Donald Phillip Verene summarizes these two moments of human nature according to Vico in this way: "through his making man can exercise his divine nature in imitation of the divine who makes by knowing, but in his making man cannot work his way up to a state of the divine. Human making done at its very limits produces heroism. The hero is the living presence of memory, the recollection of the origin pitted against the end. Vico joins the principle of pagan mythology, the Hero, with that of Christian mythology, the Fall."[7] Like the heroes of epic poetry, human beings in the age of humans can serve others with justice and piety. Heroic mind is an image for "a productive desire for wisdom" (*HM* 233) of the philosopher who is neither Stoic nor Epicurean, but acknowledges the responsibility of the philosopher to cooperate with providence for the good of the human race. "Heroic mind" does not mean near divine knowledge as much as it reinforces the essential fruit of such knowledge, which is the giving of gifts to the human race.

This active dimension of the philosophical hero explains why Vico would warn the students against philosophers who have as their only goal "the love of learning itself" (*HM* 229). Vico says that not all but "almost all of them" are so caught up in learning that they "pass their whole lives withdrawn from the public light in order to get the full enjoyment from the tranquil working of their minds and nothing else" (*HM* 230). These philosophers, such as the Stoics and Epicureans, fail to meet the criterion set in the *New Science* for philosophy which is "useful to the human race" (*NS* 129). Vico reminds the students that something more is expected of them than learning for selfish gain; and something more was expected by Plato as well, who is counted among the philosophers who meet the *New Science's* standard (*NS* 130).

Vico tells the students that after their university education they must return to the Cave, to use Plato's image. In Vico's own image, they must become heroes for the rest of humanity. Who is the philosopher Plato describes returning to the Cave if not a hero? The philosopher comes back with the wisdom to free the prisoners from their illusions, which is the greatest gift; yet he knows that since this will be extremely painful, the ones he wishes to help may even try to kill him. Plato has Socrates always before him when he writes (as Vico says about his authors), and there is poignancy in Plato speaking from personal experience about the suffering of philosophical heroes, or would-be philosophical heroes.

Vico, too, knows what a difficult task he is giving the students, as well as his readers centuries later; and his attempts to embody heroism in his own life were often thwarted. Begetting true virtue in one's soul is to take the difficult not the easy road (*NS* 1411). Vico's insight resonates with the description of the path out of the Cave as "rough and steep" (*R.* 515e; cf. 364d, 621c). Vico agrees that the philosophical hero must endure trials as Hercules, be as wily as Odysseus, and be as courageous as Achilles. He honestly admits to the students that they are right to suspect that what he asks is beyond human capacity (*HM* 230). The goal of the hero is to occupy that region between the human and the divine. As a professor of eloquence, Vico seeks to stir his audience to have a passion for such high ideals, just as he said in the *New Science* that philosophy would have to be joined to eloquence in order to achieve the purpose for which providence ordained it (*NS* 1101).

In a study which has descended through the layers of Platonism to discover the true nature of Vico's Platonism, it is fitting to end with Socrates. Vico makes it an axiom that an origin reveals something's nature. Both the image of the frontispiece of the *New Science* in Vico and of Socrates in Plato aid our memory in tracing the development of philosophy from its poetic origins and grasping the nature of philosophical heroism. Each of the circles of the spiral of the family of Plato recalls to memory an aspect of Vico's Platonic metaphysics and moral philosophy: from Pico he learned the dignity of the human mind, from Augustine, the corrective piety in the face of providence, and from Plato's dialogues, the idea of the philosophical heroism.

Socrates, as philosophical hero, is the "father of all the philosophers" (*HM* 240), the philosophical falconer holding the center together. Socrates courageously confronted the limits of his self-knowledge until the day he died. Socrates even wondered in jail whether a dream he had could be interpreted that the gods had wanted him to compose poetry instead of pursuing his philosophical quest, so at the end of his life he began to compose poetry (*Phd.* 60d–61a). Given the ancient quarrel of poetry and philosophy, this is a remarkable anecdote. Socrates made his own life his masterpiece, and even died rather than betray his teaching that "no harm can come to a good man" (*Crit.* 53c, 48b). The discovery of the intelligible universal is a momentous gift to humanity (*NS* 1040), but as a result of the intellectual focus of Socrates's quest for wisdom, he slighted the power of the imagination, as Vico points out (*AW* 180). The heroism of Socrates's life did stir *eros* in others to become good like him, but he did not write to instruct, to delight, and to move. Socrates was not a poet, yet his heroism is memorialized by Plato, who is "the Homer of the philosophers."

Plato harmonized the philosophical and the poetic in his life and work, and so too Vico sought to balance his gifts of imagination and intellect. As W. B. Yeats observed, the greatest poets and prose writers are "those who were a little weary of life . . . and who cast their imagination to us, as a something they needed no longer now that they were going up in their fiery chariots."[8] Both Plato and Vico possess the heroic mind characteristic of such rare human beings who have endured Herculean trials to the point of melancholy, and yet have had the courage not to abandon weak and fallen human beings, but to raise us up to share their experience of joy through the example of their piety and wisdom.

Notes

Introduction

1 Iris Murdoch, *The Fire and the Sun: Why Plato Banished the Poets* (New York: Viking Penguin, 1990), 20–21.

2 Giambattista Vico, *The Autobiography of Giambattista Vico*, trans. Max Harold Fisch and Thomas Goddard Bergin (Ithaca: Cornell University Press, 1983), 139; *Autobiografia*, vol. 5 of *Opere di G. B. Vico*, ed. Fausto Nicolini, 8 vols. in 11 (Bari: Laterza, 1911–41). Further citations will be inserted parenthetically in the text with the abbreviation *A* and the page number of the English translation.

3 For instance, see J. J. Chambliss, "Giambattista Vico's Imaginative Universals and Plato's Quest for the Good," *Educational Theory* 38 (1988): 311–20; Aviezer Tucker, "A Platonic Reinterpretation of Vico," *Idealistic Studies* 23 (1993): 139–150; Italian translation: "Platone e Vico: Una Reinterpretazione Platonica di Vico," trans. Daniela Rotoli, *Bollettino del Centro di Studi Vichiani*, 24–25 (1994–95): 97–115.

4 G. L. C. Bedani, *Vico Revisited: Orthodoxy, Naturalism and Science in the Scienza nuova* (New York: St. Martin's Press, 1989), 246. Cf. Donald Phillip Verene, *Man and World* 4 (1971): 344; "Introduction" to Giambattista Vico, *On the Most Ancient Wisdom of the Italians Unearthed From the Origins of the Latin Language*, trans., L. M. Palmer (Ithaca: Cornell University Press, 1988), 39, n. 5.

5 See Enrico De Mas, "Vico's Four Authors," in *Giambattista Vico: An International Symposium*, ed. Giorgio Tagliacozzo and Hayden V. White (Baltimore: Johns Hopkins University Press, 1969), 3–14; Guido Fassó, *I' quatro autori'del Vico: Saggio sulla genesi della 'Scienza nuova'* (Milan: Giuffré, 1949).

6 Heraclitus, quoted and translated in *The Presocratic Philosophers*, 2nd ed., G.S. Kirk, J. E. Raven and M. Schofield (Cambridge: Cambridge University Press, 1983), 192, fragment 207.

7 Giambattista Vico, *The New Science of Giambattista Vico*, trans. Thomas Goddard Bergin and Max Harold Fisch (Ithaca, NY: Cornell University Press, 1983); *La scienza nuova seconda* vol. 4 of *Opere di G. B. Vico*, ed. Fausto Nicolini, 8 vols. in 11 (Bari: Laterza, 1911–41), paragraph 122. Further citations will be inserted paren-

thetically in the text with the abbreviation *NS* and the paragraph number common to the Italian and English editions.

8   Aristotle, *The Complete Works of Aristotle: The Revised Oxford Translation*, Bolligen Series LXXI, ed. Jonathan Barnes, 2 vols. (Princeton: Princeton University Press, 1984); Loeb Classical Library (Cambridge: Harvard University Press), *Nicomachean Ethics*, 1106a25–1107a25. Further references to Aristotle's works will be inserted parenthetically in the text with the standard classical abbreviations.

9   Giambattista Vico, *On the Most Ancient Wisdom of the Italians Unearthed From the Origins of the Latin Language*, trans., L. M. Palmer (Ithaca: Cornell University Press, 1988), 109; *De antiquissima Italorum sapientia*, vol. 1 of *Opere di G. B. Vico*, ed. Fausto Nicolini, 8 vols. in 11 (Bari: Laterza, 1911–41). Further citations will be inserted parenthetically in the text with the abbreviation *AW* and the page number of the English translation.

10 See Isaiah Berlin for the origin of the historicist interpretation of Vico, *Vico and Herder: Two Studies in the History of Ideas* (London: Hogarth Press; New York: Viking Press, 1976). For example, Berlin writes that "this marks the birth of full-fledged modern historicism—a doctrine that in its empirical form has stimulated and enriched, and in its dogmatic, metaphysical form, inhibited and distorted the historical imagination" (36) and that "this is the whole doctrine of historicism in embryo" (38).

11 See Donald Phillip Verene, who states explicitly that "Vico is not a historicist," in "Vichian Providence," *Archivo di Filosofia* 63 (1995), 265, 270. See the similar argument in "Imaginative Universals Narrative Truth," *New Vico Studies* 6 (1988): 1–19.

12 Alasdair MacIntyre, "Imaginative Universals and Historical Falsification: A Rejoinder to Professor Verene," *New Vico Studies* 6 (1988): 25.

13 In this study, I will point out the Platonic elements of Vico's thought which reveal that he is not an historicist. For a direct critique of historicism, including MacIntyre's own historicism, see Carl Page, *Philosophical Historicism: The Betrayal of First Philosophy* (University Park: The Pennsylvania State University Press, 1995).

14 MacIntyre, 24–25.

15 See Donald Phillip Verene, "Giambattista Vico and the New Art of Autobiography" on "the genetic method," (The Institute for Vico Studies, Emory University, unpublished manuscript), 2–6.

16 MacIntyre, 27.

17 Ibid.

18 Peter Burke, *Vico* (Oxford: Oxford University Press, 1985), 8.

19 John Milbank, *The Religious Dimension in the Thought of Giambattista Vico 1668–1744: Part 2 Language, Law and History* (Lewiston, New York: Edwin Mellon Press,

1992), 5–6. See also *Part 1, The Early Metaphysics* (Lewiston, New York: Edwin Mellon Press,1991), 219–20.

20 "Introduction," *A* 44. But contrast "it was not worldly caution that moved him, but pious scruple; for whatever his youthful vagaries had been, he was now a devout Catholic," 43.

21 "Introduction," *A* 36. "Affetti di un disperato," in vol. 5 of *Opere di G. B. Vico*, ed. Fausto Nicolini, 8 vols. in 11 (Bari: Laterza, 1911–1941); trans. H. P. Adams, *The Life and Writings of Giambattista Vico* (London: Allen and Unwin, 1935), 223–26.

22 Frederick Vaughn, *The Political Philosophy of Giambattista Vico: An Introduction to La Scienza Nuova* (The Hague: Martinus Nijhoff, 1972), xi. For Vaughn's debt to Leo Strauss, see xi, n. 2.

23 Ibid. Cf. Bedani, who explicitly accepts a modified version of Vaughn's thesis, 2–3. See also Gustavo Costa review, *New Vico Studies* 8 (1990), 91.

24 See Leon Pompa, *Vico: A Study of the New Science*, 2nd rev. ed. (Cambridge: Cambridge University Press, 1990), 186–221.

25 Pompa, 208.

26 Pompa, 212.

27 Berlin, 66.

28 Berlin, 41.

29 Fausto Nicolini, *La giovenezza del Giambattista Vico* (Laterza: Bari, 1932), 118. My trans.

30 Giambattista Vico, "On the Heroic Mind," trans. Elizabeth Sewell and Anthony C. Sirignano, in *Vico and Contemporary Thought*, ed. G. Tagliacozzo, M. Mooney, and D. P. Verene (Atlantic Highlands, NJ: Humanities Press, 1979), 240; *De mente heroica*, vol. 7 of *Opere di G. B. Vico*, ed. Fausto Nicolini, 8 vols. in 11 (Bari: Laterza, 1911–1941). Further citations will be inserted parenthetically in the text with the abbreviation *HM* and the page number of the English translation.

31 The phrase is from Marsilio Ficino who in his letter on the life of Plato referred to his academy as "we, the family of Plato." *The Letters of Marsilio Ficino*, trans. members of the Language Department of the School of Economic Science, London, 5 vols. (London: Shepheard-Walwyn, 1975–94), 1: 48.

32 Paul O. Kristeller, *Renaissance Thought and its Sources* (New York: Columbia University Press, 1979), 50–51.

33 "A Second Coming," in *Yeats's Poems*, ed. A. Norman Jeffares (New York: Gill and Macmillan, 1989), line 1. See also "Blood and the Moon": "I declare this tower is my symbol; I declare/ This winding, gyring, spiring treadmill of a stair is my ancestral stair" (lines 18–20).

34 See W. B. Yeats, *A Vision* (London: Macmillan, 1937), 207, 261.

35 *A Vision*, 267–300.

36 For the claim regarding philosophy see *NS* 131, and for Plato specifically, see *A* 138.

37 Ken Wilber, "The Way Up is the Way Down" in *Sex, Ecology, Spirituality: The Spirit of Evolution* (Boston: Shambala, 1995), 319–20. I would like to thank Jim Goetsch, author of *Vico's Axioms* (New Haven: Yale University Press, 1995), for this reference.

38 I am grateful to Donald Livingston for the idea of philosophical alchemy.

Part One

1 Giambattista Vico, *On the Study Methods of Our Time*, trans. Elio Gianturco (Ithaca, NY: Cornell University Press, 1990), 90, n. 8; *De nostri temporis studiorum ratione* in vol. 1 of *Opere di G. B. Vico*, ed. Fausto Nicolini, 8 vols. in 11 (Bari: Laterza, 1911–41). Further citations will be inserted parenthetically in the text with the abbreviation *SM* and the page number of the English translation. Vico was presumably successful, since Doria wrote an attack on Descartes in 1724 as well as Locke in 1732–33.

2 Giambattista Vico, *On Humanistic Education (Six Inaugural Orations, 1699–1707)*, trans. Giorgio A. Pinton and Arthur W. Shippee, intro by D. P. Verene. (Ithaca: Cornell University Press, 1993); *Le orazioni inaugurali, I–VI*, Gian Galeazzo Visconti (Bologna: Mulino, 1982). Further citations will be inserted cited parenthetically in the text with the abbreviation *IO* and the oration and paragraph number common to the Italian and English editions.

3 Pico della Mirandola, *Conclusiones nongentaei le novecento tesi dell'anno 1496*, ed. Albano Biondi (Florence: Olschki, 1995). See Paul O. Kristeller, *Renaissance Thought and its Sources* (New York: Columbia University Press, 1979), 206–07.

4 On Vico's jurisprudential writings and the *New Science*, see Donald Phillip Verene, *The New Art of Autobiography: An Essay on the 'Life of Giambattista Vico Written by Himself* (Oxford: Clarendon Press, 1991), 137–47.

5 Gianfrancesco Pico, *The Life of Pico*, trans. Thomas More, *Early English Books* (Ann Arbor, Mich.: University Microfilms). On Gianfrancesco Pico's writings, see Charles B. Schmitt, *Gianfrancesco Pico della Mirandola (1469–1533) and his Critique of Aristotle* (The Hague: Nijhoff, 1967), Appendix A, section 1. Compare Vico's claim to be an autodidact, "a pupil acting as his own teacher" (*A* 112), and "Vico blessed his good fortune in having no teacher whose words he had sworn by" (*A* 133).

Chapter One

1 See D. P. Walker, *Ancient Theology* (London: Duckworth, 1972); Charles Trinkaus, "*Theologia Poetica* to *Theologia Platonica*" in *In Our Image and Likeness: Humanity and Divinity in Italian Humanist Thought*, 2 vols. (London: Constable, 1970), 2: 683–721; Paul O. Kristeller, *Renaissance Thought and its Sources* (New York: Co-

lumbia University Press, 1979); Frances Yates, *Giordano Bruno and the Hermetic Tradition* (Chicago: The University of Chicago Press, 1964); Charles B. Schmitt, "Perennial Philosophy: From Agostino Steuco to Leibniz," *Journal of the History of Ideas* 27 (1966): 505–32.

2 Brian Vickers, "Rhetoric and Poetics," in *The Cambridge History of Renaissance Philosophy,* ed. Charles B. Schmitt and Quentin Skinner (Cambridge: Cambridge University Press, 1988), 715–45.

3 Yates, 42–43.

4 Giovanni Pico della Mirandola, *Oration on the Dignity of Man* in *The Renaissance Philosophy of Man,* ed. Ernst Cassirer, Paul O. Kristeller, John Herman Randall, Jr. (Chicago: The University of Chicago Press, Phoenix books, 1959); *De hominis dignitate, Heptaplus, De ente et uno,* ed. Balbino Giuliano, and Enrico Castelli (Florence: Vallecchi, 1942). Further citations will be inserted parenthetically in the text with the abbreviation *O* and the page number of the English translation.

5 See for example Kristeller, *Renaissance Thought and its Sources.* For a sustained critique of this oversimplification of Pico's *Oration* and his thought as a whole, see William G. Craven, *Giovanni Pico della Mirandola: Symbol of His Age, Modern Interpretations of a Renaissance Philosopher* (Geneva: Droz, 1981).

6 Lothario Dei Segni (later Pope Innocent III), *De Misere Hominis Conditionis, On the Misery of the Human Condition,* trans. Margaret Mary Dietz (Indianapolis: Bobbs-Merrill, 1969). See Charles Trinkaus *Adversity's Noblemen: The Italian Humanists on Happiness* (New York: Columbia University Press, 1940). See also Jill Kraye's "Moral Philosophy," in *The Cambridge History of Renaissance Philosophy,* 306–16.

7 Kraye, 306.

8 Brian P. Copenhaver and Charles B. Schmitt, *Renaissance Philosophy,* vol. 3 of *A History of Western Philosophy* (New York: Oxford University Press, 1992), 166. See also, Craven, 37.

9 Gianfrancesco Pico, *The Life of Pico,* trans. Thomas More, *Early English Books* (Ann Arbor, Mich.: University Microfilms), 7–8.

10 Giovanni Pico della Mirandola, *Commentary on a Poem of Platonic Love,* trans. Douglas Carmichael (Lanham: University Press of America, 1986); *Commento alla Canzone d'amore* in *Heptaplus, De hominis dignitate, De ente et uno,* ed. Balbino Giuliano, and Enrico Castelli (Florence: Vallecchi, 1942).

11 *Commentary on a Poem of Platonic Love,* 52.

12 *Commentary on a Poem of Platonic Love,* 80, 88, 106–07.

13 Francesco Petrarch, *Rerum Familiarum Libri* I–VIII, trans. Aldo Bernardo (Albany: State University of New York, 1975), 69–70; *Le familiari di Francesco Petrarca,* ed. Vittorio Rossi and Umberto Bosco, vols. 10–13 (Florence: Sansoni, 1933–42), 10. 4. See Giuseppe Mazzotta, *The Worlds of Petrarch* (Durham, NC: Duke University Press, 1994), 155–57.

14 Francesco Petrarch, *Invective contra medicum*, ed. Pier Giorgio Ricci (Rome, 1950), 71–72; selection trans. by Trinkaus, 2: 692.

15 Boccaccio, *Boccaccio on Poetry: Being the Preface and the Fourteenth and Fifteenth Books of Boccaccio's Genealogia Deorum Gentilium in an English Version with Introductory Essay and Commentary*, trans. Charles G. Osgood, (Princeton: Princeton University Press, 1930), 39, 42, 49, 52, 59, 79, *et passim*.

16 Marsilio Ficino, *"Argumentum"* of *Poimander*, *Omnia Opera*, (Basel, 1576), 1836.

17 Ficino, *Opera*, 386. See Yates, 15; Emanuele Riverso,"Vico and the Humanistic Concept of *Prisca Theologia*," in *Vico: Past and Present*, ed. Giorgio Tagliacozzo (Atlantic Highlands, NJ: Humanities Press, 1981), 58; James Hankins, *Plato in the Italian Renaissance*, 2 vols. (Leiden: Brill, 1990), 2: 463–64; and Schmitt, 510.

18 Boccaccio, 46.

19 *The Letters of Marsilio Ficino*, trans. members of the Language Department of the School of Economic Science, London, 5 vols. (London: Shepheard-Walwyn, 1975–94), 1: 48, 53.

20 Yates, 6.

21 Eugenio Garin, "Vico and the Heritage of Renaissance Thought," in *Vico: Past and Present*, ed. Giorgio Tagliacozzo (Atlantic Highlands, NJ: Humanities Press, 1981), 111.

22 René Descartes, *The Philosophical Works of Descartes*, trans. Elizabeth Haldane and G. R. T. Ross, 3 vols. (Cambridge: Cambridge University Press, 1972–91), 1: 211.

23 See Fausto Nicolini, *Giambattista Vico: Opere* (Milan and Naples: Ricciardi, 1953), 729; see also Andrea Battistini,*Vico Opere*, 2 vols. (Mondadori, 1990) I: 811.

24 Plato, *Collected Dialogues of Plato*, ed. Edith Hamilton and Huntington Cairns (Princeton: Princeton University Press, 1961); Loeb Classical Library (Cambridge: Harvard University Press), *Theatetus*, 179e. Further references to Plato will be to these editions unless otherwise noted, and will be inserted parenthetically in the text with the standard classical abbreviations and Stephanus numbers.

25 Plotinus, *Enneads*, Loeb Classical Library (Cambridge: Harvard University Press), I. 6. 8.

26 See Nicolini, ibid.

27 E. R. Thiele, *The Mysterious Numbers of the Hebrew Kings* (Grand Rapids, W. B. Eerdman Publishing Co., 1983), 33; quoted by David M. Rohl, *Pharaohs and Kings: A Biblical Quest* (New York: Crown Publishers, Inc, 1995), 8.

28 See Hankins for the Renaissance link between chronology and geography, 2: 464.

29 Quoted in Yates, 38.

30 Quoted in Yates, 242.

31   Riverso, 64.

32   Yates, 398–431.

Chapter 2

1   Nicholas of Cusa, *Nicholas of Cusa on Learned Ignorance*, trans. Jasper Hopkins, 2nd ed. (Minneapolis: Arthur J. Banning Press, 1985), 31. On Nicholas of Cusa see Ernst Cassirer, *The Individual and the Cosmos in Renaissance Philosophy*, trans. Mario Domandi (Philadelphia: The University of Pennsylvania Press, 1963).

2   Giovanni Pico della Mirandola, *Heptaplus* in *On the Dignity of Man, On Being and the One, Heptaplus*, ed. Charles Glenn Wallis, Paul J. W. Miller, and Douglas Carmichael, (Indianapolis: Library of Liberal Arts, Bobbs Merrill, 1965); *Heptaplus, De hominis dignitate, Heptaplus, De ente et uno*, ed. Balbino Giuliano, and Enrico Castelli (Florence: Vallecchi, 1942). Further citations will be inserted parenthetically in the text with the abbreviation *H* and the page number of the English translation.

3   *The Cambridge History of Renaissance Philosophy*, ed. Charles B. Schmitt and Quentin Skinner (Cambridge: Cambridge University Press, 1988), 553.

4   Giovanni Pico della Mirandola, *De ente* in *On the Dignity of Man, On Being and the One, Heptaplus*, 52; *De dignitate, Heptaplus, De ente et uno*, ed. Balbino Giuliano, and Enrico Castelli.

5   Peter Burke, *Culture and Society in Renaissance Italy* (New York: Scribner, 1972), 29.

6   Although the attribution of divinity to the human mind is argued primarily on Platonic grounds, Vico's justification for calling us "gods" resembles Lucretius's reasoning in *De Rerum Natura*. Lucretius explains that philosophers as bearers of wisdom are gods since their gifts are more essential than the gifts of wine and grain that made Ceres and Bacchus into gods. See Lucretius, *De Rerum Natura*, trans. Humphries (Bloomington: Indiana University Press, 1968), 158. Vico reasons similarly in *IO* 1.12.

7   Salutati is another possible source for Vico's ideal of the heroic mind. "The myth of Hercules—the central theme of Salutati's *De laboribus Herculis*—recurs in humanist celebrations of man's constructive capacities and of the dignity which raises him to the level of the stars, that is, to the level of a divinity" (Antonino Poppi, "Fate, Fortune, Providence and Human Freedom," in *The Cambridge History of Renaissance Philosophy*, 645).

8   See Giuseppe Mazzotta, *Dante's Vision and the Circle of Knowledge* (Princeton, N.J.: Princeton University Press, 1993), 4.

9   See Eugenio Garin, *Storia della filosofia italiana*, 3 vols. (Turin, Einaudi, 1962), 2: 930–31. See also Visconti, "Commentario," who agrees with Garin, and adds a specific reference to Pico's *Oration* (Bologna: Mulino, 1982), 223–24, n. 1.

10   Marsilio Ficino, *Theologie Platonicienne de l' immortalité des ames*, trans. Raymond
     Marcel, 2 vols. (Paris, 1964), I: 226; selection trans. by Charles Trinkaus, "Humanist
     Themes in Marsilio Ficino's Philosophy of Human Immortality" in *In Our Image
     and Likeness: Humanity and Divinity in Italian Humanist Thought* 2 vols. (London:
     Constable, 1970), 2: 470.

11   Giambattista Vico, "The Academies and the Relationship between Philosophy and
     Eloquence," translated by D. P. Verene, found in the English translation of *On the
     Study Methods of Our Time* (Ithaca: Cornell University Press, 1990). Further cita-
     tions will be inserted parenthetically in the text with the abbreviation *PE* and the
     page number of the English translation.

12   Cassirer, *The Individual and the Cosmos in Renaissance Philosophy*, 40. Cassirer is
     here taking Cusa as the epitome of Renaissance thought.

13   Cicero, *De Officiis*, Loeb Classical Library (Harvard: Harvard University Press),
     1.153. Further citations will be inserted parenthetically in the text with standard
     abbreviations and the English page number of the Loeb edition.

Chapter 3

1   See Michael Mooney, *Vico and the Tradition of Rhetoric* (Princeton: Princeton Uni-
    versity Press, 1984); Donald Phillip Verene, *Vico's Science of the Imagination* (Ithaca,
    NY: Cornell University Press, 1981), ch. 6, and *The New Art of Autobiography: An
    Essay on the Life of Giambattista Vico Written by Himself* (Oxford: Clarendon Press,
    1991), ch. 4, especially 134, 149; James R. Goetsch, *Vico's Axioms: The Geometry of
    the Human World* (New Haven: Yale University Press, 1995).

2   Brian Vickers, "Rhetoric and Poetics" in *The Cambridge History of Renaissance Phi-
    losophy* ed. Charles B. Schmitt and Quentin Skinner (Cambridge: Cambridge
    University Press, 1988), 731.

3   The letters of Pico to Ermolao Barbaro and the responses by Barbaro and
    Melanchthon are found in Quirinus Breen, "Document: Pico della Mirandola on
    the Conflict of Philosophy and Rhetoric," *Journal of the History of Ideas* 13 (1952):
    392–426; *De hominis dignitate; lettera a Ermolao Barbaro*, ed. Giovanni Semprini
    (Rome: Antor, 1986), 71–80; *Ermolao Barbaro: Epistles, Orationes, et Carmina* ed.
    V. Branca (Florence, 1943), vol. 1, Ep. 68, 84–87, Ep. 80, 100–01, Ep. 81, 101–
    09; *Philippi Melanthonis Opera*, ed. Carolus Gottlieb Bretschneider, *Corpus
    Reformatorum*, 28 vols. (New York: Johnson Reprint, 1963; Schwetschke, 1842),
    9: 687–703.

4   Barbaro's reply, Breen, 402. See Hanna Gray for a summary of the letters, "Renais-
    sance Humanism: The Pursuit of Eloquence," *Journal of the History of Ideas* 31
    (1972): 199–216.

5   See Jerrold E. Seigal, *Rhetoric and Philosophy in Renaissance Humanism: The Union
    of Eloquence and Wisdom, Petrarch to Valla* (Princeton: Princeton University Press,
    1965), 16–17.

6   This angle of philosophy's weakness when not wedded to eloquence will be taken up most strongly by Lorenzo Valla, and Melanchthon leans in that direction as well. See P. O. Kristeller, "Humanism," *The Cambridge History of Renaissance Philosophy*, 122–23.

7   Pico's Letter, Breen, 395.

8   Ibid.

9   Ibid. Taken out of context, these claims have generated the misapprehension that Pico simply rejects the humanist ideal of joining wisdom and eloquence.

10 Pico's Letter, Breen, 401.

11 Ibid.

12 Ibid.

13 Most scholars miss Pico's irony, generating a common set of oversimplifications. For instance, Breen summarizes that "Pico had wanted to divorce rhetoric from wisdom. Barbaro had wanted to make wisdom express itself rhetorically. To Melanchthon philosophical wisdom pertains to practical life . . . it is apparent that this thinking lie in the Isocratean tradition rather than the Platonic and Aristotelian," 413. Though many scholars used to stop with Pico's criticisms of rhetoric as mere adornment and external form, most recent interpretations acknowledge there is more to Pico's letter than it may seem "at first sight, "as Gray suggests, 210. Even so, only a few locate the extent of Pico's irony. Vickers says that "where the standard interpretation of Giovanni Pico della Mirandola's dispute with Ermolao Barbaro has seen it as a straight attack on rhetoric, it can now be read as a mock one, parodying extremist logicians," 744. This is not entirely correct, because, as Barbaro points out, Pico makes his scholastic too much of a rhetorician in his defense. Ernesto Grassi says that his will not be the traditional interpretation, but he does not cite the most obvious evidence in the letter for his conclusions. See Ernesto Grassi, *Rhetoric as Philosophy: The Humanistic Tradition* (University Park: The Pennsylvania State University, 1980), 55–60.

14 Pico's Letter, Breen, 402.

15 See Gray, 200.

16 Barbaro's Reply, Breen, 408.

17 Barbaro's Reply, Breen, 407.

18 Ibid.

19 Ibid.

20 Melanchthon's Reply, Breen, 426.

21 See Seigal's introduction on Plato and Aristotle, 9–15.

22 Melanchthon's Reply, Breen, 416.

23   Ibid.

24   Melanchthon's Reply, Breen, 423.

25   See Vickers, who says that "one way of handling Plato's attack on rhetoric was to turn it around against him, as Cicero did" (732). In *Renaissance Eloquence*, ed. James J. Murphy, (Berkeley: University of California, 1983), John Monfasani similarly claims that "in eloquently arguing his case, Plato proves the great power and worth of rhetoric" (180).

26   Melanchthon's Reply, Breen, 414, emphasis added.

27   See Grassi, 55–60.

28   See Gray, who notes that the Ciceronian tradition connects heroism and oratory, 206.

29   See Donald Phillip Verene, "The Rhetorical Proof of Vico's *New Science*" (The Institute for Vico Studies, Emory University, unpublished manuscript), 2–3.

30   Verene, "Rhetorical Proof," 3.

31   For a contrasting opinion, see Andrea Battistini, "Vico as Agonistic Lector," *New Vico Studies* 12 (1994): 32–46.

32   Ernst Cassirer, "Giovanni Pico della Mirandola: A Study in the History of Renaissance Ideas," *The Journal of the History of Ideas* 3 (1942): 126.

33   Ibid.

34   Cesare Vasoli, "The Renaissance Concept of Philosophy," in *The Cambridge History of Renaissance Philosophy*, 68–69.

35   See Bergin and Fisch introduction, G1–4, on the use of "new" in Vico's title.

36   Alasdair MacIntyre, "Imaginative Universals and Historical Falsification: A Rejoinder to Professor Verene," *New Vico Studies* 6 (1988): 25.

37   Karl-Otto Apel, *Die Idee der Sprache in der Tradition des Humanismus von Dante bis Vico*, 2nd ed. (Bonn: Bouvier Verlag Herbert Grundmann, 1975), 320–21.

38   MacIntyre, 26.

39   Ernst Cassirer, "Giovanni Pico della Mirandola: A Study in the History of Renaissance Ideas," *The Journal of the History of Ideas* 3 (1942): no. 2: 123–44; no. 3: 319–46; 124.

40   Cassirer, 125.

41   Ibid.

42   Cassirer, 127

43   Ibid.

44   Ibid.

45   Cassirer, 128.

46 Ibid.

47 Ibid.

48 Cassirer, 129.

49 Seigal, 3.

50 William G. Craven, *Giovanni Pico della Mirandola: Symbol of His Age, Modern Interpretations of a Renaissance Philosopher* (Geneva: Droz, 1981), 1.

51 John Addington Symonds, *Renaissance Italy* (London: Smith & Edler, 1877), 329. See also Pico, *Commentary,* ix.

Part Two

1 "Corrections, Meliorations, and Additions," in vol. 5 of *Opere di G. B. Vico,* ed. Fausto Nicolini, 8 vols. in 11 (Bari: Laterza, 1911–41), 5: 377.

2 "In onore de Sant'Agostino," *Versi d'occasione e scritti di scula,* in vol. 3 of *Opere di G. B. Vico,* ed. Fausto Nicolini, 8 vols. in 11 (Bari: Laterza, 1911–41), 3: 117. See Ada Lamacchia, "Vico e Agostino: La presenza del *De civitate Dei* nella *Scienza nuova,*" in ed. G. Santinello, *Giambattista Vico: Poesia, logica, religione* (Brescia: Morcelliana 1986).

3 Cf. Nancy Streuver, "Vico in Post-Modern Italian Philosophy," a review article on *Recoding Metaphysics: The New Italian Philosophy* by Giovanna Borradori (Evanston: Northwestern University Press, 1988), *New Vico Studies* 8 (1990): 56–61.

4 Bergin and Fisch, "Introduction," *A* 44.

5 See *NS* 349 for the directive to the reader to remake the *New Science* for oneself.

6 Frederick R. Marcus, a book review of Peter Gimpel's *The Carnevalis of Eusebius Asch,* (Beverly Hills, California: Red Heifer Press, 1999), *New Vico Studies,* 17 (1999), 131–34.

7 On the atmosphere of Inquisition, see Donald Phillip Verene, *The New Art of Autobiography* (Oxford: Clarendon Press, 1991), 10.

8 See Frederick R. Marcus, "Vico and the Hebrews," for a reading of the *New Science* from the point of view of the role of the Hebrews, *New Vico Studies* 13 (1995): 14–32.

9 "Discoverta del Vero Dante Ovvero nuovi princípi di critica Dantesca," *Vico Opere,* ed. Nicolini, (Milan and Naples: Ricciardi, 1953), 950–54; "The Discovery of the True Dante," in *Critical Essays on Dante,* ed. Giuseppe Mazzotta (Boston: G. K. Hall, 1991).

10 Cf. Donald Phillip Verene, for the sense in which their projects can be seen as analogous, *The New Art of Autobiography: An Essay on the Life of Giambattista Vico Written by Himself,* (Oxford: Clarendon Press, 1991), ch. 3, especially 95–96. Unlike Verene, who persuasively explores the connections between Augustine's *Confessions* and Vico's *Autobiography,* I will consider the parallels between Augustine's *City of God* and Vico's *New Science.*

11 Vico also used this idea in *Il diritto universale*, in vol. 3 of *Opere di G. B. Vico*, ed. Fausto Nicolini, 8 vols. in 11(Bari: Laterza, 1911–41), chs. 42, 43. See also *La scienza nuova prima*, vol. 4 of *Opere di G. B. Vico*, ed. Fausto Nicolini, 8 vols. in 11 (Bari: Laterza, 1911–41), 4: 25.

12 The question of law, natural and divine, is not something that simply can be relegated to jurisprudential readings of Vico. In the context of the kinship of Vico and Augustine, however, I will draw attention to different aspects of governing in the *New Science* than would a study written from the jurisprudential perspective.

13 Augustine, *The City of God Against the Pagans*, trans. Henry Bettenson (London: Penguin Books, 1984). Further references will be inserted parenthetically in the text with the abbreviation *CG* and the page number of this English translation.

Chapter 4

1 See Peter Brown, *Augustine of Hippo: A Biography* (Berkeley and Los Angeles: University of California Press, 1967), 302.

2 Cf. Donald Phillip Verene, *Vico's Science of Imagination* (Ithaca: Cornell University Press, 1981), 70–71.

3 Augustine, *Confessions*, trans. F. J. Sheed (Indianapolis: Hackett, 1993), Book 7, ch. 9, 116. Further references will be inserted parenthetically in the text with the abbreviation *CG* and the page number of this English translation.

4 See Michael Mooney, *Vico in the Tradition of Rhetoric* (Princeton: Princeton University Press, 1984), 206–32.

5 See Fausto Nicolini, *Commento Storico alla seconda Scienza nuova*, 2 vols. (Rome: Edizione di Storia e Letteratura, 1978), I: 124–25.

6 The editors rightly refer the reader to the *City of God*, Book 6, for the main exposition of Varro's types, but as has already been shown, much of Part One is relevant, especially Books 2–4, 6–8. Also, the translators move Vico's parenthesis, which belongs before Vico introduces the third type, in order to break up Vico's long sentence.

7 Vico uses "vulgar"(*volgare*) and "common"(*comun*) which usually refer to poetic wisdom in a non-technical way to describe Varro's error. The error of ascribing allegorical interpretations to poetry is a philosophical error, not a vulgar or common one in the general sense. The error is common among the philosophers, and perhaps that is what Vico means to convey by calling it "the vulgar common error."

Chapter 5

1 See Peter Brown, *Augustine of Hippo: A Biography* (Berkeley and Los Angeles: University of California Press, 1967), 312.

2 See entry for "rough hew" in *The Oxford English Dictionary*, 2nd edition, vol. 14, 140.

3 Cf. Brown, 317.

4 See Donald Phillip Verene, *Vico's Science of Imagination* (Ithaca and London: Cornell University Press, 1981), 127–58.

5 I follow the correction by Bergin and Fisch that Vico means axiom 16, when he says "Propositions XV[I]–XXII will give us the foundations of the certain."

6 *De universi juri uno principo et fine uno liber unus*, 1720, vol. 2 of *Opere di G. B. Vico*, ed., Nicolini, 8 vols. in 11 (Bari: Laterza, 1911–41), 2: 26.

7 Ficino explicitly states all three of Vico's principles of humanity in *Letter 19*, in *The Letters of Marsilio Ficino*, 5 vols (London: Shepheard-Walwyn, 1975–94), I: 45.

8 See Verene, "Imaginative Universals and Narrative Truth," *New Vico Studies* 6 (1988), 9, and *The New Art of Autobiography: An Essay on the Life of Giambattista Vico Written by Himself* (Oxford: Clarendon Press, 1991), 139–140, 229.

9 Cf. Verene, *Vico's Science of Imagination*, 64.

10 *La scienza nuova prima*, I.12., 16–17. See Verene, *The New Art of Autobiography*, 137–47.

11 "I know" (*oida*) is the perfect tense of "I see" (*orao*). "Idea" is a participle meaning something seen, and thus by extension something known, that is, seen by the eye of the mind.

12 In the section "Method," Vico names a history of human ideas second, and treats philosophy of authority as the third aspect. In the "Corollaries concerning the principal aspects of this science" Vico orders them as follows: 1. a rational civil theology of divine providence (*NS* 385), 2. a philosophy of authority (*NS* 386), 3. a history of human ideas (*NS* 391), 4. a philosophical criticism (*NS* 392), 5. an ideal eternal history (*NS* 393), 6. a system of the natural laws of the gentes (*NS* 394), and 7. the principles of universal history (*NS* 399).

13 Contrast Alasdair MacIntyre, "The Relationship of Philosophy to its Past" in *Philosophy in History*, ed. Richard Rorty, J. B. Scheewind, Quentin Skinner (Cambridge: Cambridge University Press, 1984), 31–48.

14 See Verene, *Vico's Science of Imagination*, 65–95.

15 See Verene *Vico's Science of Imagination*, 36–64.

16 Thomas Hobbes, *Leviathan* (London: Penguin, 1985), I.13,14, 183–201.

17 Hobbes, II. 18, 239.

18 See Verene, *Vico's Science of Imagination*, 137.

19 Immanuel Kant, "Preface to Second edition," *Critique of Pure Reason*, trans. N. Kemp Smith (New York: St. Martin's Press, 1965), B xxiv–xxx.

20 Immanuel Kant, *Religion within the Limits of Reason Alone*, trans. T. M. Greene and H. H. Hudson (Chicago: Open Court, 1934). Cf. Nicholas Wolterstorf, *Reason within the Bounds of Religion* (Grand Rapids, Mich.: Eerdams, 1984).

21 See William James, *Pragmatism* (Indianapolis: Hackett, 1981), 14–15.

22 See Verene, *Vico's Science of Imagination*, 43–44.

23 See Ernesto Grassi, *Rhetoric as Philosophy: The Humanist Tradition* (University Park: Pennsylvania State, 1980), dedication.

24 See Donald Phillip Verene, "Giambattista Vico's 'Reprehension of the Metaphysics of René Descartes, Benedict Spinoza, and John Locke': An Addition to the *New Science* (Translation and Commentary)" *New Vico Studies* 8 (1990), 2–18. See especially Vico's comment on Locke as Epicurean and Descartes as Stoic, 3, §1215.

25 Donald Phillip Verene, "Philosophical Memory" *AA Files* 16: 57–62; *Vico's Science of Imagination*, 96–126.

Chapter 6

1 See Ann Hartle, *Death and the Disinterested Spectator* (Albany: State University of New York, 1986), 85–135. See also note 8 on Augustine and Platonism, 232–34.

2 See Hartle who, drawing on *Confessions* VII.5, links moral and intellectual error, 104.

3 T.S. Eliot, *The Four Quartets*, "The Dry Salvages," 5, in *The Complete Poems and Plays: 1909–1950* (New York: Harcourt, Brace & World, 1971), 136–37.

4 See Peter Brown, *Augustine of Hippo: A Biography* (Berkeley and Los Angeles: University of California Press, 1967), 113, 121, 134–35, 264–69.

5 Crinito, *De Honesta Disciplina Libri* 25, (Basil, 1532), 80. See D. P. Walker, *Ancient Theology* (London: Duckworth, 1972), 49.

6 John O'Meara, "Introduction," *CG* xvi–xvii.

7 Cf. Jean-Jacques Rousseau, *The First and Second Discourses*, ed. Roger Masters, trans. Roger and Judith Masters (New York: St. Martin's Press, 1964), I, 64. Cf. Michel de Montaigne, "Of Pedantry," *The Complete Essays of Montaigne*, trans. Donald M. Frame (Stanford: Stanford University Press, 1976), 97–106.

8 See Hartle, 104.

9 Heraclitus of Ephesus, fragment 200, in *The Presocratic Philosophers*, eds. G. S. Kirk, J. E. Raven, and M. Schofield, 2nd edition (Cambridge: Cambridge University Press), 188.

10   O'Meara, "Introduction," xvi–xvii; *CG* 10.29, 415.

11   Friedrich Nietzsche, *Beyond Good and Evil: Prelude to a Philosophy of the Future* (New York: Random House, 1966), 3.

Part Three

1   Werner Jaeger, *Paideia: The Ideals of Greek Culture*, 3 vols. (Oxford: Oxford University Press, 1971), 2: 210.

2   See Andrea Battistini, *Vico Opere*, 2 vols. (Milan: Mondadori, 1990), 2: 1262.

3   See Alexander Bertland, "The Significance of Tacitus in Vico's Idea of History," *Historical Reflections* 22 (1996): 517–35.

4   Alexander Pope, "An Essay on Criticism II," *Norton Anthology of Poetry*, ed. Allison, Barrows, Blake, Carr, Eastman, and English, 3rd ed. (New York: W. W. Norton, 1983), 402, lines 255–56.

Chapter 7

1   Contrast Andrea Battistini, "Vico as Agonistic Reader," *New Vico Studies* 12 (1994), 33.

2   On the three versions of the *New Science*, 1725, 1730, and 1744, see Max Fisch's introduction to the *Autobiography*.

3   For the acknowledgment by Plato of cyclopes as first fathers, see *NS* 296, 338, 503, 522, 547, 950, 962, 982, 1005.

4   Rousseau, *Emile: or On Education*, trans. Allan Bloom (New York: Basic Books, 1979), 40. I would like to thank Jim Goetsch for this reference.

5   Plato, *The Republic*, trans. Richard W. Sterling and William C. Scott (New York: W. W. Norton & Company, 1985). Further quotations from this translation will be inserted parenthetically in the text with the abbreviation *R.* and the Stephanus numbers.

6   Plato, *The Laws of Plato*, trans. Thomas Pangle (Chicago: The University of Chicago Press, 1988). Further quotations from this translation will be inserted parenthetically in the text with the abbreviation *Leg* and the Stephanus numbers.

7   Michael Morgan reads Plato's political thought in a similar fashion. Morgan states that "some commentators are willing to acknowledge Platonic realism as emerging only much later, in the *Laws*, but they are wrong. The power and poignancy of realism are already present in the *Republic*." *Platonic Piety* (New Haven: Yale University Press, 1990), 157; cf. 149–50, 154. Morgan also rightly states that the *Republic* itself is "about eternity and history, about transcendence and everyday life, and the account of justice, virtue, and philosophy that it produces must ignore neither of these twin dimensions of Platonic piety," 127.

8   Cf. Jean-Jacques Rousseau, *First and Second Discourses*, Roger D. and Judith R. Masters (New York: St. Martin's Press, 1964), I: 46–54.

9   From the point of view of the *Statesman* myth, in the rest of the *Republic* Socrates is only considering cities under the rule of Zeus not Chronos, but I do not want to digress too far from the *Republic* here.

10   Werner Jaeger, *Paideia: The Ideals of Greek Culture*, 3 vols. (Oxford: Oxford University Press, 1971), 3: 197–212.

11   See Thomas L. Pangle, "Interpretive Essay," *Plato's Laws* (University of Chicago Press, 1988) for Rousseau and *Laws* 3, 423.

12   See Andrea Battistini, *Opere Vico* 2 vols. (Milan: Mondadori, 1990), 296.

13   Cf. Jaeger, 3: 231–238. Note especially: "Plato thinks that spiritual self-discipline will gradually break down into complete licence, and finally into the savagery of the Titans, who were the monsters before the cave-men" (238).

14   See Pangle, 521, n. 9.

15   See Vittorio Mathieu, for how Plotinus's ideas of individuals and the Baroque sense of history make Vico's idea of history possible in "Truth as the Mother of History," in *Giambattista Vico's Science of Humanity*, ed. Giorgio Tagliacozzo and Verene (Baltimore: Johns Hopkins University Press, 1976), 113–24, especially 113.

16   See Fausto Nicolini, *Commento storico al seconda scienza nuova* 2 vols. (Rome: Edizioni de Storia e Letteratura), 2: 144.

17   See Joseph Anthony Mazzeo, "Genesis, *Timaeus* and Vico's Conception of History," *Yale Italian Studies* 2 (1978): 169–81.

Chapter 8

1   See Iris Murdoch, *The Fire and the Sun: Why Plato Banished the Poets* (New York: Viking Penguin, 1990), 20–21, 87.

2   On the critique of the analogy of God and a craftsman, see Ann Hartle, *Death and the Disinterested Spectator : An Inquiry into the Nature of Philosophy* (Albany: State University of New York Press, 1986), 105.

3   See A. Pagliaro, "Lingua e poesia secondo G. B. Vico" and "Omero e la poesia populare in G. B. Vico" in *Altri saggi di critica semantica* (Messina and Florence: D'Anna, 1961), 299–474.

4   Nicholas of Cusa, *On Learned Ignorance*, trans. Jasper Hopkins, 2nd ed. (Minneapolis: Arthur Banning Press, 1985).

5   See Francis M. Cornford for comparison of the *Sophist* to *Republic* 10 in *Plato's Theory of Knowledge: The Theatetus and the Sophist of Plato translated with a running commentary* (London: Routledge & Kegan Paul, 1935), 198–99.

6   Cornford, 323.

7 Stanley Rosen, *Plato's Sophist* (New Haven: Yale University, 1983), 147.

8 Ibid.

9 For a detailed summary, see Cornford's chart of the division, 324.

10 Cornford, 199.

11 Michele Le Doeuff, *The Philosophical Imaginary* (Stanford: Stanford University Press, 1989).

12 On Horace's commonplace see, Brian Vickers, "Poetic and Rhetoric" in *The Cambridge History of Renaissance Philosophy*, eds. Charles B. Schmitt and Quentin Skinner (Cambridge: Cambridge University Press, 1988), 718.

13 Donald Phillip Verene, "Vico's Frontispiece and the Tablet of Cebes," in *Man, God and Nature in the Enlightenment*, ed. E. D. Braun, Donald C. Mell, and Lucia Palmer (East Lansing, Mich.: Colleagues Press, 1988): 1–11.

14 Marsilio Ficino, *Ficino and the Phaedrean Charioteer*, trans. Michael B. Allen (University of California Press, 1981), 76.

15 Giuseppe Mazzotta, *Dante's Vision and the Circle of Knowledge* (Princeton: Princeton University Press, 1993), 171.

16 *Metafisica e teologia civile in Giambattista Vico*, ed. A. Lamacchia (Bari: Levante, 1992) is an exception; it uses the upper half of the frontispiece on its cover.

17 For Vico's image of the relationship of modern metaphysics and the natural world, see Verene, "Vico's 'Ignota latebat,'" *New Vico Studies* 5 (1987): 77–98.

Chapter 9

1 Cf. Michael Morgan, *Platonic Piety* (New Haven: Yale University Press, 1990), 114, 150.

2 See Hardy Hansen and Gerald M. Quinn, *Greek: An Intensive Course*, 2nd ed. (New York: Fordam University, 1992), 72. Homer said that Achilles had *arete* in his legs, meaning physical excellence, and then in philosophy *arete* comes to mean virtue in both moral and intellectual senses. I have already mentioned *oida* (I know) which is the perfect tense of I see (*orao*), and so there is an etymological basis for the image of "the mind's eye."

3 Benedetto Croce, *The Philosophy of G. B. Vico*, trans. R. G. Collingwood (New York: Macmillan, 1913), 82. W. B. Yeats underlined this sentence connecting the ethic of Vico and Plato in his copy of Collingwood's translation (the private library of Anne Yeats, Dalkey, Co. Dublin). I would like to thank Miss Anne Yeats for allowing me to spend an afternoon in her father's library.

4 See Marsilio Ficino, *The Letters of Marsilio Ficino*, trans. members of the Language Department of the School of Economic Science, London, 5 vols. (London: Shepheard-Walwyn, 1975–94), 1: 34.

5   See Werner Jaeger, *Paideia: The Ideals of Greek Culture*, 3 vols. (Oxford: Oxford University Press, 1971), 2: 19.

6   See Ernesto Grassi, *Rhetoric as Philosophy: The Humanist Tradition* (University Park: Pennsylvania State, 1980), dedication.

7   Donald Phillip Verene, *Vico's Science of the Imagination* (Ithaca: Cornell University Press, 1981), 122. Given the special claims Vico makes about the Hebrews, it is not quibbling to amend this formulation to say that Vico incorporates the notion of the Fall found in *Genesis* from the Hebrew tradition rather than the Christian.

8   W. B. Yeats, "Rosa Alchemica," in *Mythologies* (London: Papermac, 1992), 282.

Index

Achilles, 217, 223, 230, 234
Acquaviva, Matteo, 16
Adam, 41–43, 45, 47, 54, 138, 200
Aeneas, 182, 232
Aglaophemus, 24
Alfarabi, 46
Anacharsis, 26
Apuleius, 89
Aquinas, see Thomas Aquinas
Aristotle (Aristotelian), 15, 112, 127,
    190, 215;
    and the divine, 135, 218;
    on the hero, 227;
    on history, 21, 197;
    on human nature, 54–55;
    on the mean, 2;
    on poetry, 222;
    on rhetoric, 4, 62–64;
    on the senses, 113, 230;
    and Vico's preference for Platonic
        metaphysics, 152
Asaph, 43
Atticus, 158
Augustine, xi, 8–12, 151, 234;
    and the Bible, 104, 196;
    on divine providence, 80, 104–11,
        116, 194, 196;
    on divine grace, 109, 137–38, 146;
    Augustinian theology, 4;
    on Plato's critique of Homer, 31, 95,
        199;
    critique of Platonic pride, 80, 129–
        36, 140, 145, 147;

and frontispiece, 213–14;
on history, 21, 79, 110, 120, 195;
on Varro's types of theology, 24, 81–
    91, 93–94, 102, 122–23;
praise of the Platonists and Plato,
    90, 99, 130;
Vico's "particular protector," 77–78,
    91, 136;
works of:
    Confessions, 104, 130, 135;
    The City of God, 8, 11, 24, 31,
        79–91, 95, 97–100, 104–10,
        119, 125, 130–36, 138, 141;
    La Beata Vita, 143

Bacon, Francis (Lord Verulam), 2, 95,
    113, 154–55
Barbaro, Ermolao, 59–64, 66
Bayle, Pierre, 141
Bedani, G. L. C., 1
Bergin, Thomas Goddard, 4
Berlin, Isaiah, 6
Bessarion, 25
Boccaccio, Giovanni, 24
Bruno, Giordano, 25, 35
Burke, Peter, 4, 47

Calvin, John, 109, 137
Cassirer, Ernst, 56, 70–73
Cato, 158
Causabon, Isaac, 25, 33, 36
Censorinus, 35
Cicero (Ciceronian),

on eloquence, 60–68;
on Euhemerism, 98;
as syncretic, 73;
on wisdom, 56, 81, 211;
on Socrates, 49, 100;
on providence, 81, 119;
on philosophy, 143;
on Plato's Republic, 158
Confucius, 26
Cornford, Francis, 204
Croce, Benedetto, 229
Cusanus, Nicholas, see Nicholas of Cusa

Dante, 78–79, 130, 135, 165, 195,
    214–16
Democritus, 25
Demosthenes, 65
Descartes, René (Cartesian),
    as confused with Plato, 2, 17, 49;
    as against Renaissance ideals, 15–16,
        65, 71–73, 124–25;
    in contrast to method of Vico, 49,
        68, 118;
    tree of knowledge, 29;
    and Vico's inaugural orations, 16–17
Dio Chrysostom, 106
Doria, Paolo Mattia, 3, 16, 211
Duns Scotus, 62

Eliot, T. S., 132
Epicurus (Epicurean), 19, 81, 119, 146;
    excluded by axiom 5, xii, 5–6, 9, 68,
        99, 103, 125, 213, 226, 233;
    on chance, 57, 103, 107, 120, 193;
Euhemerus, 84, 88, 98, 122

Facio, Bartolomeo, 22
Ficino, Marsilio,
    and frontispiece, 214;
    and Pico, 17, 23, 53–54;
    Platonic Theology (Theologia
        Platonica), 19, 24;
    and poetic theology, 24–25, 31;
    as source of phrase "the family of
        Plato," 7, 9–10, 12, 136, 156,
        219, 234;

Vico's praise of, 16
Fisch, Max Harold, 4, 100

Garin, Eugenio, 25, 73
Gimpel, Peter, 78
Grotius, Hugo, 2, 154

Hegel, G. W. F., 4, 8
Heraclitus, 2, 30, 143, 198
Hercules (Herculean), 35, 51, 83, 231,
    234–35
Herder, Johann Gottfried, 4, 8
Hermes Trismegistus (Thrice Great,
    Hermes, Hermetica), 21, 23–
    26, 33–36, 40, 89
Herodotus, 34–35
Hesiod, 153, 164–65, 183, 223
Hobbes, Thomas, 119–20
Homer,
    allegorical interpretation of, 23, 25,
        30–31, 89, 95, 224;
    critique of, 31, 95, 199, 222–24;
    and Dante, the Tuscan Homer, 78–
        79, 215;
    discovery of the true, 9, 19, 21–22,
        30, 37, 84, 96–97;
    on frontispiece, 215, 217;
    and heroism, 223–24, 226, 234;
    and ideal eternal history, 92, 101,
        172, 177–79, 182–83;
    Plutarch on, 155–56;
    as teacher of Greece, 142, 151, 221–
        22, 224;
    works of:
        Iliad, 19, 177, 182, 191;
        Odyssey 19, 31, 179, 223–24
Horace, 66, 210, 216–17, 235

Iamblichus, 25, 35–36, 200

Kant, Immanuel (Kantian), 1, 4, 72,
    124
Kristeller, Paul O., 7–8

Locke, John, 65, 115
Lotario Dei Segni, Pope Innocent III,
    22

Lucretius (Lucretian), 5, 62

Machiavelli, Nicolo, 191
MacIntyre, Alasdair, xi, 3–4, 71
Manetti, Giannozzo, 22
Marcus, Frederick R., 77–78
Mazzoni, Giacopo, 16
Mercury, 52, 214–15
Medinaceli, Duke of, 16
Melanchthon, 63–64
Milbank, John, 4
Moses, 21, 25, 35, 47
Murdoch, Iris, 1

Nicholas of Cusa, 39, 202
Nicolini, Fausto, 6–7, 30–31, 191
Nifo, Agostino, 16

Odysseus (Ulysses), 23, 31, 217, 223–
    24, 230, 232, 234
Oracle at Delphi (Delphic, Temple of
    Delphi), 51, 55, 116, 228
Orpheus, 21, 24–25, 95
Oziosi, Academy of, 55, 66, 77, 228

Parmenides, 198
Patrizi, Francesco, 16
Paul, 89–90, 98, 104, 120, 130, 132–
    33, 147
Pelagius (Pelagian), 45, 109, 137
Petrarch, Francesco, 22, 24–25, 73, 95
Philolaus, 24
Piccolomini, Alessandro, 16
Pico della Mirandola, Giovanni, xi, 7, 9,
    12, 15–19, 55, 91, 93, 125,
    151;
    and the New Science, 69–70, 80,
        129;
    on angels, 43–45, 55–56;
    and eloquence, 59–64, 71–74;
    on human dignity, 10, 47, 134–35,
        145, 234;
    "maker and molder of thyself," 39–
        48, 53–54, 57, 80, 134, 206;
    on piety, 46;
    on moral philosophy, 43–44, 52;
    on poetic theology, 21–37;

works of:
    De Ente, 44–45;
    Heptaplus, 39–40, 42, 45–47, 55;
    Oration on the Dignity of Man, 8,
        10, 22–25, 27, 39–49, 52–53,
        69–70, 80, 129, 134, 206,
        214;
    Letter to Ermolao Barbaro, 59–64,
        66;
    Poetic Theology, 95;
    Nine Hundred Theses, 18

Pico della Mirandola, Gianfrancesco
    (nephew of Giovanni), 23, 47
Plato (see also, Vico, Giambattista,
    critique of Plato and praise of
    Plato), xi–xii, 1–12, 151–235;
    on eikon, 11, 200, 204–05, 207–08,
        210, 216, 221, 223;
    on Eros, 25, 214–15, 218, 225–26;
    on eros, 39, 199, 205, 207, 214–15,
        218–19, 225–28, 232, 235;
    on moderation, 173–74, 210, 225–
        26, 232;
    and the quarrel with Homer, 11, 32,
        95, 142, 199, 217, 222–23,
        234;
    on paideia, 11, 218;
works of:
    Alcibiades (Alc. I), 25, 54–55, 91;
    Apology (Ap.), 31, 228;
    Charmides, 25;
    Cratylus (Crat.), 30, 154–56,
        165–66, 200–01, 215, 226;
    Critias (Criti.), 158, 166, 170–
        73, 177, 180–83, 185–86,
        188–89, 192;
    Crito (Crit.), 116, 234;
    Gorgias, 60;
    Laws (Leg.), 159, 161, 165–66,
        172;
    and the New Science, 153,
        158, 173, 176–83, 191–92,
        194, 196;
    on Nestor, 174–75;
    on seriousness and poetry,
        199–200, 223;

on moderation, 173–74, 225–
  26, 232;
on providence, 203–04, 227;
Phaedo (*Phad.*), 234;
Phaedrus (*Phadr.*), 60, 63, 71,
  111, 159–66, 195, 206–07,
  214;
Republic (*R.*), xii, 42, 53, 62;
  on the Cave, 100, 203, 207,
  233–34;
  and the *City of God*, 83;
  and Er, myth of, 224, 230;
  on health and justice, 229–30;
  and history, 153, 158, 177–
  83, 185–89;
  on the Divided Line, 196,
  205, 207;
  on moderation, 210;
  and philosopher-kings, 48,
  159–64, 167–68, 173–76,
  182, 188, 194;
  on poetry, 31–32, 95, 199–
  200, 203;
  and pre-political times, 157,
  172;
  and Vico, 143, 158, 163, 182,
  191, 194–96;
Seventh Letter, 158, 173, 176;
Sophist (*Sph.*), 30, 142, 197–99,
  202–05, 207–08, 216, 229–
  30;
Statesman (*Politicus*) (*Plt.*), 153,
  159, 164–66, 172, 177, 180,
  182–89, 191–92, 194, 196,
  203, 222;
Symposium (*Smp.*), 25, 39, 44,
  175, 199, 202, 205–07, 214,
  218, 223, 225–28, 232;
Theatetus, 30;
Timaeus (*Ti.*), 78, 89, 105, 126,
  152–53, 196–97, 199–200;
  and the Atlantis story, 168–
  73, 177, 180–81, 183, 185,
  189;
  and *Republic*, 166–68;
  and Vico, 158, 194, 196–97,
  216, 218

Platonism, xi, xii, 1, 7–9, 80, 99, 151;
  Italian Platonists (Renaissance
    Platonists), 15–17, 19, 21,
    40, 45, 49, 54, 78–79, 125,
    147;
  and the conceit of scholars, 22,
    26–28, 31–33, 36–37, 96;
  and poetic theology (*prisca
    theologia*), 21–37, 117;
Neoplatonism, 7;
  allegorical interpretation of
    poetry, 21, 30–31, 192, 199,
    224;
  and Augustine, 88–90, 146;
  and Christianity, 25, 35, 39, 78,
    135–36, 147;
  and ideas in God's mind, 190
Pletho, 24
Plotinus, 7, 16, 31, 90, 104, 138, 224
Plutarch, 139–40, 155–56
Poliziano, Angelo, 74
Polybius, 123, 141
Pompa, Leon, 5–6
Pope, Alexander, 155
Porphyry, 89–90, 131, 137, 195
Proclus, 25
Protagoras, 114, 204
Pseudo-Dionysius, 78
Pythagoras, Pythagorean, 24–27

Renan, Joseph Ernest, 73
Richardus, 109
Riverso, Emanuele, 36
Rousseau, Jean-Jacques, 160

Savanarola, 135–36
Scaevola, Q. T., 83–85, 143
Scheffer, Johann, 34
Scotus, see Duns Scotus
Seneca, 70, 87
Seutonius, 24
Shakespeare, 106
Socrates,
  Cicero on, 49, 100;
  on the chronological table, 15;
  as the father of all philosophers, 7,
    12, 156;

as philosophical hero, 8, 156, 219,
    221–35;
on place in ideal eternal history, 8–
    9, 151;
on Plato's portrait of, 11, 176, 208,
    219, 221–35;
and self-knowledge, 55, 71, 116,
    210, 216–17, 228;
and Varro, 89;
and Vico, 49, 67, 100, 152, 207,
    232
Solon, 116, 168–70, 172, 177
Spinoza, Baruch (Benedict), 6
Steuco (Steuchio), Agostino, 16, 25
Stoics (Stoicism), 21, 31, 146;
    excluded by axiom 5, xii, 5–6, 9, 68,
        99, 103, 125, 213, 226, 233;
    on fate, 5–6, 57, 103, 107, 120,
        193;
Strauss, Leo, 5

Tacitus, 2, 15, 153–54, 190, 192
Terence, 95
Thiele, Edwin, 32
Thomas Aquinas, 46

Varro, Marcus Terentius, 34, 222;
    on natural theology as Platonic, 88–
        91, 99;
    and naturalistic explanations of
        poetry, 87, 96–98;
    on the Platonists as the best
        philosophers, 91, 99, 130;
    and the types of theology in City of
        God, 24, 81–91;
    and Vico on types of theology, 91–
        102
Vasoli, Cesare, 70
Vaughn, Frederick, 5
Verene, Donald Phillip, xi, 69, 233
Vickers, Brian, 59

Vico, Giambattista, xi–xii, 1–12;
    on ars topica and ars critica, 121–22;
    on axiom 5, xii, 5, 57, 68, 99, 103,
        111–13, 125, 129, 137–38,
        213, 226–27;

on the barbarisms of sense and
    reflection, 140, 172, 179–80,
    232;
on the certain and the true, 8, 112–
    15, 120, 123, 126–27, 139,
    142, 218;
and Christianity, 3–4, 18–19, 35,
    39, 77–80, 144–48;
on chronology, 32–37, 97;
on the conceit of nations (ax. 4), 26,
    32, 36–37;
on the conceit of scholars (ax. 3), 4,
    7, 26–28, 36–37, 78, 91, 96,
    116, 120, 124, 182, 188;
on corso e ricorso, 8–9, 35, 78–79,
    92–93, 101, 116, 123, 142,
    145, 148, 151, 196, 217, 222;
on coscienza and scienza, 111–15,
    166, 202;
critique of Plato,
    ignorance fall of man, 152, 194–
        96;
    misleading about Homer, 30–32,
        37, 221;
    believing in golden age philoso-
        pher-kings, 159, 182, 188;
on desire (eros), 37, 52, 68, 74, 215,
    218–19, 228;
on divine providence, 5, 37, 98–101,
    103–27, 139–40;
    as common to all religions, 146,
        196;
    and divine grace 109, 111, 126–
        27, 136–38, 145–46;
    as poetic providence, 115–20;
    on the rational civil theology of,
        4, 81–103, 111, 113;
    on the remedies of, 140–41;
    on the truth of, 120–27;
    on Vichian providence, 111–27;
and dogmatism, 3–4, 9;
on the Egyptians, 27–28, 33–36,
    169;
and eloquence, 10, 15–16, 19, 53,
    56–57, 59–74, 110, 125–26,
    129, 136, 138, 140, 145–47,
    216, 231, 234;

on *fantasia*, 28–29, 50, 115, 118,
    122, 216;
the four authors of, 1–2, 6, 10, 15,
    18, 95, 151, 153–55;
and the Hebrews, 35, 77–78, 92–
    94, 100, 110, 169;
on the heroic mind, 12, 50–51, 68,
    74, 215, 219, 221, 229–30,
    232–33, 235;
and historicism, xi, 2, 3;
on human nature, 1, 5, 39–40, 48,
    53–56, 129–48, 189–190;
    man as is and ought to be, 31, 52,
        153, 157–58, 176, 179, 190;
    by nature social, 91, 106, 164;
    as fallen, 11, 52–53, 55, 57, 68,
        104, 119, 129–48, 213, 218,
        227, 229, 233, 235;
on ideal eternal history, 5, 8, 21,
    101, 126;
    and the Egyptians, 33–36;
    and philosophy's place, 120,
        125–26, 136, 140;
    and Plato's place, 151, 222;
    and Plato's philosophy of history,
        157–98;
    as a Platonic form of history,
        190–98;
on imaginative universals, 27–28,
    31, 97–99, 116–17, 120–121,
    123–24, 126, 156, 232;
    and intelligible universals, 27–28,
        97–99, 116, 126, 156, 230,
        234;
    on Jove as first, 116–18, 121,
        123, 126, 139, 193, 203;
and Inquisition, 5, 78;
on Lady Metaphysic, 68, 99, 106,
    136, 138, 141, 146, 196,
    211–19;
on his "metaphysics compatible with
    human frailty," 3, 6, 18, 49,
    80, 124, 129, 136–37, 210–11;
on method, 69, 126, 138, 143, 155;
    on the new critical art, 4, 137;
    and philosophy examining philo-
        logy, 7–8, 100, 115, 120, 137;

on moderation, xi, 2–3, 5, 52, 210,
    219, 227–28;
on *paideia*, 10–11, 39–40, 48, 51,
    53–57, 59, 68, 77, 80, 125,
    133, 141–43, 226;
on philosophical heroism, 11–12,
    217–35;
on philosophy, 55;
    on the origin of, 228, 230;
    and philology, 4, 18, 115, 120–
        22, 124, 137, 197;
    on its place in human affairs,
        129;
    and religion, 125, 140–48;
    on its role in barbarism, 125–26,
        140–41;
    on Vico's humbling of, 136–48;
on piety, 3, 5, 12, 35, 74, 78–79,
    81, 123–25, 136–46, 189–90,
    203, 219, 234;
praise of Plato, 158;
    as best philosophy when
        combined with Christian
        faith, 79;
    as discovering divine providence,
        99;
    as an entire university, 67, 155;
    as the ideal philosopher, 151–56;
    as the imaginative universal for
        philosophy, 31;
    as the inventor of philosophical
        heroism, 221, 228;
    as meriting the epithet "divine,"
        56, 103;
    as the prince of divine philoso-
        phers, 152;
    as the prince of Greek wisdom,
        154;
    as the prince of political
        philosophers, 155;
    as proving true the immortality
        of human souls, 114;
on the principles of humanity, xii,
    112–16, 118, 120, 123–26,
    139, 142, 217–18, 227;
on *sapienza poetica*, 22–31, 91–92,
    94, 97, 99, 101;

on *sapienza riposta*, 91–92, 94–97,
99–100;
on self-knowledge, 17, 48, 49, 51,
55–56, 59, 71, 80, 116, 143,
219;
on *sensus communis*, 121, 124;
on theology,
Christian, 77–81, 92–94, 100–
03, 123;
rational civil, 4, 81–82, 91–103,
111, 113;
and skepticism, 3, 5, 9, 124–25, 140;
on the *verum-factum* principle, 3, 69,
99, 116, 126, 201–03, 209;
works of:
"The Academies and the
Relation between Philosophy
and Eloquence" (*PE*), 17, 55,
66, 77;
Autobiography (*A*), 2, 15, 17, 19,
65, 67, 69, 70, 74, 148, 169,
187, 195, 201–02, 229;
on anger, 147;
on Augustine, 109;
on Christianity, 79;
on natural theology, 100;
on Plato, 79, 151–56, 194–
95, 221–22;
on self-love, 144;
on Socrates, 207, 232;
"On the Heroic Mind,"(*HM*) 17,
50–51, 66, 70–71, 110, 156,
218–19, 228–29, 231–34;
Inaugural Orations (*IO*), 17, 48–
57, 59, 66–67, 70, 79, 80, 129,
135–36, 144–45, 147, 200;

*On the Most Ancient Wisdom of
the Italians* (*AW*), 3, 6, 49, 80,
99, 102, 129, 136–37, 200–
02, 210–11, 235;
*The New Science of Giambattista
Vico* (1744) (*NS*), as a whole,
1, 5–6, 9–10, 15–19, 21–22,
25–26, 32, 51, 67–71, 74,
77–82, 91–94, 101, 103, 110,
112, 114–16, 120–21, 125–
26, 129, 136–37, 142–44,
146, 148, 153, 156–57, 197,
215;
Chronological Table of, 15,
32–33, 169;
Frontispiece of, 11, 32, 208–
219, 221, 234; illustration,
212;
Conclusion of, 166, 190–96;
*On the Study Methods of Our
Time* (*SM*), 18, 49, 65–67,
70, 121;
Universal Law, 17

Villarosa, 148
Virgil, 79, 89, 135, 153

Whitehead, Alfred North, 9
Wilbur, Ken, 9

Xenophanes, 88

Yates, Frances, 25, 36
Yeats, W. B., 8, 235

Zoroaster, 21, 24–26